*More Love for Marlene Koch's*

# EAT *what you* LOVE
## COOKBOOKS

Thank you for your wonderful cookbooks! Since I started using your cookbooks I have lost 57 pounds. I have tried different types of diets in the past with little success. Your books do not feel anything like the unspeakable word "diet," but instead a great life change. Thank you again, I cannot wait for the next one!

MARCINE SUTTLES, *Easley, South Carolina*

Marlene, I can't begin to tell you how much we love your books. I bought them to help me with my weight watcher program, but had no idea my entire family would benefit—or love the food so much! I have lost 50 pounds, my husband 30 pounds, and both of my kids are fitter than ever. They actually fight over which Eat What You Love dish we are going to have for dinner! If that weren't enough the recipes are easy and have me excited about cooking again. Thank you from all of us!!!!

BELINDA JONES *(and family), Atlanta, Georgia*

Marlene, thank you so much for making a big change in our lives. I have congestive heart failure and type 2 diabetes, but since my husband and I have been eating from your books my diabetes is in remission! We both recommend your books constantly, give them as gifts, and use them to make family dinners.

JOSIE WHITE, *Houston, Texas*

I can't wait until your next book comes out. With the help of your recipes, and I haven't found a bad one yet, I have lost 80 pounds. I plan to continue using your recipes for the rest of my life. They are my new way of cooking, and I love it!

DONNA ROY, *Newington, Connecticut*

LOVE, LOVE, LOVE!!! I have all three of your *Eat What You Love* cookbooks and absolutely love them. They are now the only cookbooks I use on a daily basis. The recipes are so easy, and so delicious! I mark each recipe I would make again and the books are now overflowing with tags. We bought them to eat healthier. Who knew it was the taste we would fall in love with? Your restaurant makeovers are even better than those we used to order when we ate out!

JANELLE FISCHER-TORRES, *Belmont, California*

Running Press
Hachette Book Group
1290 Avenue of the Americas, New York, NY 10104
www.runningpress.com
@Running_Press

Printed in Canada

Originally published in 2016 by Running Press in the United States of America

Revised Edition: January 2018

Published by Running Press, an imprint of Perseus Books, LLC, a subsidiary of Hachette Book Group, Inc. The Running Press name and logo is a trademark of the Hachette Book Group.

The publisher is not responsible for websites (or their content) that are not owned by the publisher.

Food styling by Carole Haffey
Food styling for air fryer chapter and page 136 by Lisa Cherkasky

Prop styling by Mariellen Melker
Prop styling for air fryer chapter and page 136 by Kristi Hunter

Print book cover and interior design by Susan Van Horn

Library of Congress Control Number: 2015950650

ISBNs 978-0-7624-9281-7 (paperback), 978-0-7624-5784-7 (hardcover), 978-0-7624-5827-1 (ebook)

10  9  8  7  6  5  4  3  2  1

# Eat *what you* LOVE
# QUICK & EASY

## MARLENE KOCH

*Food Photography by*
### STEVE LEGATO

RUNNING PRESS
PHILADELPHIA

*To family, friends, colleagues,
and my amazing "kochbook" fans:
Your love and support make **my** life
more delicious.*

# CONTENTS

## EAT WHAT YOU LOVE: QUICK & EASY RECIPES

# INTRODUCTION

QUICK, EASY, HEALTHY, AND BEST OF ALL, TASTY! When it comes to creating guilt-free goodness, this culinary quartet hits all the right notes. Welcome to my world, and to *Eat What You Love Quick & Easy*, the fourth book in my "Eat What You Love" cookbook series. If this is the first time you've encountered an Eat What You Love book, I'm thrilled to have you here. If you've ever tried giving up the foods you love for the sake of your health, you know just how difficult it can be, but in my world, you don't have to! I believe everyone should be able to enjoy the great taste of the foods they love, and good health. Just ask Miriam, or John, Barbara, or any of the countless readers who have been kind enough to share their incredible stories as to how they simply cooked (and happily ate) their way to better health. It truly warms my heart every time a reader shares their story of "effortless" weight loss or "defeating" diabetes—and it delights me to no end when I hear that "healthy-hating" husbands and finicky teens that are gladly gobbling down healthy meals!

If you are adding this latest volume to your Eat What You Love "kochbook" collection, thank-you, I can't wait to share all that is new! You might think that quick and easy recipes would be, well, quick and easy to create; however such is not the case. I learned that lesson pretty fast—especially when I refused to compromise on flavor. But the results were worth the effort! From 5-Minute Shrimp Salsa and 10-minute Amazing Garlic Butter Chicken to 5-ingredient Black Bean Soup, Everyday Marinated Steak (that's done in 30 minutes), and the Easiest-Ever Blueberry Pie, I've already added dozens of the mouthwatering made-in-minutes dishes in this book to my own go-to recipe collection and I am confident you will be doing the same once you've tried them.

With this book, for the first time, I offer you a peek inside my own kitchen in a section I call the Quick and Easy Kitchen. In it you will find a pantry list for the most common ingredients used in the book (including multiple choices for sweeteners) to keep you well stocked and ready to cook in a flash. There's also a list of the tools I love and can't live without that help to make fast cooking fun and easy. And because so many readers have asked, I've also included two pages packed full of cooking tips and tricks for eating what you love when you're cooking just for two (or even just you)!

Also new to this book is one of the simply sweetest dessert chapters ever—an entire chapter of Easy No-Bake Desserts. The scrumptious-yet-speedy recipes range from a luscious 15-Minute Coconut Cream Candy Bar Pie to No-Bake Cherry Topped Cheesecake Cupcakes, Chocolate Hazelnut Nutella Mousse, and a 2-Minute Chocolate Cupcake (just) for one. Did I mention the desserts average a mere 150 calories a serving? It's a chapter not to be missed! Another first-timer is a whole chapter devoted to do-it-yourself dressings, spice mixes, and sauces. The recipes are great healthy basics and will not only save you time, but money.

As in my previous books you will find portion sizes that are real, not skimpy, and nutrition information you can count on. Speaking of good nutrition, if you are following the trend to eat less meat, simply swim on over to the fish, seafood, and meatless mains chapter and try one of the marvelous meatless recipes like Creamy Vegetable Enchiladas or Steak-Style Portobellos. I guarantee no one will miss the meat.

On the other hand, if what you love about my cookbooks are my beloved decadent-tasting restaurant makeovers—and their equally amazing sugar, fat, calorie and sodium savings—look no further than the deep, dark Double Chocolate Pancakes, Chili's-Style Cajun Chicken Pasta, or creamy crispy Fried Macaroni and Cheese. All are quick, easy, healthy, and utterly delicious!

From start to finish, this book will have you cooking the foods you love in a snap—breakfasts are as easy as 5-Minute Breakfast Pizzas, family suppers are a cinch with favorites like Good 'n Easy Turkey Chili, and last minute guests are a delight to feed when armed with speedy 5-Ingredient Spinach Stuffed Salmon and Last Minute Roasted Reds. In many ways this was the most challenging book I have ever written, but now that it's finished (and in your hands), I am elated to say that quick, easy, healthy, and tasty are a culinary quartet worth singing about!

My best to you and yours,

*Marlene*

P.S. If you love air-frying, you are going to love the "bonus" chapter. Tasty, healthy, easy, and QUICK!

# EAT WHAT YOU LOVE:
# Your Easy Guide to Healthy Eating

F AT IS BAD FOR YOU, fat is good for you. You can't eat eggs, you should eat eggs! Are sugar and salt really that bad? With so many conflicting messages, and different "diets," it's hard to know what to believe. And more importantly, amidst all of the chatter, how's a hungry better-health-seeking food lover to know what's best to eat?

I'm happy to say that I can help. As I shared in my introduction, I believe everyone deserves to eat the foods they love—*and* enjoy good health. As a nutritionist and a mom of two food-loving boys and a stepdaughter with diabetes, I also know that eating healthfully is not always easy—especially since we are pre-destined to love the very foods we're often told not to eat!

In this book you will find over 180 incredible tasting recipes that have been carefully crafted with great taste and good nutrition in mind, allowing you and yours to enjoy the creamy, cheesy, crunchy, salty, and yes, sweet foods you love without worry or guilt. As a bonus, every recipe is also quick and easy to make—so you'll always have time for a healthy meal—even when you're rushed for time! To make healthy shopping and cooking easier I've included lots of tips throughout (like how to fit beloved butter into a healthy diet!), and last but not least in the pages that follow you will find the nutrition principles that guide me as I create my simply delicious recipes, along with tools to help you look and feel your very best.

Eating more healthfully? Piece of cake!

## CALORIES COUNT

We know it's not good to eat too many of them, but what exactly *is* a calorie? A calorie is simply a measure of the amount of energy a food provides. This energy fuels the body and enables it to grow, move, and think. We need calories! The problem lies not with the calories themselves, but the excess weight caused by consuming too many of them, which is *really* easy to do! Here is some more information about calories and health:

**The best thing you can do for your health is to maintain a healthy weight.** Nothing trumps a healthy weight when it comes to looking and feeling your best. Most people on average "burn" between 1,800 and 2,400 calories a day.* If you eat more calories than you expend, you will gain weight. If you eat fewer calories than you need, you will lose weight.

**For weight control, the type of calories you eat matters less than the total number of calories.** While eating nutrient-rich food is better overall for your health, and *highly* recommended, numerous studies have demonstrated that you will in fact lose more weight eating 1,000 calories a day of Twinkies than 1,500 calories of fish.

**Cutting calories has a bigger impact on weight loss than expending them.** Studies estimate that what you eat accounts for a resounding 75% of weight loss. It is not surprising when you consider that slashing just 100 calories equals running an entire mile! Be active for your health (and to maintain a healthy weight), but curb calories if you want to slim your waist.

THE BOTTOM LINE: Calories count, and one of the best ways to get more bang for your calorie buck is to cook. Every recipe in this book has been carefully crafted to help you enjoy great tasting food while you effortlessly curb excess calories. (Be sure to check out the "Dare to Compare"s found on many of the recipes to see the colossal calorie savings you can reap!)

* For a personalized estimate of your caloric needs go to marlenekoch.com/tools/ and click on the Personal Calorie Calculator.

## FAT MATTERS

The headline next to the stick of butter reads, "Fat is Back!" After years of classifying fats as a dietary four-letter word, it appears we had it all wrong—or did we? Let me start by saying that from a culinary standpoint, it's hard to beat the flavor, aroma, and creamy or crispy texture that fat adds to foods. And from a nutritional standpoint, fats are vital for good health (and good looks). That said, it's important to note that all fats are not created equal, nor is adding more fat to your diet necessarily healthy. Here are some quick facts about fat:

**Some fats are substantially better than others.** Heart- and brain-healthy mono- and polyunsaturated fats come primarily from fruits and vegetables, like avocados, corn, and olives, as well as nuts, seeds, and fish. Conversely, less healthful saturated fat is found primarily in animal products such as butter, meat, and full-fat dairy products. Eating more plant-based fats and less "sat" fat is undisputedly better for your health. Trans fats—found most often in commercial baked goods, snacks, and some stick margarines—are not healthy, and should be avoided.

**Fats are calorie heavyweights.** All fats (healthy and not) have nine calories per gram—more than twice the calories per gram of protein and carbohydrates—making most foods that are high in fat also high in calories. An oh-so-healthy cup of olive oil has over 1,900 calories! Eating all fats in moderation helps curb excess calories.

**Low- or no-fat foods are not always the healthy choice.** Replacing fat with sugar, as many food manufacturers do to reduce fat, does not make a product more healthful. Reduced fat foods should have fewer calories and ideally, less sugar.

THE BOTTOM LINE: How much and what type of fat you eat matters. In this book you will find rich tasting, creamy, "fried," and cheesy foods—all with a fraction of the customary fat. Healthy fats, like those found in canola oil and nuts, are featured throughout the book and less healthy fats (see page 58 for more on beloved butter), have stealthfully been reduced.

## CARB CONSCIOUS

Although carbs often take a bad rap, the truth is there's plenty to love about carbs. First, while it's true that all carbohydrates, with the exception of fiber, break down into glucose, that's actually a good thing as glucose is the preferred fuel for our bodies and brain. Second, there are different types of carbohydrates—some healthy and some not. Third, as with fats, both the type and the amount of carbs you eat matters. Here's what to consider when it comes to carbs:

**Complex and un-refined or minimally processed carbs are good for you.** These types of carbs, which include whole grains, veggies, fruit, and beans, promote good health, as they are chock-full of vitamins, minerals, antioxidants, and phytochemicals. They also come packaged with fabulous fiber, which slows the breakdown of carbohydrates and their impact on blood sugar.

**Simple and refined carbohydrates offer little more than calories.** While they are a quick source of energy, these type of carbohydrates, which include sugar and soda, fruit juices, cakes and pastries, un-enriched white bread, and white rice, contain few nutrients. Additionally, their rapid breakdown can spike blood sugar and contribute to weight gain and trigger a higher risk for diabetes and heart disease. (For more on sugar see page 36.)

**Fiber is a no-calorie carbohydrate with great health benefits.** Even though fiber is classified as a carbohydrate, it can't be digested, hence it has no calories and does not raise blood sugar. Fiber is broken down into two categories. Insoluble fiber helps keep your system moving; soluble fiber traps fat and cholesterol and can help reduce your risk for heart disease, type 2 diabetes, high blood pressure, and obesity. Soluble fiber also makes you feel fuller longer.

THE BOTTOM LINE: It pays to be conscious of the type of carbs you eat and how much, especially for those with diabetes or on weight loss diets. All of my recipes are what I call "carb-conscious." Slow-burning complex carbs such as fiber-rich oats, beans and non-starchy veggies, along with fresh fruit take center stage, while refined carbs and added sugars have been curbed. Moreover, the total carbs have been kept in check so that even those on carbohydrate- or blood sugar-sensitive diets can eat the foods they love!

## SUGAR SMARTS

It's hard *not* to love sugar, especially since we are born with an affinity for its sweet taste. But as the evidence in the case against added sugars in our diet and its detrimental effect on health continues to grow, there's simply no sugarcoating the havoc eating excess sugar can reap on your health. (Added sugars are not those naturally found in foods such as fruit, milk, and vegetables, but sugars *added* to processed foods to make them sweeter.) Here's the scoop on added sugars:

**Sugar can have major health consequences.** Sugar, unlike more complex carbohydrates, offers little more than calories and enters the bloodstream rapidly, which spikes blood sugar and insulin levels. Consuming too much sugar has been found to contribute to heart disease, obesity, type 2 diabetes, liver damage, some cancers, and even premature aging. Research shows that drinking a single 12-ounce can of regular soda a day—which contains 10 teaspoons of sugar—can increase your risk for type 2 diabetes by 18%!

**The recommended allowance for added sugar is 6 teaspoons a day for women and 9 for men.** The average American consumes 22 teaspoons of added sugar a day, or 170 pounds per year, far more than is healthful. The number one contributor of added sugar is sweetened beverages, followed by candy, sweet desserts, fruit drinks, and sweetened cereals. While natural, honey, molasses, maple syrup, and agave nectar are also added sugars.

**Using alternative sweeteners in place of added sugars.** The healthiest way to satisfy a sweet tooth is with nature's candy—fresh fruit. That said, studies show that sugar substitutes, including those that are all natural, can help reduce the amount of added sugars, along with the calories and the numerous health concerns they carry, in the foods you eat. (See page 36 for more information.)

THE BOTTOM LINE: Minimizing the use of added sugars is smart for everyone. This book lets you and yours enjoy all the sweet foods you love—and stay healthy too. From beverages to desserts I've trimmed the sugar, with virtually every recipe delivering a teaspoon or less of added sugar. Best of all, you would never know it, and that's sweet indeed!

## PROTEIN PROWESS

Of the three macronutrients, protein is arguably the most powerful. Protein is a component of every part of your body and contributes to every function. Without adequate protein your muscles and immune system are weakened, your hair is thin, and your nails become brittle. Powerful protein also reduces appetite and has the ability to make you feel full faster and stay fuller longer—making it great for weight control. Here's how to harness the power of protein:

**Maximize the power of protein at every meal.** Research shows the best way to maximize protein synthesis and retain muscle mass is to consume 30 grams of protein at every meal, starting with breakfast. Moreover, a high-protein breakfast helps curbs your appetite not only until lunch, but until you go to bed! Eating more protein than that only adds calories.

**Choose lean when selecting protein.** To keep unhealthy fat and calories in check, remove the skin from poultry and steer yourself toward lean meats (and for good health, include fish on your menu twice each week). Lean cooked meat, poultry, fish or other seafood, on average, provides 7 grams of protein per ounce.

**Don't overlook meatless sources of protein.** Cottage cheese and Greek yogurt are excellent sources of protein with 14 and 11 grams per one-half cup, respectively. A cup of low-fat milk or 1-ounce of reduced-fat cheese clocks in at 8 grams per serving, and both have the bonus of calcium. Plant-based foods are also an excellent source of protein and contain lots of antioxidants, fiber, and absolutely no fat! These include dried cooked peas (20 grams per cup), beans (12 to 15 grams per cup), frozen peas (8 grams per cup), quinoa (8 grams per cup), nuts (6 grams per ounce) and cooked spinach or raw broccoli (6 grams each per cup).

THE BOTTOM LINE: To maintain a strong, lean body and to keep hunger at bay, pay heed to eating adequate protein in equal amounts at each meal. From breakfast smoothies made with Greek yogurt, to protein-rich soups made from beans and the leanest of meats, to sandwiches, easy poultry, beef and seafood entrees, and meatless mains in this book you'll find plenty of generously portioned quick 'n easy protein-rich recipes to power your day!

## SALT SENSE

Every chef knows that salt makes just about everything taste better. (If you need proof, check out the sodium content of any restaurant menu!) In addition to adding a flavor of its own, salt (sodium chloride) enhances sweet flavors and tones down those that are bitter. Unfortunately, when eaten in excess, sodium also has the ability to raise blood pressure, making a love for salt not so sweet. Here's what's important to know about sodium:

**Eating too much sodium is bad for your health.** As we age, our blood pressure tends to rise. This, coupled with the fact that sodium causes fluid retention, which can also increase blood pressure, makes eating too much salt a serious concern. High blood pressure increases your risk for heart disease, kidney disease, strokes, and osteoporosis.

**The current recommended allowance for sodium is 2,300 mg of sodium a day.** This equals about 1 teaspoon of table salt a day and is considerably less than the 3,500 milligrams we now average.

In the US, 77% of the sodium we eat comes from processed and restaurant foods which can have thousands of milligrams of sodium in a single serving. To compare, only 11% of the salt we eat is attributed to salt added during cooking or at the table.

**The effects of sodium can be countered by increasing other foods in your diet.** A diet high in fruits and vegetables combined with nonfat or low-fat dairy, beans and nuts, and a healthy 2,300 milligrams of sodium, has been shown to naturally lower blood pressure. In addition, foods high in potassium, like bananas, tomatoes, citrus fruits, potatoes, beans, spinach, peas, and yogurt have a positive blood pressure-lowering effect.

THE BOTTOM LINE: It pays to be sensible with the amount of salt you eat and the easiest way to do so is to cook! In creating my recipes I use lower sodium cooking techniques, like draining and rinsing canned foods, and in my healthy pantry (see page 23) and in my recipes you'll find a vast array of flavorful lower sodium ingredients. To save BIG on sodium, be sure to check out my chapter on Quick and Easy Basics (page 22) and use the freezer guide on page 100 to make your own pre-prepared "packaged meals".

## Easy Guide to Healthy Eating at a Glance

+ Strive to maintain a healthy weight by balancing the calories you eat and drink with those you "spend" each day.

+ Choose foods with healthy fats, limit foods with saturated fats, and avoid foods with trans fat. Limit the total amount of fat you consume to help keep calories in check.

+ Choose good carbs. Fill your plate with a variety of vegetables, fruits, and whole grains.

+ Eat fewer starchy and refined carbohydrates and more fiber.

+ Limit all sources of added sugar.

+ Eat lean protein in similar amounts at each meal.

+ Moderate your sodium intake and counter its effects by eating more fruits, vegetables, beans, nuts, and nonfat or low-fat dairy.

# Your Easy Guide to Eating with Diabetes

Having diabetes can be difficult, but I believe that eating when you have diabetes can be easy, and even fun! My food-loving stepdaughter Colleen was diagnosed with type 2 diabetes just before she entered college. Like most people with type 2 diabetes, she was given medication to take, but that wasn't the hard part. After being told what she should and, most of all, what she shouldn't eat, the hardest part for her was facing the buffet tables in the dining hall three times a day! Last week Colleen was here for a visit and she, my husband, my two hungry college-age boys, and I had a lovely Sunday dinner—and much of the menu was from this book. There was no talk of what she should or shouldn't eat. Instead, there was simply delicious food for all!

There is no greater reward than to hear that my books make life easier for some and more delicious for others and I am very grateful to those who have taken the time to share with me how my books have helped them control their blood sugar, lose weight, and, in some cases, even reverse type 2 diabetes!

Throughout this book you will find lots more information to help you, or someone you love, take charge of diabetes. From 3-Ingredient Chocolate Caramel Biscuit Donuts (*really*), to Quesadilla Burgers, pizza, pasta, and No-Bake Cherry Topped Cheesecake Cupcakes, the great news is that there isn't a "shouldn't" recipe in this book! Carbs, fat, and sodium have all been curbed and all of the nutrition information you need is listed with every recipe. Eating what you love with diabetes has never been quicker or *easier!*

## WHAT IS DIABETES?

Diabetes is defined and diagnosed when a person has higher-than-normal blood glucose levels. To understand diabetes it is important to know about two things that normally circulate in your blood—glucose and insulin. When a person eats carbohydrates, they break down into glucose, which then enters the bloodstream. Insulin, a hormone produced in your pancreas, acts as a key to allow glucose to move from your blood into your cells where it is used for needed energy. In type 1 diabetes, the pancreas produces little or no insulin. In type 2 diabetes, the body produces insulin, but either not enough and/or or the body's cells become resistant to it. No matter what the cause, too much sugar in your blood can result in both short-term and long-term negative health consequences.

PREVALENCE: An estimated 29 million people in the United States have diabetes, and that number is rising. Among those 20 and older, a new case of diabetes is diagnosed every 19 seconds with type 2 diabetes accounting for 90 to 95% of cases. Another 86 million Americans are estimated to have pre-diabetes. With pre-diabetes, your blood sugar is higher than normal, but not quite high enough to be classified as diabetes—yet. If left unchecked, the majority of people with pre-diabetes go on to develop type 2 diabetes.

PREVENTION: While one unfortunately has no control of the onset of type 1 diabetes, there are many lifestyle factors within one's control that contribute to type 2 diabetes. The good news is that 8 out of 10 cases of type 2 diabetes can actually be prevented or delayed with weight loss (if you are overweight), physical activity, and a healthy diet. If you have pre-diabetes, the combination of modest weight loss (as little as 5 to 7% of your body weight) and exercise (walking 30 minutes a day five days a week) can delay or even prevent the onset of diabetes all together.

## EATING WHAT YOU LOVE WITH DIABETES

Whether you want to reduce your risk for diabetes, push back pre-diabetes, or keep diabetes in check, rest assured you *can* enjoy the foods you love—and the mouthwatering recipes in this book (and all of my books) can help. With less sugar, unhealthy fats, carbs, and sugar, they're the perfect plate (and glass and bowl) partners for helping you meet better health goals. Beyond the recipes, you'll find plenty of healthy eating and shopping tips, and a nutritional analysis for every recipe that makes menu planning quick and easy (see page 16 for more on meal planning).

The truth is there is no such thing as a one-size-fits-all "diabetes diet." Persons with diabetes should follow the same healthy eating guidelines we all should follow (see page 13), while also ensuring carbs are kept in check. Here are some extra tips for managing your blood sugar:

+ Avoid skipping meals.
+ Eat breakfast, lunch, and dinner at regular times.
+ Eat a similar amount of food at each meal.
+ Set a carb budget (page 19) and spend it evenly throughout the day.
+ Eat the protein on your plate before the carbs.

## EAT WHAT YOU LOVE:
# Your Easy Guide to Meal Planning

The beauty of this book is that very little planning, time, or effort is required to make any of the delectable recipes. Moreover, as with my previous *Eat What You Love* cookbooks, all you have to do is get cooking to enjoy the "better-for-you" benefits that have been built into each and every recipe. In fact, the majority of my wonderful "kochbook" fans simply cook for themselves and their families from my books with the confidence that every recipe has been carefully crafted to deliver good health—with great taste!

That said, knowing what you are going to make and eat ahead of time not only eliminates the dreaded "what's for dinner?" question, but it can also save time and money. And as we all know, when hunger strikes, the best of intentions can quickly fly off the plate! This is another reason that meal planning can be key to successfully adopting healthier eating habits or maintaining an eating plan that can help achieve health goals such as weight loss or keeping blood sugar in check. In this section, you will find an array of information on meal planning, ranging from the quickest and easiest way to balance a healthy meal (hint: all you need is a plate) to how to use calorie, carbohydrate, or food exchanges to achieve or maintain your healthiest best. Concluding the section are details concerning how the nutritional information for each recipe was calculated, in addition to useful tidbits on serving sizes, garnishes, and optional ingredients.

## EASY MEAL PLANNING WITH YOUR PLATE

When it comes to meal planning, there is no quicker or easier tool than the plate method. All you need to do to eat better is follow the instructions on how to portion your plate and you're on your way to better health. My plate (aka "Marlene's Plate") differs just slightly from the government's USDA "MyPlate," as I find that a slightly higher portion of protein, less starch, and more non-starchy vegetables are even better for satiety, weight control, and blood sugar management.

To create a healthy meal that is moderate in both carbs and calories, use a 9-inch dinner plate (no larger) as your guide. Fill half the plate with non-starchy vegetables and salad, and then fill one-quarter of the plate with a starchy side or bread. The remaining quarter should be comprised of any lean meat, poultry, or seafood entrée (like the dozens in the book!). If you're

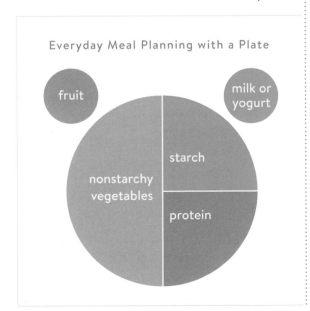

Everyday Meal Planning with a Plate

dining on pasta, pizza, or another dish that combines a starch and a protein (like my Good 'n Easy Turkey Chili), dish up one serving and fill the rest of the plate with salad and more non-starchy veggies. To complete your meal, add one 8-ounce glass of skim or low-fat milk or yogurt and for dessert, add a single serving of whole fruit. (If you need to keep tighter control of your carbs or prefer to finish your meal with one of my sweet treats, then save either your dairy or fruit servings for snacks.)

## MEAL PLANNING WITH CALORIE SMARTS

A guaranteed way to keep weight in check is to balance the number of calories you eat each day with what you expend. I believe that it's nutritionally smart for everyone to know how many calories they require. Yet, according to a recent survey by the International Food Information Council Foundation, only 9% of Americans are able to accurately estimate the number of calories they need. If you don't know how many calories you need, the number of calories in any food or dish has little meaning. For example, when you know that your daily calorie needs (or budget) is 1,800 calories, the fact that the breakfast in front of you has 1,500 calories (or 75% of your entire days budget!), has far more significance.

To plan meals, either per meal, per the day, or per the week using calorie smarts; you first need to know how many calories you require. To assist you in determining your personal calorie needs, you will find a Personal Calorie Calculator at www.marlenekoch.com (click on the

Nutrition Tools tab). Once you know how many calories you need each day, you can set a budget based on your goals (whether you want to lose, maintain, or gain weight). To look and feel your very best, remember to spend your calorie budget wisely on filling nutrient-dense foods such as those high in water, fiber, and protein.

The recipes in this book are calorie bargains. Every one of them has been designed to deliver more taste with fewer calories (hello 120-calorie Dark Chocolate Strawberry Smoothie!) and, even better, the calorie reduction comes not from the sneaky trick of reducing the serving size, but by trimming the excess fat and sugar none of us need. I guarantee you'll be thrilled by how deliciously far this book can make your "budget" stretch!

*A calorie budget for weight maintenance for a moderately active woman is between 1,800 and 2,200 calories per day, and for a man, 2,200 to 2,700 calories. Subtract 500 calories from each day for an estimated weight loss of one pound per week.*

## USING FOOD EXCHANGES

The exchange system—which groups similar foods, such as starches or fruit, into "exchange lists"—is a traditional meal planning tool for weight loss and diabetes. The foods within each list contain a comparable amount of calories, carbohydrates, protein, and fat, and they affect blood sugar similarly. This allows a food in a particular group to be "exchanged" or traded for another. By creating a meal plan that designates the number of servings allowed from each of the various food groups, the exchange system ensures all your nutrient needs are met and that carbs, fat, and calories are well balanced.

As an example, the value of a starch exchange is 80 calories, 15 grams of carbohydrate, and 1 to 2 grams of fat. In the starch group this equates to a single slice of bread, one-half cup of cooked oatmeal, or a quarter of a large bagel. So when you follow a meal plan based on the exchange system, you can "exchange" a slice of toast for a half cup of cooked oatmeal or a quarter of a bagel. The number of servings you are allowed to choose from each group at each meal or snack is based on your individual needs and is best determined by a qualified professional such as a registered dietitian or certified diabetes educator.

Food exchanges are included in every recipe and based on those set forth by the Academy of Nutrition and Dietetics and the American Diabetes Association. The individual food groups include:

+ **Starch** (*breads, pasta, rice, beans, potatoes, and corn*)

+ **Vegetable** (*all non-starchy vegetables*)

+ **Fruit** (*fruits and fruit juices*)

+ **Milk** (*nonfat and low-fat yogurt*)

+ **Meat** (*lean meats, cheese, and eggs*)

✦ **Fat** (*oil, butter, margarine, nuts, and other fats*)

✦ **Carbohydrate** (*sugar and desserts*)

# CARBOHYDRATE COUNTING

A healthy diet for anyone—including people with diabetes—is one that contains wholesome, good-for-you foods, including carbohydrate-rich fruits and vegetables, whole grains, and low-fat dairy. That said, of all the nutrients you eat carbohydrates have the greatest impact on blood glucose, and as such, controlling the amount of carbs you eat can help keep blood sugar in check. Carbohydrate counting, or carb counting, is a meal-planning tool that helps you control the amount of carbohydrates you consume.

To count carbs, you simply add up all of the carbohydrates you're eating, whether it be a meal or a snack, and strive to keep the total within a designated budget. As with calories, the amount of carbohydrates we each require varies. To help you determine a personal carbohydrate budget, you will find a Carbohydrate Calculator at *www. marlenekoch.com* (click on the Nutrition Tools tab). It's also good to keep in mind that while all carbs are counted equally, no matter what their source (be it whole wheat bread or brownies), it's best for your health if you fill your plate with nutrient-rich, not empty, carbs (non-starchy veggies are carb bargains!).

Every recipe in this book has been designed with carb counting in mind. From pancakes and sandwiches to pasta, pizza, and sweet, satisfying desserts, you'll not find a single recipe that doesn't fit easily into any healthy carb budget. And the counting is on me!

> *A carbohydrate budget for diabetes or weight loss averages 45 grams of carbohydrates per meal for most women and 60 grams for most men. In addition, 2 to 3 snacks are usually allowed each day ranging between 15 and 22 grams of carbohydrate.*

## USING CARB CHOICES

At the end of every recipe in the nutrition section you will find "Carbohydrate Choices." I find it easy to work with the total number of carbohydrates when controlling carb intake, but another way to count carbs is to break down the total amount of carbs into to 15-gram carbohydrate servings, or "choices," of carbohydrate. Many common food servings average 15 grams of carbohydrate, including a single slice of bread, a single serving of fruit, and a cup of milk. To calculate carb choices from the total number of carbohydrates in a food, the carb total is simply divided by 15. Thus, a cup of oatmeal with 27 grams of carbohydrate = 2 Carb Choices, and a small apple with 15 grams of carb = 1 Carb Choice. The conversion chart on the next page makes easy work of the math.

A last note on carbohydrate counting: Even with the right information in hand, keeping within a carbohydrate budget can be very challenging, especially when you want to eat the traditional carbohydrate-rich foods you love. The recipes in this book are fantastic for getting the most satisfaction out of and s-t-r-e-t-c-h-i-n-g your carbohydrate budget. If you need more information on carbohydrate counting or a personalized menu plan, a registered dietitian nutritionist or certified diabetes educator can help you.

| Grams of Carbohydrate | Carbohydrate Choices |
|:---:|:---:|
| 0–5 | 0 |
| 6–10 | ½ |
| 11–20 | 1 |
| 21–25 | 1½ |
| 26–35 | 2 |
| 36–40 | 2½ |
| 41–50 | 3 |
| 51–55 | 3½ |
| 56–65 | 4 |

Most women average 3 carbohydrate choices per meal and men 4 carbohydrate choices per meal. Snacks average 1 to 1 ½ carb choices.

## GUIDE TO THE NUTRITION INFORMATION IN THIS BOOK

+ A nutritional analysis complements every recipe so you can easily select recipes based on your personal needs. The information was calculated using ESHA Nutrition Food Processor software in conjunction with manufacturers' food labels.

+ **Food Exchanges** follow the guidelines of the American Diabetes Association. Values have been rounded to the nearest one-half for ease of use. For more information, see page 18.

+ **Carbohydrate Choices** have been calculated in accordance with the American Diabetes Association. For more information, see page 19.

+ **Weight Watchers®** and **SmartPoints®** are registered trademarks of Weight Watchers International, Inc. All comparisons use the most current information available.

## SERVING SIZES

I pride myself in offering realistic portion sizes that satisfy. There is nothing worse than getting excited about the nutrition numbers only to find they relate to a mere bite! I also use common sense when it comes to serving measurements. For example, in an entrée with four chicken breasts and a pan sauce (that serves four), each person gets one chicken breast and an equal portion of sauce. I do not give the exact amount of sauce as the amount is not precisely consistent, and measuring it is messy and tedious. Just divide such items evenly and you're good to go. For casseroles that are messy and/or easier to divide by simply portioning in the pan, like lasagna, I find it more practical to list the serving simply as "one-fourth or one-sixth of the dish." I am also aware that appetites and caloric needs vary. Feel free to adjust the serving sizes to your own or your family's needs and desires. Here are more helpful tidbits:

+ **Garnishes that are meant to be eaten (e.g., sprinkled green onions or powdered sugar) are included in the nutritional analysis.**

+ **Optional ingredients are not included in the nutritional analysis.**

+ **Items that are added "to taste" are not included. If a choice is given, the first item listed was used for the nutritional analysis.**

Last, I've created these recipes so you and yours can eat what you love without worry or guilt. Use the numbers if you need to, but remember to sit back, savor, and enjoy!

# The Quick & Easy Kitchen

As a busy mom and author I have always taken pride in creating not only healthy, but deliciously easy recipes. So it is with great pride that I offer you my quickest easiest collection of recipes yet! In order to create them I found myself having to dig deeper than ever into my culinary tricks. No stone was left unturned when it came to finding the perfect blend of short-cut ingredients, the most streamlined techniques, or the most efficient equipment.

The key to effortlessly whipping up incredible recipes in no time flat is to keep a well-stocked pantry. To help you do that, this section includes a pantry list of the most commonly used ingredients in the book. You will also find further details on many of the ingredients that specifically help me create not good, but great tasting better-for-you recipes along with information on sweeteners, light products, and substitutions you can make when needed or desired. I'm also excited to give you a peek into my "kochbook" kitchen by listing the best tools to have when you need to get dinner (or breakfast or lunch) on the table in a hurry. Having all of them is not necessary to create the recipes in this book, but I guarantee they will make your make your time in the kitchen easier and get you out quicker! Last, by popular demand, I have included two full pages of information and tips on how to eat what you love with ease when cooking just for two. Are you ready to cook?

# EAT WHAT YOU LOVE QUICK & EASY INGREDIENTS

A well-stocked pantry takes the stress out of meal planning and streamlines prep. Below is a list of the basic ingredients I like to keep on hand. With them you can simply "shop the pantry" and whip up meals on a whim with just a few fresh or added ingredients. Stock up by buying items when they are on sale and be sure to replenish when you use them up. You'll find more detailed information about the ingredients marked with an * starting on page 24.

## IN THE CUPBOARD

### Baking Basics
- ☐ Applesauce, unsweetened (4-ounce cups)
- ☐ Baking Powder and Baking Soda
- ☐ *Baking Spray
- ☐ *Cocoa Powder (Dutch-processed and regular)
- ☐ Extracts (almond, coconut, vanilla)
- ☐ *Flour (all-purpose, cake flour, white whole wheat, Wondra instant)
- ☐ Shortening
- ☐ Sugar (brown, granulated, powdered)
- ☐ *Sweeteners (Truvia for Baking, no-calorie granulated sucralose, plus packets)

### Flavorful Condiments
- ☐ Barbeque sauce
- ☐ Hot Sauce (Tabasco, Sriracha, Buffalo Sauce)
- ☐ Ketchup
- ☐ Liquid Smoke
- ☐ *Mayonnaise, light
- ☐ Mustard (Dijon, yellow)
- ☐ Salsa, jarred
- ☐ Soy Sauce, reduced-sodium
- ☐ Worcestershire Sauce

### Great Grains
- ☐ Bread (variety of light and whole wheat)
- ☐ Bread Crumbs (plain, panko)
- ☐ Brown Rice, quick-cooking (I use Uncle Ben's)
- ☐ Cornmeal, yellow
- ☐ Couscous, plain
- ☐ *Oats (quick, old-fashioned)
- ☐ *Pasta (whole grain blend or preferred in a variety of shapes)

### Miscellaneous
- ☐ Bacon Bits (real crumbled)
- ☐ Beans, canned, reduced sodium (black, garbanzo)
- ☐ Broth, reduced sodium (chicken, beef)
- ☐ *Cooking Spray
- ☐ Cornstarch
- ☐ Evaporated Milk, low fat
- ☐ Fish, canned (tuna, salmon)
- ☐ Honey
- ☐ Jam, low-sugar (strawberry, orange marmalade)
- ☐ Maple-flavored syrup (light or sugar-free)
- ☐ Marinara, jarred
- ☐ *Oils (canola, extra-virgin olive oil, sesame)
- ☐ Peanut Butter
- ☐ Pumpkin, 100% pure solid packed
- ☐ Spices, dried (variety)
- ☐ Tomatoes (diced, fire-roasted, paste, pureed)
- ☐ Vinegar (apple cider, balsamic, rice wine)

### Fridge

- ☐ Bacon, center cut
- ☐ *Butter
- ☐ Cheese, reduced-fat (cheddar, mozzarella)
- ☐ Chocolate Fudge Topping (sugar-free or light)
- ☐ *Cottage Cheese
- ☐ *Cream Cheese (light, nonfat)
- ☐ *Eggs, large
- ☐ Garlic, jarred, minced
- ☐ Ginger, jarred, minced
- ☐ Half-and-half, nonfat
- ☐ *Margarine
- ☐ *Milk, low fat (or alternative)
- ☐ Parmesan Cheese
- ☐ Sour Cream, Light
- ☐ *Tortillas (high fiber, corn)
- ☐ *Yogurt, Greek plain (nonfat or low fat)

### Frozen

- ☐ *Beef, ground, 93% lean
- ☐ Chicken Breasts (skinless, boneless breasts)
- ☐ Corn kernels
- ☐ Fruit (blueberries, strawberries)
- ☐ Ice Cream, vanilla (light or no-added sugar)
- ☐ Peas
- ☐ Shrimp
- ☐ Spinach
- ☐ Tilapia (or other white fish)
- ☐ *Whipped Topping, light

## Here's a little more information about some of my favorite ingredients:

### Bread

"Light" breads generally have one-half the calories and carbs (about 45 and 9 per piece, respectively), and more fiber and protein per ounce than traditional breads. Sourdough bread is a good traditional white choice that raises blood sugar slower than regular white.

### Buttermilk

Buttermilk adds great flavor to recipes and lightens and tenderizes baked goods. To make your own, place 1 tablespoon of vinegar or lemon juice in a measuring cup; pour in enough low-fat milk (or soy or almond "milk") to make 1 cup, let it sit for 5 to 10 minutes, and then stir before using. Alternately, mix 1/2 cup nonfat or low-fat plain yogurt with 1/2 cup of milk.

### Cocoa Powder

I prefer Dutch processed cocoa powder. The Dutch process reduces cocoa's natural acidity and bitterness and mellows the cocoa, imparting a richer darker color. Hershey's brand Special Dark cocoa powder can be found next to the regular cocoa powder in most markets. Regular unsweetened cocoa powder can be substituted.

### Cooking and Baking Sprays

The difference between a cooking and baking spray is that a baking spray also contains flour making greasing *and* flouring a pan a snap (especially those hard-to-coat spots). If you don't have baking spray and the recipe calls for it, dust the pan with flour after using cooking spray. Remember, lightly spraying with either one—for two to three seconds— is all it takes.

## Cottage Cheese

Cottage cheese is one of my favorite sneaky ingredients for cutting calories and fat while adding protein to recipes—especially when it's creamed. To cream it, blend with an immersion blender or in a food processor until no curds are left (think thick sour cream). Small curd low-fat or 2% cottage cheese is my preferred choice.

## Cream Cheese

While there are some good store brands, Philadelphia brand cream cheeses are reliable go-to's, especially for the reduced fat and nonfat varieties. Neufchatel cheese can be used in place of light tub-style cream cheese in any of the recipes. Nonfat cream cheese has fewer calories, but does not have the taste or texture to stand on its own, so I don't recommend using it by itself.

## Milk and Non-Dairy Milk Alternatives

I prefer reduced- or low-fat dairy products over nonfat products. One percent milk is richer and has better body than skim and reduced-fat cheeses have more flavor and meltability than nonfat. If you prefer to substitute a non-dairy beverage or milk alternative, such as soy or almond "milk," these can be used in most recipes with little to no adjustment. Light soymilk will yield the closest taste results. To make up for the loss of body in sauces and soups, stir in 1/4 to 1/2 teaspoon of cornstarch. (Note: nondairy "milks" cannot thicken instant pudding mix.)

## Eggs and Egg Substitutes

To maintain the great taste and texture of real whole eggs in most recipes I prefer to use a higher ratio of egg whites to yolks (or use only egg whites when appropriate) instead of liquid egg substitute. This technique gives the best results, particularly in baking. There are some recipes, though, such as smoothies and egg casseroles, where a liquid egg substitute works perfectly well.

$$\text{1 large egg} = \text{2 large egg whites} = \text{1/4 cup liquid egg substitute}$$

## Flours

All-purpose flour is the gold standard. It has the perfect amount of protein for structure and creates a light texture. Cake flour has less protein and as such creates a lighter, more tender crumb. To make your own cake flour, use 2 tablespoons of cornstarch and enough all-purpose flour to fill a one-cup measure for each cup of cake flour needed. For whole grain goodness, white whole wheat flour is my pick. It has lighter taste than whole wheat flour but as much fiber. The most common brand is King Arthur. You can replace white whole wheat flour with all-purpose flour or use a 50/50 blend of white and wheat flour. For gluten-free baking I like Cup4Cup brand gluten-free flour blend.

## Lean Ground Beef, Turkey, and Pork

Lean ground beef, turkey, and pork, make it possible to keep meat on a healthy table. I prefer 93% lean ground beef and turkey and 95% lean ground pork. I find meat with less fat than that is dry and mealy. (Tip: 93% lean beef is actually 39% fat (not 7% as is easy to assume); the "%

lean" you see on the label refers to the percent of fat based on weight, not calories.)

## Whipped Topping

Light whipped topping has a fraction of the calories and fat of heavy cream. Lite Cool Whip, sold in the freezer section, is my topping of choice. Be sure to thaw it before using (tip: place it in the fridge when you bring it home). I prefer light, *not* nonfat whipped topping. The minimal calorie savings are not worth the difference in taste and texture. For garnishing, light real whipped cream sold in aerosol cans is a calorie bargain (just don't overdo it!). It does not work, however, as a substitute for light whipped topping that is to be mixed into a recipe.

## Margarine or Butter

Smart Balance Original Buttery Spread (in the tub, 67% fat). It has 65% less saturated fat of butter, and no trans fats. Soft and tub margarines with less than 65 % fat by weight do not work well in cooking or baking as their water content is too high. I prefer to use butter when a small amount makes a noticeable taste difference. Use it where and when it suits you best.

## Mayonnaise

At 1,440 calories per cup, regular mayonnaise packs a weighty punch. Fortunately, I've found that a 50/50 blend of light mayonnaise and low-fat (or non-fat) plain yogurt makes a great replacement. You may add additional light mayo or light sour cream for the yogurt if you prefer. I do not recommend low-fat mayonnaise; it is not as tasty as the light variety.

## Nonfat Half-and-Half

Nonfat or fat-free half-and-half has the creaminess of regular half-and-half without the fat. Reasonable substitutes are 2% or nonfat evaporated milk or real half-and-half (which of course adds extra fat and calories). Nonfat milk is not a good substitute.

## Oats

Old-fashioned oats, rolled oats, and the quick-cooking variety may be interchanged. Instant oatmeal is not a suitable replacement for any of them.

## Oils

All liquid oils contain the same amount of fat so it's the flavor, or lack of, that determines what I use for a particular recipe. For cooking, canola oil is heart healthy and works well. The distinct flavor of more expensive extra virgin olive oil breaks down under heat, so is best reserved for dressings and drizzling versus cooking. Distinctly flavored sesame oil (made from sesame seeds) can be found in the Asian section of most markets, and has no equal substitute.

## Pasta

From traditional semolina pasta and whole grain "blend" pastas to those higher in fiber and protein, or now, gluten-free, there are plenty of pastas to choose from. For fewer calories and more nutrients, check labels and look for a pasta that provides at least 5 grams of fiber per serving. Whole wheat pasta is one choice, but there are now many others that offer additional fiber and protein without the whole wheat taste. My favorite gluten free pastas are those blended with corn. Pasta shape can be varied with what you have on hand.

## Sweeteners

### No- and Low-Calorie Granulated Sweeteners

*The choice is yours.* Every recipe has been tested with both no-calorie sucralose-based sweeteners and low-calorie natural stevia-based products including Truvia for Baking (made with 25% real sugar). No-calorie granulated sucralose measures 1:1 for sugar, and has the least carbohydrates and calories. Most stevia- or sucralose/sugar blends measure 1:2—as they have twice the sweetening effect. When using one, or another sweetener of choice, follow package directions for sugar equivalent measure

If you prefer to use packets for sweetening beverages, keep in mind all sweetener packets have the sweetness equivalant of 2 teaspoons of sugar.

### Regular Sugar Substitution

When using regular sugar in baked goods, omit ¼ teaspoon of baking soda per cup of sweetener and expect to increase baking time by as much as 7 to 10 minutes for cakes, 5 minutes for muffins, and 3 to 5 minutes for cookies. Check all baked goods according to the recipe's test for doneness. (Tip: The normal substitution for sugar is 1:1 for measured granulated no-calorie sweetener, however you can cut one-fourth of the sugar called for in most baked goods with the only effect being slightly reduced sweetness.)

## Yogurt

I specify plain Greek yogurt in many of the recipes, but you can use regular yogurt if you prefer. Thick and creamy Greek yogurt averages half the carbs and sugar and twice the protein of traditional American-style yogurts. Either non-fat or low-fat (2%) Greek yogurt can be used (I like Fage brand). Tip: To ensure the yogurt is truly "Greek," check the label to make sure the only ingredients are milk and active cultures and it has over 20 grams of protein per cup.

## Tortillas

Tasty reduced-carbohydrate, low calorie, high-fiber tortillas are widely available and found next to the regular tortillas. Mission Carb Balance and La Tortilla Factory Smart and Delicious Wraps are two I like. (Mission Carb Balance flour tortillas

| | Granulated Sucralose (Any Brand) | Stevia/Sugar Baking Blend (Truvia Baking Blend) | Sugar |
|---|---|---|---|
| Equivalent Measure | 1 cup | ½ cup | 1 cup |
| Calories | 96 | 190 | 784 |
| Carbohydrates | 24 | 47 (usable) | 190 |
| Recipe Adjustments | None | May need a few more minutes baking time | See "Granulated sugar" above |

* All sugar substitute packets are equivalent to the sweetness of 2 teaspoons of sugar. Do not measure packets contents. The contents are far more intense than measurable products.

are the perfect swap for pizza crusts and air-fryed creations). When shopping for high fiber tortillas look for wraps that offer over 9 grams of fiber each. 100% corn tortillas are a great gluten free substitute.

## EAT WHAT YOU LOVE QUICK & EASY COOKING ESSENTIALS

Here's a list of my favorite fast-prep tools and equipment to help you make the recipes in this book, and to get you in-and-out of the kitchen—fast!

**Measuring Spoons.** At least 2 sets. Nothing slows you down more than searching for a clean measuring spoon or having to clean a dirty one. I prefer stainless steel. A slim design will ensure you can dip them into spice jars and a flat top is perfect for easy leveling.

**Measuring Cups.** Two sets of dry measuring cups (I prefer stainless steel), and 1, 2, and 4- cup microwave safe glass cups. Glass measuring cups can double duty when mixing liquid ingredients for muffins and pancakes and heating jams and sauces eliminating extra bowls.

**Mixing Spoons, Spatulas and Whisks.** I keep a bucket of these on my counter for grab and mix use at all times. Heat-proof spatulas can go from bowl to skillet.

**Small glass mixing or "mise en place" bowls.** A good set of mixing bowls goes without saying, but I find an extra set of small ones is helpful for for prepping ingredients so they are ready to go when you make the dish (also known as a *mise en place*).

**Sharp Knives.** Not only do they make the job go faster, they are safer. I can't imagine having to cook without my chef's knife (a knife sharpener is a good investment, too).

**A V-Slicer.** You don't need an expensive mandoline to make perfectly sliced tomatoes, cucumbers, or onions in a jiffy. Inexpensive V-slicers work wonders. Be sure to use the food guard at all times. The blades on these gadgets are sharp!

**Kitchen Scale.** For accuracy in making a dish (and to ensure accuracy in the nutritionals) nothing is more valuable than a food scale. Once you have one, I guarantee you'll use it more than you ever thought you would.

**4-1 Box Grater.** While I love (and also recommend) sharp handheld microplane graters, a good old-fashioned standup box grater is oh-so-versatile.

**Garlic and Handheld Citrus Presses.** A garlic press makes quick work of "mincing" garlic while a handheld citrus press makes quick work of that 2-tablespoons of lime juice.

**Tongs.** Several pairs with metal tips. Tongs are like having an extra hand (that can take the heat!) and can be used for flipping meat, chicken, and bacon, to serving pasta and sides.

**Fine Mesh Strainers.** While I love a good in-sink standing colander for pasta, I find myself reaching for these even more often as they come in all sizes (I have several) and double duty as speedy sifters for flour and powdered sugar.

**Non-stick Skillets.** 8, 10, and 12-inch. These are the workhorse pans in my quick-cook kitchen. With little fat required you just cook, wipe out, and go! Be sure you have lids that fit, either from your other pots to be used for steaming, or purchase a large universal lid.

**Non-stick Grill Pan.** Want to grill in a hurry? Just set one of these no-fuss pans on your stovetop and you're set to go—year round. I frequently purchase these as gifts.

**Instant Read Thermometer.** There's no better way to determine the doneness of meat. See page 228 for more information and a cooked-to-perfection temperature chart.

**Slow-Cooker.** Fix-it-and-forget-it defines this popular piece of cooking equipment. From soups to chilis to stews (and even lasagna), a slow cooker can help you cook fast!

**Air Fryer.** Who knew that this piece of equipment would become a quick and easy favorite? Nothing works better for producing crispy crave-worthy foods with less fat, in less time. Add the quick cleanup convenience, and I'm in love.

*Eat What You Love*

# { COOKING FOR TWO }

The very last page of every *Eat What You Love* cookbook includes instructions on how to reach me. It doesn't matter whether you have a question, a comment, or a concern, I *love* hearing from you. One question I often receive is whether I would consider writing a cookbook with recipes just for two. Because I feel passionately that *everyone* should be able to eat the foods they love—and my readers have families of various sizes—I have not considered such (yet). Instead, I offer recipes with a variety of yields, which also make practical sense. For example, beverages and smoothies and on-the-go breakfast sandwiches almost always serve one, casseroles serve six to eight, and desserts range from those that serve one (for last minute cravings) to those that serve twelve or more (for entertaining). For most entrees, as with most cookbooks, the common serving size is a comfortable four.

I can, however, fully appreciate the desire for recipes for two. My husband and I are now empty nesters much of the time, as are many of our friends. None of us need to make large meals nor do we want too much waste or numerous leftovers. That's why I am thrilled to tell you that this book has the most recipes of all my books already scaled for two (or just you). There are over three dozen of them, including scrumptious dishes and desserts in every chapter including: Pumpkin Pie French Toast (page 73), Loaded Philly Cheesesteaks (page 134), Teriyaki Salmon and Spinach Salads (page 156), Buttons, Bowties and Blue Cheese Pasta (page 169), Easiest-Ever Corn on the Cob (page 189), Amazing Smashed Garlic Butter Chicken (page 207), Pan Seared Filet Mignon with Red Wine Sauce (page 235), 4-Ingredient Sweet and Spicy Pork Chops (page 237), Bacon-Wrapped Rosemary Cod (page 255), Steak Style Portobellos (page 265), Chocolate Caramel Cheesecake Cupcakes (page 298), Chicken Spinach Artichoke Dip Sandwiches (page 332), and Chocolate Soufflés for Two (page 344).

I am also happy to share that when creating recipes I often start with making one-half of a recipe and that the ingredients in recipes that serve four can simply be divided in half to serve two, with no loss of quality. On the following page you will find lots of tips for using the recipes in this book to make cooking and eating quicker, easier, healthier, cheaper, and tastier for two.

# Tasty Cooking-for-Two Tips

Having fewer mouths to feed means less worry about who likes what and more opportunities for lovable leftovers! Here are tips for shopping and cooking for two (or even just you):

**Make a plan.** Planning meals for the week reduces impulse buying and allows you to grab bargains with confidence. And don't forget to plan for leftovers. Cook meals that require perishable produce like mushrooms, fresh spinach, and berries soon after shopping, and save those with longer lasting veggies like cabbage, carrots, and peppers for later in the week.

**Shop for two.** It's easy to succumb to "buy more, get more, and family pack" savings, but you don't save when you throw food out. Keep to a list, especially with perishable items. Bulk bins and salad bars can help when you need a small amount, and bouillon paste (like Better than Bouillon) is perfect when less than a can of broth is needed.

**Cook once, eat twice.** "Batch" cooking is built right in when you make a recipe that serves four! I find nothing is better than "banking" a great meal for an effortless lunch or dinner. Most meat and pasta entrees last at least 3 days when covered and stored in the refrigerator and stir-fry leftovers can't be beat. Don't care for leftovers? Re-purpose them. Place a leftover chicken entrée on a salad of fresh veggies, stuff meat into tortillas for tacos, or turn salmon cakes into salmon burgers.

**Make friends with your freezer.** Soups, stews, chilis, and slow cooker dishes are all perfect for freezing as are muffins and cookies (see page 100 for more freezer tips).

**Scale down.** All of the recipes in this book that serve four can be halved to make just two servings. Chicken entrees with crumb coatings and fish dishes lend themselves particularly well to being halved, and half of a recipe of the filling for any of the no-bake pies fills four individual ready-to-eat graham cracker crusts. To divide an egg in half, whisk and measure 2 tablespoons or use 2 tablespoons liquid egg substitute. Remember to also scale down pan and pot sizes one size.

| TO DIVIDE A RECIPE IN HALF: | |
| --- | --- |
| **RECIPE SAYS:** | **USE:** |
| 3/8 tsp. | 1/4 tsp. |
| 1 Tbsp. | 1 1/2 tsp. |
| 1/4 Cup | 2 Tbsp. |
| 1/3 Cup | 2 Tbsp. + 2 tsp. |
| 2/3 Cup | 5 Tbsp. +1 tsp. |
| 3/4 Cup | 1/4 Cup + 2 Tbsp. |

# EAT *what you* LOVE
# QUICK & EASY
# RECIPES

# BEVERAGES & BREAKFAST TREATS

## beverages & breakfast treats

# For the Love of
# { SUGAR }

Cooking—and especially baking—with less sugar can be challenging. That's why I'm happy to say that today there are more no-calorie and reduced-calorie sweetening options than ever, including those that are all-natural. After putting every sweetener on the market to the test, I have found the following to be easy to find (at most grocery stores), economical, safe, and deliciously sweet for cooking and baking.

*Every recipe that calls for a "sweetener" was tested with each of the sweeteners below. Please use the information provided to select a sweetening choice that suits you and yours best.*

**SUCRALOSE:** All recipes were tested and analyzed with no-calorie, sucralose-based sweeteners. "Granulated" sucralose measures 1:1 for sugar. It is the measurable sweetener that delivers the best-tasting results with the least calories and carbohydrates. Generic brands are identical to better-known brands. (Sucralose/sugar blends may also be used; per package directions, use ½ as much. Baking times will increase slightly.)

**ALL-NATURAL STEVIA:** There are many types and brands of all-natural stevia-based sweeteners; they differ, however, in sweetness, taste, calories, and safeness. All recipes were tested with Truvia Baking Blend, made with 25% real sugar. It has 75% fewer calories and carbs when compared to sugar, and no aftertaste (as is common with stevia). The blend is twice as sweet as sugar, so you *simply use half as much as the amount of sweetener called for in any recipe* (see chart below). Baking time may need to be extended slightly. In the recipes in this book, the caloric difference averages less than 10 additional calories per serving versus using a no-calorie sweetener. (50/50 sugar/stevia blends also work well with slightly more calories and carbs.)

**GRANULATED SUGAR.** Even when made with sugar, my reduced-fat recipes are healthier than their higher-calorie counterparts. When using regular sugar in baked goods, omit ¼ teaspoon of baking soda per cup of sweetener and expect to increase baking time by 7 to 10 minutes for cakes, 5 minutes for muffins, and 3 to 5 minutes for cookies. Check all baked goods according to the recipe's test for doneness. (Tip: The normal substitution for sugar is 1:1 for granulated no-calorie sweetener. However, you can cut one-fourth of the sugar called for in most baked goods with the only effect being slightly reduced sweetness.)

| | Granulated Sucralose (Any Brand) | Stevia/Sugar Baking Blend (Truvia Baking Blend) | Sugar |
|---|---|---|---|
| **Equivalent Measure** | 1 cup | ½ cup | 1 cup |
| Calories | 96 | 190 | 784 |
| Carbohydrates | 24 | 47 | 190 |
| Recipe Adjustments | None | May need a few more minutes baking time | See "Granulated Sugar" above |

*\*Note: All sugar substitute packets, which are great for beverages, are equivalent to the sweetness of 2 teaspoons of sugar. Do not measure packets contents. The contents are far more intense than measurable products.*

# Apple-licious Green Smoothie

*DRINKING YOUR GREENS IS A GREAT WAY TO ADD EXTRA NUTRIENTS to your diet, but the appearance, taste, and price of "green" drinks can be anything but appealing. Fortunately, this big 16-ounce smoothie, packed with nutrients, looks and tastes terrific—and it costs just pennies to make! Baby spinach has the mildest flavor and you don't need to remove the stems; with regular spinach or kale, ditch the stems and use only the leaves. For a twist, try orange juice instead of apple.*

MAKES 1 SERVING

½ medium apple, cored

½ small banana

½ cup packed spinach leaves or kale

½ cup light apple juice

1 teaspoon lemon juice

¾ cup crushed ice

1. Place all the ingredients except the ice in a blender. Blend to mix.

2. Add crushed ice and blend on high until the ice is completely incorporated. Pour into a tall glass and serve immediately.

**DARE TO COMPARE:** Save your bucks! A single Starbucks Sweet Greens Smoothie made with apple, lemon juice, and a handful of fresh greens will set you back more than $7.00.

**NUTRITION INFORMATION PER SERVING:** Calories 120 | Carbohydrate 31g (Sugars 25g) | Total Fat 0 g (Sat Fat 0g) | Protein 1g | Fiber 4g | Cholesterol 0mg | Sodium 30mg | Food Exchanges: 2 Fruit, ½ Vegetable | Carbohydrate Choices: 2 | Weight Watcher Smart Point Comparison: 6

# Blueberry Citrus Sparkler

*SO LONG SODA! Muddled blueberries mingle with orange juice and a touch of lemon in this all natural, no-added sugar, sun-kissed sparkling beverage. Swapping a single 12-ounce can of Sunkist orange soda for this sparkler not only saves you more than a recommended day's worth of added sugar, it also adds a fresh boost of vitamin C to your day. See "Marlene Says" for directions on how to make it by the pitcherful.*

MAKES 1 SERVING

¼ cup frozen blueberries, thawed*

½ cup light orange juice

1 teaspoon lemon juice

¼ teaspoon lemon zest

½ cup crushed ice

½ cup club soda

1. Place the blueberries in a medium glass. Using a wooden spoon, press on, or "muddle," the berries, partially smashing them so they release their juice. Stir in orange juice, lemon juice, and zest.

2. Place the ice in a tall glass. Pour juice mix over the ice, top with club soda, and give one quick stir.

**Marlene Says:** *To make a pitcherful, muddle 1 cup blueberries in a one-quart container; stir in 2 cups orange juice, 4 teaspoons lemon juice, and 1 teaspoon lemon zest. Place 2 cups of ice in a 2-quart pitcher. Add juice mix, top with 2 cups of club soda, and stir.*

*Note: Frozen blueberries release more juice. Feel free to garnish with fresh berries.

**NUTRITION INFORMATION PER SERVING:** Calories 45 | Carbohydrate 10g (Sugars 9g) | Total Fat 0g (Sat Fat 0g) | Protein 1g | Fiber 1g | Cholesterol 0mg | Sodium 25mg | Food Exchanges: ¾ Fruit | Carbohydrate Choices: ¾ | Weight Watcher Smart Point Comparison: 2

# Peachy Sweet Tea Freeze

*THIS SLUSHY SIPPER IS A FRUITY TWIST on the refreshing Arnold Palmer—the classic 50/50 mix of iced tea and lemonade. Thanks to black tea and real peaches, a glass provides 130% of the daily value for vitamin C as well as a bucketful of antioxidants. Best of all, it tastes like a million bucks when compared to the sugar-laden, artificially-flavored bottled peach iced teas, and that's pretty peachy!*

MAKES 1 SERVING

1 cup cold unsweetened black tea

½ cup frozen peach slices

1 ½ tablespoons granulated sweetener (or 2 packets)*

¾ cup crushed ice

1. Place the tea, peach slices, and sweetener in a blender. Blend to mix.

2. Add ice and blend on high until the ice is completely incorporated. Serve immediately.

**Marlene Says:** *A strongly flavored black tea will ensure the tea flavor shines through. Steeping a single bag in one cup of boiling water for at least 5 minutes, or steeping 2 tea bags for 3 minutes, does the trick.*

* See page 36 for sweetener options.

**NUTRITION INFORMATION PER SERVING:** Calories 45 | Carbohydrate 10g (Sugars 6g) | Total Fat 0g (Sat Fat 0g) | Protein 1g | Fiber 1 g | Cholesterol 0mg | Sodium 0mg | Food Exchanges: ¾ Fruit | Carbohydrate Choices: ½ | Weight Watcher Smart Point Comparison: 2

# Almond Joy Smoothie

*INSPIRED BY THE FAMOUS CANDY BAR, this quick-fix smoothie boasts the same beloved classic combination of coconut, chocolate, and almond—boosted with the flavor of almond milk. Perfect for those who are lactose or dairy intolerant, almond milk is also lower in calories and carbohydrates than cow's milk. Of course, regular low-fat milk or soymilk can be used in this very nourishing smoothie. When shopping for almond or soymilk, look for those that are unsweetened.*

MAKES 1 SERVING

⅔ cup unsweetened vanilla almond milk

⅓ cup plain nonfat Greek yogurt

½ medium frozen banana

1 tablespoon cocoa powder

4 teaspoons granulated sweetener (or 2 packets)*

½ teaspoon coconut extract

¼ teaspoon almond extract

¾ cup crushed ice

1. Place all the ingredients except the ice in a blender. Blend to mix.

2. Add crushed ice and blend on high until the ice is completely incorporated. Serve immediately.

**DARE TO COMPARE:** Jump for joy! This 14-ounce smoothie delivers 10 grams of protein, 25% of your daily calcium needs, and 17% of your daily vitamin E requirement. Compare that to a 1.76-ounce Almond Joy candy bar that instead packs 220 calories, 12 grams of fat, and 20 grams of added sugar.

* See page 36 for sweetener options.

**NUTRITION INFORMATION PER SERVING:** Calories 120 | Carbohydrate 19g (Sugars 12g) | Total Fat 2g (Sat Fat 0g) | Protein 10g | Fiber 4g | Cholesterol 0mg | Sodium 110mg | Food Exchanges: ¾ Low-fat Milk, ½ Fruit | Carbohydrate Choices: 1 | Weight Watcher Smart Point Comparison: 4

# Dark Chocolate Strawberry Smoothie

*ATTENTION CHOCOLATE LOVERS: This super decadent tasting, chocolate-covered-strawberry-in-a-glass smoothie is perfect any time of day! You just can't go wrong with vitamin, fiber-rich fresh frozen strawberries and antioxidant-rich cocoa powder packed into a slim, satisfying 120 calories. Feeling inspired? Replace the strawberries with frozen raspberries or dark cherries. Any way you make it, this drink does a body good!*

MAKES 1 SERVING

¼ cup warm water

3 tablespoons granulated sweetener (or 4 packets)*

1 tablespoon cocoa powder

½ cup low-fat milk

¾ cup frozen strawberries

½ cup crushed ice

1. Place warm water, sweetener, and cocoa in blender. Blend to mix.

2. Add remaining ingredients and blend until the ice is completely incorporated and the shake is thick and creamy. Serve immediately.

**Marlene Says:** *I prefer to use Dutch-processed cocoa powder, like Hershey's Dark, in this recipe as it dissolves more easily and provides the darkest color and the smoothest flavor, but any unsweetened cocoa powder can be used.*

* See page 36 for sweetener options.

**NUTRITION INFORMATION PER SERVING:** Calories 120 | Carbohydrate 20g (Sugars 14g) | Total Fat 2g (Sat Fat 1g) | Protein 6g | Fiber 4g | Cholesterol 5mg | Sodium 65mg | Food Exchanges: 1 Fruit, ½ Low-fat Milk | Carbohydrate Choices: 1 | Weight Watcher Smart Point Comparison: 5

# Oatmeal Cookie Breakfast Smoothie

*IF YOU LIKE DUNKING OATMEAL COOKIES into a cold glass of milk, you're sure to love this breakfast-in-a-glass smoothie that makes "eating" a healthy breakfast a breeze. It takes less than 5 minutes to make and delivers the whole grain goodness of oats, a half serving of fruit, 70% of your daily requirement of calcium, and a whopping 17 grams of keep-you-full-till-lunchtime protein. Wow! Oats not only thicken this smoothie, but also add the perfect cookie taste and subtle texture. Quick (not instant) oats work best.*

MAKES 1 SERVING

1/3 cup low-fat milk

3 tablespoons quick oats

1 tablespoon raisins

1/2 cup nonfat Greek yogurt

2 tablespoons granulated sweetener (or 3 packets)*

1/2 teaspoon cinnamon

1/2 teaspoon vanilla extract

1 cup crushed ice

1. Place the milk, oats, and raisins in a blender and let soak for 3 to 4 minutes.

2. Add remaining ingredients and blend on high until the ice is completely incorporated and the smoothie is creamy. Serve immediately.

**Marlene Says:** *The powerful combination of oats and milk provides protein and fiber along with 9 key nutrients, including potassium for maintaining healthy blood pressure and B vitamins to help convert your breakfast into energy to fuel your day.*

* See page 36 for sweetener options.

**NUTRITION INFORMATION PER SERVING:** Calories 190 | Carbohydrate 27g (Sugars 15g) | Total Fat 2g (Sat Fat 0.5g) | Protein 17g | Fiber 2g | Cholesterol 5mg | Sodium 40mg | Food Exchanges: 1½ Low-fat Milk, ½ Starch, ½ Fruit | Carbohydrate Choices: 1½ | Weight Watcher Smart Point Comparison: 6

# McMarlene's Mocha Frappe

*IT'S BEEN SAID THAT ONE BELOVED RECIPE can justify the cost of an entire cookbook. Miriam, who lost over 100 pounds cooking from my books, said for her, my Frosty Caramel Frappe (in Eat More of What You Love) was such a recipe. If you prefer the Mocha Frappé at McDonald's, this is that recipe. It has 80% fewer calories, 85% less sugar, and 90% less fat than the original, plus there's no waiting in line. With less than 100 calories per serving, I'm so loving it!*

MAKES 1 SERVING

1½ teaspoons cocoa powder

1 teaspoon instant coffee powder

¼ cup light no sugar-added vanilla ice cream

¼ cup low-fat milk

2 tablespoons granulated sweetener (or 3 packets)*

¾ cup crushed ice

Light whipped cream and sugar-free chocolate syrup (optional)

1. In a blender, place ¼ cup warm water, cocoa, and coffee powder, and blend briefly. Add remaining ingredients except the ice, and blend to mix.

2. Add crushed ice and blend on high until the ice is completely incorporated. Pour into a tall glass and top with light whipped cream and drizzle of chocolate syrup, if desired. (Two tablespoons of canned light whipped cream and 1 teaspoon drizzle adds 25 calories.)

**DARE TO COMPARE:** Of all the drinks on McDonald's McCafé menu, none are less healthy than the frappes. A medium Mocha Frappé, with 540 calories, 22 grams of fat, and 71 grams of sugar, has more fat than an order of medium fries, more sugar than four chocolate chip cookies, and more calories than a double cheeseburger.

* See page 36 for sweetener options.

**NUTRITION INFORMATION PER SERVING:** Calories 85 | Carbohydrate 10g (Sugars 8g) | Total Fat 3g (Sat Fat 1g) | Protein 4g | Fiber 2g | Cholesterol 5mg | Sodium 55mg | Food Exchanges: ½ Low-fat Milk | Carbohydrate Choices: ½ | Weight Watcher Smart Point Comparison: 3

# Thick and Creamy Strawberry Shake

*IF YOU'RE A FAN of my earlier* Eat What You Love *cookbooks, you already know my thick and creamy pudding shakes are a reader favorite. So it caught me by surprise when (strawberry lover me) realized I had yet to create a strawberry milkshake. Well, it was worth the wait! This luscious shake is thick and creamy and full of fresh strawberry flavor, and, as usual, has a mere fraction of the customary sugar, fat, and calories. Top it with squirt of light whipped cream and a cherry for only 25 extra calories and get ready to head to strawberry heaven.*

**MAKES 1 SERVING**

²/₃ cup low-fat milk

1 tablespoon sugar-free instant cheesecake or vanilla pudding mix

½ cup frozen unsweetened strawberries

2 teaspoons granulated sweetener (or 1 packet)*

½ cup light, no-sugar-added vanilla ice cream

¼ cup crushed ice

Light whipped cream (optional garnish)

Cherry (optional garnish)

1. Place the milk and pudding mix in a blender, blend to mix, and let set for 1 minute.

2. Add strawberries, sweetener, ice cream, and ice blending until ice is fully incorporated and shake is thick and creamy. Pour shake into a tall glass and top with whipped cream and cherry, if desired.

**DARE TO COMPARE:** A "Love It" sized strawberry milkshake at Cold Stone Creamery clocks in at 1,130 calories, 66 grams of fat, and a whopping 117 grams of sugar (or more than 2 days' worth!).

**NUTRITION INFORMATION PER SERVING:** Calories 200 | Carbohydrate 30g (Sugars 17) | Total Fat 5g (Sat Fat 2g) | Protein 9g| Fiber 6g| Cholesterol 5mg | Sodium 350 mg | Food Exchanges: ½ Low-fat Milk, ½ Fruit, 1 Carbohydrate | Carbohydrate Choices: 2 | Weight Watcher Smart Point Comparison: 8

# Skinny Pumpkin Spice Latte

*TO BE HONEST, I've never been a big fan of pumpkin spice lattes—that was until I created this recipe! Made with real pumpkin (instead of sugary pumpkin flavoring), this is warm and creamy and has just the right amount of sweet and spice. I fell in love with this coffeehouse favorite in the fall, but I plan to enjoy it all year long. To make your own Pumpkin Pie Spice, see page 313.*

MAKES 1 SERVING

3/4 cup low-fat milk

2 tablespoons canned pumpkin

1/4 teaspoon pumpkin pie spice

4 teaspoons granulated sweetener (or 2 packets)*

1/2 cup freshly brewed coffee

2 tablespoons light whipped cream

1. Whisk together the milk, pumpkin, pumpkin pie spice, and sweetener in a microwave-safe mug. Microwave on high for 1½ minutes or until warmed through (do not boil).

2. Remove mug from the microwave and add the coffee. Top with whipped cream and enjoy!

**DARE TO COMPARE:** Skip the trip! A Starbucks Grande Pumpkin Spice Latte also made with low-fat milk has 390 calories, 13 grams of fat, and 49 grams (12 teaspoons worth) of sugar.

* See page 36 for sweetener options.

**NUTRITION INFORMATION PER SERVING:** Calories 110 | Carbohydrate 14g (Sugars 11g) | Total Fat 3.5g (Sat Fat 1g) | Protein 8g | Fiber 1g | Cholesterol 15mg | Sodium 115mg | Food Exchanges: 3/4 Low-fat Milk, 1/2 Vegetable | Carbohydrate Choices: 1 | Weight Watcher Smart Point Comparison: 4

# Banana-Oat Breakfast Cookies

*COOKIES FOR BREAKFAST? Count me in! With the delicious taste combination of peanut butter and banana, these dump-and-stir nutritious goodies deliver gold-star nutrition thanks to whole grain flour and hearty oats. Plus, you'll find 6 grams of protein and 3 grams of fiber, not to mention a mere 1/2 teaspoon of added sugar, in each. They're super tote-able and freeze well, making it super easy to start (or even finish) your day in a deliciously healthy way.*

**MAKES 12 SERVINGS**

1 cup mashed banana

1/2 cup smooth peanut butter

1 large egg white

1 teaspoon vanilla

1/3 cup granulated sweetener*

2 tablespoons brown sugar

2 cups old-fashioned oats

1/2 cup white whole wheat flour

1 teaspoon baking soda

1/2 teaspoon nutmeg

1. Preheat the oven to 350°F. Line a baking sheet with a baking mat or spray with a nonstick cooking spray.

2. In a large bowl, combine the first 6 ingredients (banana through brown sugar). In a medium bowl, stir together the remaining ingredients and then stir the oat mixture into the banana mixture.

3. Spoon cookie batter onto baking sheet using 3 tablespoons for each cookie. Flatten each with a wet glass or your fingertips to 1/4-inch thick (or 3 inches across). Bake for 10 to 12 minutes, or until cookies are lightly browned.

**Marlene Says:** *Once cooled, store cookies in a baggie or air-tight container and freeze for up to a month. They thaw quickly at room temperature or can be re-heated in the microwave for 30 to 45 seconds.*

\* See page 36 for sweetener options.

**NUTRITION INFORMATION PER SERVING:** (1 cookie) Calories 160 | Carbohydrate 21g (Sugars 6g) | Total Fat 6g (Sat Fat 1.5g) | Protein 6g | Fiber 3g | Cholesterol 0mg | Sodium 115mg | Food Exchanges: 1 Carbohydrate, 1 Fat | Carbohydrate Choices: 1 | Weight Watcher Smart Point Comparison: 4

# 3-Ingredient Chocolate Caramel Biscuit Donuts

*THREE INGREDIENTS AND 20 MINUTES TO WOW! These easy-to-make homemade "donuts," covered with chocolate and drizzled with caramel are a treat. Even the salt in the biscuits, which can be a bit much on its own, adds a positive flavor note when mingled with chocolate and caramel. Perfect for a special Sunday morning, these clock in with 50% fewer calories and a fraction of the sugar found in a donut shop chocolate and caramel-coated donut.*

MAKES 8 SERVINGS

1 package reduced-fat canned biscuits (8 biscuits)

3 tablespoons sugar-free chocolate fudge topping (like Smuckers)

3 teaspoons sugar-free caramel ice cream topping

1. Preheat the oven to 350°F. Place biscuits on an ungreased cookie sheet 2 inches apart. Gently flatten each biscuit into a 3-inch circle. With a 1-inch cookie cutter (or the top of an empty 16-ounce water bottle), cut out the center of each biscuit.* Bake 13 to 15 minutes, or until golden brown.

2. While the "donuts" are still warm, top each with 1½ teaspoons fudge topping and spread until smoothly coated. Let the fudge topping set (4 to 5 minutes) and then drizzle each donut with ½ teaspoon of the caramel topping.

**DARE TO COMPARE:** A Dunkin' Donuts Chocolate Caramel Donut has 370 calories, six times the fat and four times the sugar you'll find in these!

\* You can also bake the donut holes. Each plain hole has 30 calories and 6 grams of carbohydrates. A dusting of powdered sugar (2 teaspoons in total), only adds 2 calories per donut hole.

**NUTRITION INFORMATION PER SERVING: (1 donut)** Calories 160 | Carbohydrate 28g (Sugars 4g) | Total Fat 4g (Sat Fat 1g) | Protein 4g | Fiber 1g | Cholesterol 0mg | Sodium 460mg | Food Exchanges: 2 Carbohydrate | Carbohydrate Choices: 2 | Weight Watcher Smart Point Comparison: 5

# 100-Calorie Blueberry Bran Muffins

*THESE ARE MY EASIEST, SLIMMEST, HEALTHIEST blueberry muffins yet! Made with applesauce and buttermilk, they're low in fat, yet deliciously tender and moist. They also have four grams of healthy fiber, are a good source of iron, and an excellent source of several B vitamins. I prefer to make them with fresh blueberries, but frozen also works. These freeze well.*

MAKES 12 SERVINGS

1½ cups All-Bran cereal

1 cup low-fat buttermilk

½ cup unsweetened applesauce

½ cup granulated sweetener*

1 large egg

1 tablespoon canola oil

1 tablespoon molasses

1 cup all-purpose flour

1 teaspoon baking powder

¾ teaspoon baking soda

1 cup fresh or frozen blueberries

1. Preheat the oven to 375°F. Line 12 muffin cups with paper or foil liners, and lightly spray the liners with nonstick cooking spray. In a medium bowl, whisk together the first seven ingredients (cereal through molasses). Let set for 5 minutes.

2. In a large bowl, combine the flour, baking powder, and baking soda. Make a well in the center, and pour in the bran mixture. Using a large spoon or spatula, stir until the dry ingredients are moistened. Gently stir in the blueberries.

3. Spoon the batter evenly into the prepared muffin tins, filling each cup two-thirds full. Bake for 16 to 18 minutes or until the center springs back when lightly touched. Cool for 5 minutes before removing to a wire rack.

* See page 36 for sweetener options.

**NUTRITION INFORMATION PER SERVING:** (1 muffin) Calories 100 | Carbohydrate 20g (Sugars 6g) | Total Fat 2g (Sat Fat 0g) | Protein 4g | Fiber 4g | Cholesterol 20mg | Sodium 210mg | Food Exchanges: 1 Starch | Carbohydrate Choices: 1 | Weight Watcher Smart Point Comparison: 3

# Cinnamon Swirl Quick Cake

*IN THIS RECIPE MORE THAN HALF THE INGREDIENTS do double (or triple) duty, allowing a handful of ingredients to create a tender coffee cake both swirled and topped with sweetness and spice (lining up all the ingredients makes quick work of each component). To create the swirl, give the batter no more than one or two quick turns of your wrist after adding the swirl mixture. Don't worry about the batter at the bottom of the bowl; it will pick up the swirl effect when you spoon it into the pan.*

MAKES 9 SERVINGS

10 tablespoons granulated sweetener*, divided

2 tablespoons cinnamon, divided

2 tablespoons brown sugar, divided

2 cups reduced-fat baking mix, (like Bisquick Heart Smart), divided

2 tablespoons melted margarine or butter, divided

3/4 cup low-fat buttermilk

1 large egg, lightly beaten

1/2 teaspoon vanilla

1. Preheat the oven to 350°F. Lightly coat an 8 x 8-inch baking dish with nonstick cooking spray.

2. For the swirl: In a small bowl, combine 1/4 cup sweetener, 1 1/2 tablespoons cinnamon, and 1 tablespoon brown sugar. Set aside. For the topping: In a small bowl, combine 2 tablespoons sweetener, 1/2 tablespoon cinnamon, 1 tablespoon brown sugar, 1/4 cup baking mix, and 1 tablespoon margarine, and set aside.

3. For the cake: In a large bowl, measure remaining 1 3/4 cups baking mix, 1 tablespoon margarine, and 1/4 cup sweetener, along with the buttermilk, egg, and vanilla. Stir just until all ingredients are combined.

4. Sprinkle the swirl mixture over the cake batter. With a wooden spoon or spatula, give one big turn to swirl in about half of the mixture, and then spoon the batter into the baking dish. Sprinkle the cake with the reserved topping and bake for 14 to 16 minutes, or until the center springs back when lightly touched.

* See page 36 for sweetener options.

**NUTRITION INFORMATION PER SERVING:** (1 piece) Calories 150 | Carbohydrate 23g (Sugars 4g) | Total Fat 4g (Sat Fat 1g) | Protein 4g | Fiber 0g | Cholesterol 20g | Sodium 320 mg | Food Exchanges: 1 Starch, 1/2 Carbohydrate | Carbohydrate Choices: 1 1/2 | Weight Watcher Smart Point Comparison: 5

# Small Batch Bakery-Style Blackberry Muffins

*SHHH. . . . WITH THEIR BIG, CRACKLY, SUGARED TOPS, your family will swear you bought these at the bakery. The secret is that it takes only 10-minutes to whip up the batter and the even bigger secret is that there's only 1 teaspoon of added sugar per muffin! I really love that this recipe quickly makes a "small batch" of 6 muffins (making it perfect for when a dozen is more than you need). Frozen blackberries make it easy to bring-home-the-bakery any day of the year.*

MAKES 6 SERVINGS

½ cup plain nonfat Greek yogurt (or light sour cream)

1 large egg

2 tablespoons melted margarine or butter

1½ teaspoons orange zest

1 cup all-purpose flour

⅓ cup granulated sweetener*

2 tablespoons granulated sugar, divided

1½ teaspoons baking powder

¼ teaspoon baking soda

¾ cup fresh or frozen blackberries

1. Preheat the oven to 375°F. Line 6 muffin cups with paper or foil liners, and lightly spray liners with nonstick cooking spray.

2. In a small bowl, whisk together the first 4 ingredients (yogurt through zest). In a medium bowl, combine flour, sweetener, 1½ tablespoons sugar, baking powder, and baking soda. Add the blackberries, toss them in the flour, and then add the yogurt mixture. Stir just until the dry ingredients are moistened.

3. Spoon batter into prepared muffin cups, filling each ⅔ full. Dust muffins with remaining ½ tablespoon of sugar. Bake for 18 to 20 minutes, or until the tops are brown and the center springs back when lightly touched. Cool for 5 minutes before removing to a wire rack.

> **DARE TO COMPARE:** A piece of Starbucks Reduced-Fat Berry Coffee Cake has 350 calories, 10 grams fat, 31 grams of sugar, and 480 milligrams of sodium.

* See page 36 for sweetener options.

**NUTRITION INFORMATION PER SERVING:** (1 muffin) Calories 150 | Carbohydrate 23 (Sugars 7g) | Total Fat 4g (Sat Fat 1g ) | Protein 5g | Fiber 1g | Cholesterol 35mg | Sodium 220mg | Food Exchanges: 1½ Starch, ½ Fat | Carbohydrate Choices: 1½ | Weight Watcher Smart Point Comparison: 4

# BREAKFAST & BRUNCH

# breakfast & brunch

# For the Love of
## { BUTTER }

I *really* love butter. Let's face it, whether slathered on toast, layered into a decadent sauce, or blended into cookie batter, there's nothing like butter for adding great flavor to any food it touches. Unfortunately, there's no getting around the fact that butter is dense in calories and fat, particularly saturated fat, which increases the risk of cardiovascular disease when eaten in excess. But this doesn't mean you need to eliminate it from your diet.

The trick to incorporating butter into healthy recipes—and enjoying it as part of a healthy diet—is to use it where it shines most brightly, such as adding a small amount to a sauce right before serving, or reserving it for baking when nothing but butter will do. (If you love spreading butter on toast or warm bread, try light butter, which has all of the flavor with half the fat and calories!). To keep butter use in healthy check here are:

## THREE "BETTER-FOR-YOU-THAN-BUTTER" SWAPS:

**OILS:** Canola and olive oil are both high in monounsaturated fats, which can help improve blood cholesterol when used instead of butter. However, at 120 calories a tablespoon, both have even more calories than butter (at 100 calories per tablespoon), so also use them sparingly when looking to curb calories. For baking, oil works well for quick-method breads and muffins and cakes, but not in recipes that require "creaming" the fat with the sugar to build volume. Margarine is a better replacement in such recipes.

**MARGARINE:** Margarine often gets a bad rap, but today there are many with healthy fat profiles. I like Smart Balance Original. It has 90 calories per tablespoon, no trans fats, and one-third the saturated fat of butter. Note: Tub margarine is fine for spreading, but for baking, a spread with at least 65% fat is required. (Light butter, unfortunately, is less than 65% fat.)

**FRUIT AND VEGETABLE PURÉES:** There's no slimmer, healthier butter substitute for baking than puréed fruit and veggies when moistness is the main priority. While a cup of oil has a staggering 1,927 calories and a cup a butter has 1,627, a cup of unsweetened applesauce and pumpkin purée average a mere 100! Plus, fruit and veggies come with the added bonus of extra vitamins, minerals, fiber, and antioxidants. For best results, replace no more than half of the usual fat with a fruit or vegetable purée.

# Make-Ahead Bacon Cheddar Grab 'n Go Burritos

*I STARTED MAKING THESE SO MY SON, Stephen, could eat a nutritious breakfast on his way to work, but it wasn't long before everyone in the family was grabbing them. Healthier than the breakfast burritos at the drive-through and less expensive than those in the supermarket freezer case, these can easily be varied to suit your taste. I make a batch or two on Sunday night and we grab and go all week!*

MAKES 4 SERVINGS

4 large eggs

½ cup liquid egg substitute (or 4 large egg whites)

Salt and pepper, to taste

4 (8-inch) reduced-carb high-fiber flour tortillas

4 tablespoons salsa

4 tablespoons shredded reduced-fat cheddar cheese

4 teaspoons real bacon bits

1. In a medium bowl, whisk together the eggs and egg substitute. Spray a medium-size nonstick skillet with cooking spray and place over medium heat. Add eggs to pan and cook, stirring gently, for 2 to 3 minutes or until just set. Season with a sprinkle of salt and pepper to taste.

2. Soften 2 of the tortillas by heating them in the microwave on high for 30 seconds. Spread the middle of each tortilla with 1 tablespoon salsa, and top with about ⅓ cup eggs. Top eggs with 1 tablespoon of cheese and 1 teaspoon bacon bits. Fold bottom of tortilla over filling, then the sides, and roll up burrito-style. Repeat with remaining 2 tortillas and ingredients.

3. Wrap each burrito in plastic wrap and place in the refrigerator. When ready to eat, re-heat each (you do not need to unwrap them) for 30 to 45 seconds on high. Burritos will keep for up to 5 days in the refrigerator and may be frozen.

**DARE TO COMPARE:** These clock in with half of the fat, carbs, and sodium—and a third fewer calories—than a similar-sized McDonald's Sausage Burrito. They also have 25% more protein and 6 times the fiber! A mixture of whole eggs and liquid egg substitute or egg whites ensures good health *and* great taste!

**NUTRITION INFORMATION PER SERVING: (1 burrito)** Calories 195 | Carbohydrate 17g (Sugars 2g) | Total Fat 9g (Sat Fat 3.5g) | Protein 16g | Fiber 6g | Cholesterol 185mg | Sodium 260mg | Food Exchanges: 2 Lean Meat, 1 Starch, ½ Fat | Carbohydrate Choices: 1 | Weight Watcher Smart Point Comparison: 3

# One-Bowl Double Chocolate Pancakes

*Inspired by the sugary, carb-heavy Chocolate Chocolate Chip Pancakes at IHOP, these are a chocolate pancake lover's dream come true. In less than 15 minutes, with the quick and healthy help of a baking mix, you can whip up these amazing guilt-free cakes. They are chocolaty enough to eat alone, but I included a drizzle of chocolate syrup for good measure!*

MAKES 4 SERVINGS

1¼ cups reduced-fat baking mix (like Bisquick Heart Smart)

⅓ cup granulated sweetener*

1 large egg, beaten

1 cup low-fat milk

¼ cup cocoa powder (Dutch-processed preferred)

1 teaspoon vanilla

4 tablespoons light chocolate syrup

1. In a medium bowl, combine all the ingredients and stir just until smooth.

2. Spray a nonstick skillet or griddle with cooking spray, and place over medium heat. Pour ¼ cup of batter per pancake into the skillet and spread into a 4-inch circle. Cook the pancakes for 3 to 4 minutes, or until bubbles form on top and underside is firm. Flip the pancakes and cook until done, about 2 to 3 more minutes. Stack on a plate and cover to keep warm. Top each serving with a drizzle of chocolate syrup.

> **DARE TO COMPARE:** An order of Chocolate Chocolate Chip Pancakes at IHOP clocks in at 710 calories, 23 grams of fat, 113 grams of carbs, and 2070 milligrams of sodium. Feel free to add a squirt of light whipped cream. A two-tablespoon squirt adds only 15 calories!

\* See page 36 for sweetener options.

**NUTRITION INFORMATION PER SERVING:** (2 pancakes) Calories 240 | Carbohydrate 39g (Sugars 11g) | Total Fat 5g (Sat Fat 2g) | Protein 9g | Fiber 3g | Cholesterol 55mg | Sodium 500mg | Food Exchanges: 2½ Starch, ¼ Low-fat Milk, ½ Fat | Carbohydrate Choices: 2 | Weight Watcher Smart Point Comparison: 7

# 5-Minute Breakfast Pizzas

*ONE OF THE FIRST THINGS I REMEMBER COOKING on my own were pizzas made with English Muffins. I'd top an English muffin half with spoonful of jarred pizza sauce and a sprinkling of cheese, and voilà, pizza! Here I have brought forth that wonderful simplicity (with a few new tricks) and applied it to breakfast. With their great taste and fabulous nutritional profile, I don't know what took me so long. . . .*

MAKES 1 SERVING

1 light multi-grain
English muffin (like Thomas')

1 small tomato, sliced

1 large egg

¼ cup liquid egg substitute
(or 2 egg whites)

1 green onion, minced

Salt and pepper, to taste

2 tablespoons shredded
reduced-fat mozzarella cheese

1. Turn on the broiler. Lightly toast both sides of the English muffin halves and transfer to a baking sheet. Top each muffin with tomato slices.

2. In a small bowl, whisk together the egg, egg substitute, green onion, and salt and pepper if desired. Spray a small nonstick skillet with cooking spray and place over medium heat. Add eggs to pan and cook, stirring gently, for 2 to 3 minutes or until curds form and eggs are just set. Divide eggs evenly between muffin halves.

3. Top each "pizza" with 1 tablespoon mozzarella, and broil 1 minute, or until cheese melts and is lightly browned. Serve immediately.

**Marlene Says:** *In less than 10 minutes you get two pizzas for less than 250 calories! And, with 22 grams of protein and 9 grams of fiber, this nutritious breakfast is sure to satisfy. Just add a piece of fruit to complete your breakfast.*

**NUTRITION INFORMATION PER SERVING:** (2 "pizzas") Calories 240 | Carbohydrate 29g (Sugars 2g) | Total Fat 7g (Sat Fat 2.5g) | Protein 22g | Fiber 9g | Cholesterol 185mg | Sodium 450mg | Food Exchanges: 2½ Lean Meat, 1½ Starch, ½ Vegetable | Carbohydrate Choices: 1½ | Weight Watcher Smart Point Comparison: 4

# Cinnamon Chai Oatmeal

*FROM COFFEE SHOPS TO FAST FOOD RESTAURANTS and even smoothie shops, oatmeal is popping up on menus everywhere. And why not? Oatmeal is quick and easy to prepare, inexpensive, and low in calories—that is, until the tasty stir-ins and toppings are added! This flavor-infused bowl delivers the goodness of oats and the healthfulness of tea, along with the toasty warmth of cinnamon and spice and the sweetness of honey—all for 200 calories. No standing in line required.*

**MAKES 1 SERVING**

1¼ cups water

2 chai tea bags

½ cup old-fashioned oats

1½ tablespoons granulated sweetener (or 2 packets)*

Pinch of salt

1 teaspoon honey

1 tablespoon nonfat half-and-half

1. In a small saucepan, bring the water to a boil, remove from heat, and steep the tea bags for 3 minutes. Remove tea bags and bring tea to a boil. Add the oats, sweetener, and salt. Reduce heat and simmer for 5 minutes.

2. Remove from heat and let sit 1 to 2 minutes to thicken. Transfer to a bowl, drizzle with honey and half-and-half, and serve.

**DARE TO COMPARE:** It's amazing how quickly those tasty toppings add up. A tablespoon of brown sugar adds 50 calories (and 13 grams of sugar), a sprinkling of dried fruit adds another 100 calories (and 20 more grams of sugar), and 2 tablespoons of a nut topping adds 100 calories. Use all three and you add extra 250 calories, 9 grams of fat, and 33 grams of sugar to your bowl.

* See page 36 for sweetener options.

**NUTRITION INFORMATION PER SERVING:** Calories 200 | Carbohydrate 35g (Sugars 6g) | Total Fat 3g (Sat Fat .5g) | Protein 7g | Fiber 4g | Cholesterol 0mg | Sodium 150mg | Food Exchanges: 2 Carbohydrate | Carbohydrate Choices: 2 | Weight Watcher Smart Point Comparison: 6

# Easy Breakfast "Soufflé" for Two

*THIS RECIPE IS SO EASY, YET SO IMPRESSIVE. It looks like a tricky, time-consuming soufflé, but it's as fast and simple to make as a standard puffy omelet. Here are the secrets: 1) Adding sugar to the egg whites not only sweetens the "soufflé," it makes the egg whites more stable. 2) The addition of milk and flour to the yolks help create and maintain the large egg "puff." 3) A touch of lemon zest, a dusting of powdered sugar, and a drizzle of jam lend this egg puff soufflé style!*

MAKES 2 SERVINGS

3 large eggs, separated

1 tablespoon granulated sugar

⅓ cup low-fat milk

2 tablespoons all-purpose flour

1 teaspoon lemon zest

1 teaspoon butter

2 tablespoons low-sugar strawberry jam

2 teaspoons powdered sugar

1. Preheat the oven to 375°F. In a medium bowl, with an electric mixer, beat the egg whites on high until foamy. Add sugar and continue to beat until soft peaks form. Set aside.

2. In a separate bowl, place the egg yolks, milk, flour, and lemon zest. Beat on medium speed until smooth. With a rubber spatula, mix ⅓ of the whipped egg whites into yolk mixture. Gently fold in remaining whites. Melt butter in an 8- or 9-inch nonstick ovenproof skillet over medium heat. Pour egg mixture into the pan and cook for 1 minute, or until the edges and bottom are lightly browned.

3. Transfer to oven and bake for 10 to 12 minutes, or until soufflé is puffed and golden. While soufflé is baking, in a small microwave-safe bowl, heat the jam and 1 tablespoon water on high for 20 seconds, and stir. Remove soufflé from oven, dust with powdered sugar, and drizzle with jam.

**Marlene Says:** *For the fluffiest soufflé, use room-temperature eggs or run warm water over cold eggs to warm the whites before separating them. Be sure there is no trace of egg yolk in the whites before beating them, and do not overbeat. Egg whites should lift, then quickly curl down, when whites are lifted with beaters.*

**NUTRITION INFORMATION PER SERVING:** Calories 215 | Carbohydrate 19g (Sugars 14g) | Total Fat 9g (Sat Fat 3.5g) | Protein 12g | Fiber 0g | Cholesterol 285mg | Sodium 135mg | Food Exchanges: 1½ Lean Meat, 1 Carbohydrate, 1 Fat | Carbohydrate Choices: 1 | Weight Watcher Smart Point Comparison: 6

# Cheesy Spinach Breakfast Bake

*RISE AND SHINE! This protein-packed, Italian-inspired three-cheese bake is perfect for entertaining. The egg mixture can be made ahead of time, and while individually portioned ramekins create a beautiful presentation, you can also bake it in an 8 x 8-inch or other similar sized baking dish. Any way you make it, this easy cheesy bake will have guests saying "Bellisimo!" Sliced tomatoes pair with it perfectly.*

MAKES 6 SERVINGS

6 packed cups fresh baby or regular spinach

1 15-ounce container low-fat ricotta cheese

1/2 cup shredded low-fat mozzarella cheese

2 large eggs

1/4 cup liquid egg substitute (or 2 egg whites)

2 tablespoons dried minced onion

1 teaspoon garlic salt

3/4 teaspoon dried oregano

1/2 teaspoon black pepper

3 tablespoons grated Parmesan cheese

1. Preheat the oven to 350°F. Lightly coat six 6-ounce ramekins with cooking spray, and set aside.

2. Spray a large nonstick skillet with cooking spray and place over medium heat. Add the spinach plus 1 tablespoon water to the pan and sauté for 4 minutes, or until the spinach is slightly wilted and the water has cooked off. Let cool slightly. In a large bowl combine the next 8 ingredients (ricotta through black pepper), and stir in the spinach.

3. Transfer the mixture to the ramekins (a generous 1/2 cup each), and bake for 20 minutes. Sprinkle each ramekin with 1/2 tablespoon Parmesan and bake for 5 additional minutes, or until Parmesan is lightly browned.

**Marlene Says:** *When using an 8 x 8-inch baking dish, bake for 25 minutes before adding the cheese. If you cut it into 4 portions, a hearty quarter of the bake has 210 calories, 9 grams each of carbs and fat, and 26 grams of protein. Leftovers keep and re-heat well!*

**NUTRITION INFORMATION PER SERVING:** (1 ramekin) Calories 140 | Carbohydrate 6g (Sugars 3g) | Total Fat 6g (Sat Fat 3.5g) | Protein 17g | Fiber 1g | Cholesterol 80mg | Sodium 440mg | Food Exchanges: 2 1/2 Lean Meat, 1/2 Carbohydrate | Carbohydrate Choices: 1/2 | Weight Watcher Smart Point Comparison: 3

# Shortcut Spanish Potato Frittata

*WHEN I VISITED MY SON STEPHEN WHEN HE WAS STUDYING IN SPAIN, I was introduced to the popular egg and potato dish called "tortilla." It seemed that everyone in Spain ate slices of this delicious and versatile dish for breakfast, lunch, and dinner (both warm and at room temperature). Here, instead of cooking the potatoes in oil, as they do in Spain, I lighten it by using chicken stock. To hasten the prep, I turn to refrigerated pre-cut potatoes. The result is a minimal effort dish that's just as wildly versatile and satisfying.*

MAKES 6 SERVINGS

20 ounces packaged potato cubes with onions (I use Simply Potatoes)

1 cup reduced-sodium chicken broth

1 medium onion, chopped (1½ cups)

6 large eggs

1 cup liquid egg substitute

½ teaspoon salt

¼ teaspoon black pepper

1 tablespoon olive oil

1. Position the oven rack about 6 inches below the broiler. Place potatoes and broth in a large microwave-safe bowl, cover with plastic wrap, and microwave on high for 10 minutes. While the potatoes are cooking, spray a large nonstick ovenproof skillet with cooking spray and place over medium heat. Add onion and cook for 5 minutes, or until translucent and starting to brown.

2. In a large bowl, whisk together the eggs, egg substitute, salt, and pepper. With a slotted spoon, transfer the cooked potatoes into the egg mixture (leaving the broth behind).

3. Reduce the heat to medium low, add the olive oil to the skillet, and swirl to coat. Pour in the egg mixture, and when it starts to bubble on the edges, cover the skillet. Turn on the broiler. Continue to cook for 10 to 12 minutes on the top of the stove, or until just set around the edges. Uncover skillet and place under the broiler for 2 to 4 minutes, watching carefully, until eggs have set and tortilla has browned. Remove from oven and let cool for 10 minutes before serving.

**Marlene Says:** *If you prefer to use fresh potatoes from your pantry, use 1 pound (about 3 medium) unpeeled, red-skinned potatoes, cut into ½-inch cubes.*

**NUTRITION INFORMATION PER SERVING:** Calories 185 | Carbohydrate 17g (Sugars (3g) | Total Fat 7g (Sat Fat 2g) | Protein 13g | Fiber 2g | Cholesterol 180 mg | Sodium 320 mg | Food Exchanges: 2 Lean Meat, 1 Starch, ½ Fat | Carbohydrate Choices: 1 | Weight Watcher Smart Point Comparison: 3

# 30-Minute Skillet Strata

*I LOVE THE CONVENIENCE OF FUSS-FREE EGG DISHES, especially "stratas" with their make-ahead layers of egg and bread. The problem is that I don't always plan far enough in advance to soak the bread. The beauty of this strata is that no soaking is required. As in any strata, the middle is soft and pillowy, but with this one you also get a crunchy top! Italian sausage, mushrooms, and mozzarella cheese add savory goodness to this sensational speedy strata.*

MAKES 5 SERVINGS

4 slices sourdough bread

4 large eggs

4 large egg whites (or ½ cup liquid egg substitute)

1½ cups low-fat milk

½ cup shredded low-fat mozzarella cheese

¼ teaspoon black pepper

1/8 teaspoon salt

1 (4-ounce) link Italian turkey sausage, casing removed

2 cups sliced mushrooms

¾ cup chopped onion

¼ teaspoon Italian seasoning

1. Preheat the oven to 425°F. Toast the bread slices and cut into 1-inch squares.

2. In a medium bowl, whisk together the next 6 ingredients (eggs through salt); set aside.

3. Place a medium ovenproof skillet over medium-high heat. Crumble sausage into the skillet along with the mushrooms and onion, and sauté for 7 to 8 minutes, or until onions are translucent and the mushrooms have softened and their liquid has cooked off.

4. Add the bread squares to the pan and stir to distribute evenly (piling some of the mushroom mixture on top of some of the bread). Remove pan from heat and pour in egg mixture. Sprinkle with Italian seasoning and bake for 12 to 15 minutes, or until eggs have set.

**NUTRITION INFORMATION PER SERVING:** Calories 210 | Carbohydrate 17g (Sugars 6g) | Total Fat 7g (Sat Fat 3.5g) | Protein 21g | Fiber 0g | Cholesterol 165mg | Sodium 390mg | Food Exchanges: 2 Lean Meat, ½ Low-Fat Milk, 1 Starch, ½ Vegetable | Carbohydrate Choices: 1 | Weight Watcher Smart Point Comparison: 4

# 5-Ingredient Banana-Oat Pancakes for One

*I'M ALWAYS ON THE LOOKOUT FOR EASY, TASTY, HEALTHY RECIPES. As such, a banana-oat pancake recipe featured widely on the Internet boasting "mere minutes" and only "three healthy ingredients" caught my attention. Although the recipe did not work, it did help me create these fast, filling, five-ingredient Banana Oat Pancakes that indeed, take mere minutes to make. They also happen to be gluten and dairy-free.*

MAKES 1 SERVING

1 medium banana, mashed (about ½ cup)

1 tablespoon creamy peanut butter

¼ cup liquid egg substitute, or 1 large egg

¼ cup quick oats

¼ teaspoon baking powder

1. In a small bowl, whisk together the banana and peanut butter. Whisk in egg substitute or egg. Stir in the oats and baking powder; let sit for 5 minutes.

2. Spray a large nonstick skillet with cooking spray and place over medium heat. Pour ¼ cup of batter per pancake into the skillet. Cook the pancakes for 3 to 4 minutes on the first side. (Note: turn carefully; the pancakes will be soft.) Flip and cook for 2 to 3 minutes, or until puffed and set.

**Marlene Says:** *Quick oats are cut smaller than rolled oats and as such work great to thicken (as in my Oatmeal Cookie Smoothie) and absorb liquid (as found in this recipe). To make your own quick oats from rolled (or Old Fashioned Quaker) oats, simply process them in a food processor until smaller in size.*

**NUTRITION INFORMATION PER SERVING:** (3 pancakes) Calories 305 | Carbohydrate 43g (Sugars 22g) | Total Fat 10g (Sat Fat 2g) | Protein 14g | Fiber 6g | Cholesterol 0mg | Sodium 300mg | Food Exchanges: 1 Starch, 1 Fruit, 1½ Lean Meat, 1 Fat | Carbohydrate Choices: 3 | Weight Watcher Smart Point Comparison: 5

# Light and Fluffy Blueberry Cornmeal Pancakes

*IF CORNMEAL PANCAKES CONJURE UP the thought of heavy Southern-style "hoecakes," let me assure you that these are anything but. A generous dose of buttermilk and equal measures of cornmeal and all-purpose flour ensure these easy, home-style golden cakes are fluffy, not flat. Top them with sugar-free or reduced-sugar maple syrup, Fast-Fix Berry Sauce (page 318), or a smear of jam and additional fresh berries.*

MAKES 4 SERVINGS

½ cup cornmeal

½ cup all-purpose flour

3 tablespoons granulated sweetener*

2 teaspoons baking powder

¼ teaspoon baking soda

1¼ cups low-fat buttermilk

2 large eggs, beaten

½ cup fresh or frozen blueberries

1. In a medium bowl, combine the first 5 ingredients (cornmeal through baking soda). Make a well in the mixture, add buttermilk and eggs, and stir until just combined. Gently stir in the blueberries.

2. Spray a nonstick skillet or griddle with cooking spray and place over medium heat. Pour ¼ cup of batter per pancake into the skillet. Cook pancakes for 3 to 4 minutes on the first side or until golden on the bottom. Flip pancakes and cook until done, about 2 to 3 minutes. Stack on a plate and cover to keep warm, or serve immediately.

* See page 36 for sweetener options.

**NUTRITION INFORMATION PER SERVING:** (2 pancakes) Calories 195 | Carbohydrate 30g (Sugars 6g) | Total Fat 3.5g (Sat Fat 1.5g) | Protein 9g | Fiber 2g | Cholesterol 95mg | Sodium 450mg | Food Exchanges: 2 Starch, ½ Lean Meat | Carbohydrate Choices: 2 | Weight Watcher Smart Point Comparison: 4

# Pumpkin Pie French Toast

*WITH THIS RECIPE YOU CAN ENJOY THE DELICIOUS AROMA and mouthwatering flavor of pumpkin pie all year round—for breakfast no less! Worried about carbs or calories? With just 170 calories—and less carbs and fewer calories than in a typical bowl of cereal and milk—this scrumptious breakfast fits easily into almost any diet. (Psst . . . it's even more tempting when topped with your favorite maple-flavored syrup.)*

MAKES 2 SERVINGS

1 large egg, beaten

1/4 cup low-fat milk

1/4 cup canned pumpkin

1 tablespoon brown sugar

Scant 1/2 teaspoon pumpkin pie spice

1/4 teaspoon vanilla

4 slices French bread

1. In a medium bowl, whisk together all of the ingredients except the bread.

2. Spray a nonstick skillet or griddle with cooking spray, and place over medium heat. Gently dip French bread in the egg mixture, making sure to let excess liquid drip off and place in the hot skillet. Cook for about 2 minutes, or until golden brown on the bottom. Flip and cook another 2 minutes. Repeat if needed with remaining slices of bread.

**Marlene Says:** *If you're looking for another use for canned pumpkin, you can't go wrong with the Skinny Pumpkin Spice Latte on page 48 or 2-Minute Microwave Pumpkin Pie on page 273 (and they're both great for breakfast!). You'll find a recipe to make your own pumpkin pie spice on page 313.*

**NUTRITION INFORMATION PER SERVING: (2 slices)** Calories 170 | Carbohydrate 32g (Sugars 5g) | Total Fat 4g (Sat Fat 1g) | Protein 11g | Fiber 1g | Cholesterol 90mg | Sodium 260mg | Food Exchanges: 2 Starch, 1/2 Lean Meat | Carbohydrate Choices: 2 | Weight Watcher Smart Point Comparison: 5

# Fast-Fix Strawberry "Cheesecake" Waffle Sandwiches

*FROZEN WAFFLES HAVE NEVER TASTED BETTER!* *The trick is to put away the toaster; instead, take two waffles, stuff them with a "cheesecake" filling and jam, and then place the sandwich in a buttered skillet. Five minutes later you have a buttery, crispy, creamy, sweet waffle sensation. Once toasted, these can be wrapped, frozen, and reheated for a delicious breakfast-on-the-go.*

MAKES 4 SERVINGS

⅓ cup light tub-style cream cheese

⅓ cup nonfat plain Greek yogurt

1½ tablespoons powdered sugar

8 low-fat multi-grain frozen waffles

2 teaspoons butter

8 teaspoons reduced-sugar strawberry jam

1. In a small bowl, mix cream cheese, yogurt, and sugar until smooth.

2. Spread 2 tablespoons of the mixture on one waffle, and 1 teaspoon of jam on another waffle. Sandwich the waffles together, and repeat to make 4 waffle sandwiches.

3. Place a large skillet over medium-low heat. Add 1 teaspoon butter and swirl skillet to coat pan. Place two waffle sandwiches in the skillet. Cook for about 3 minutes on one side, flip, and cook for 2 minutes, or until golden and filling is warm. Repeat with remaining butter and sandwiches, and serve while warm.

**Marlene Says:** *Pop frozen sandwiches into a toaster or toaster oven to reheat.*

**NUTRITION INFORMATION PER SERVING:** (1 Sandwich) Calories 220 | Carbohydrate 33g (Sugars 9g) | Total Fat 7g (Sat Fat 3.5g) | Protein 9g | Fiber 3g | Cholesterol 15mg | Sodium 470mg | Food Exchanges: 2 Starch, 1 Fat | Carbohydrate Choices: 2 | Weight Watcher Smart Point Comparison: 8

# Breakfast Cheesecake!

*YEP, I'M SAYING YOU CAN HAVE CREAMY, SWEET, STREUSEL-TOPPED CHEESECAKE—for breakfast! Made with cottage cheese and Greek yogurt, this decadent tasting yet slim cheesecake delivers a big dose of protein and a hefty helping of calcium to kick-start your day. No bottom crust hastens the preparation, but do plan on making it several hours before you want to serve it. Once made, it will keep for days. Fresh fruit makes a great topping!*

MAKES 8 SERVINGS

1/2 cup rolled oats

1 tablespoon melted butter or margarine

1 tablespoon brown sugar

1/2 teaspoon cinnamon

1 1/3 cups low-fat cottage cheese

2/3 cup light tub-style cream cheese

2/3 cup granulated sweetener*

1 tablespoon cornstarch

1 large egg, beaten

2 large egg whites

2/3 cup plain nonfat Greek yogurt

3/4 teaspoon orange zest

1. Preheat the oven to 325°F. Lightly spray a 9-inch pie plate with cooking spray, and set aside. In a small bowl, combine the first 4 ingredients (oats through cinnamon), and set aside.

2. Using a food processor, blend the cottage cheese until very smooth and creamy. Add cream cheese, sweetener, and cornstarch, and pulse to blend. Scrape batter into a medium bowl and whisk in the egg, and then the egg whites. Stir in the yogurt and orange zest, pour into the pie plate, and smooth the top.

3. Place the cheesecake in the oven and bake for 25 minutes. Open the oven and sprinkle the oat topping onto the cheesecake (concealing any cracking), and bake for 10 more minutes, or until the sides are firm and the center is still slightly soft. Cool to room temperature and refrigerate at least 3 hours before serving.

* See page 36 for sweetener options.

**NUTRITION INFORMATION PER SERVING:** (1/8 of cheesecake) Calories 150 | Carbohydrate 10g (Sugars 5g) | Total Fat 6g (Sat Fat 3.5g) | Protein 11g | Fiber 1g | Cholesterol 35mg | Sodium 300mg | Food Exchanges: 1 Lean Meat, 1/2 Carbohydrate, 1/2 Fat | Carbohydrate Choices: 1 | Weight Watcher Smart Point Comparison: 4

# Quick & Easy Waffled Hash Browns

*I BET YOU NEVER KNEW THAT A WAFFLE IRON would forever change the way you make hash browns. If you love crispy hash browns, but not the time or the mess they take to make, this amazingly easy recipe is a must-try. Shred a potato (or purchase shredded potato), season it, plop it into the waffle iron, and in eight short minutes you have perfectly cooked crispy hash browns. (Tip: My husband often makes a half a recipe of these easy waffled 'browns.)*

MAKES 2 SERVINGS

1 medium (12 ounce) russet potato

2 green onions, minced

½ teaspoon reduced-sodium seasoned salt

¼ teaspoon black pepper

1. Preheat a waffle iron (to medium heat, if you have the option). Peel (if desired), and shred the potato. Place the shredded potato in a colander and press on it with a paper towel to remove moisture. You should have about 2 cups of dried potato.

2. In a medium mixing bowl, transfer the potatoes and add the remaining ingredients, tossing gently to combine. Evenly spread 1 cup of the seasoned potatoes onto the iron. Close the lid (it will not close completely) and cook for 2 minutes. Gently press down on the lid to further compress the potatoes and cook for 6 more minutes, or until the potatoes are crisp and brown (peeking is okay).

3. Repeat with remaining potatoes.

**Marlene Says:** *Russet potatoes work best for these as they are the driest potato. Simply Potatoes brand fresh shredded potatoes (usually found by the eggs), also works well. Just season and cook!*

**NUTRITION INFORMATION PER SERVING: (1 waffled hash brown)** Calories 125 | Carbohydrate 29g (Sugars 2g) | Total Fat 0g (Sat Fat 0g) | Protein 3g | Fiber 2g | Cholesterol 0mg | Sodium 280mg | Food Exchanges: 2 Starch | Carbohydrate Choices: 2 | Weight Watcher Smart Point Comparison: 4

# APPETIZERS & SNACKS

## *appetizers & snacks*

# Avocado Ranch Dip

*CREAMY AVOCADO TAKES THE FAMILIAR TASTE OF TRUSTY OL' RANCH to new heights in this crowd-pleasing dip. It's luscious with baked tortilla chips (like the Tasty Homemade Taco Chips on page 86), fresh veggies, or even as a topper for burgers (see the Southwest Beef & Bean Burger on page 135). Or, thin it out with a touch of water and you have the perfect dressing for a crispy green or taco salad. It keeps up to two days stored in the refrigerator.*

MAKES 12 SERVINGS

1 large avocado

2 teaspoons lime juice

1/2 cup light sour cream

1/3 cup light mayonnaise

1/4 cup plain nonfat Greek yogurt

2 tablespoons green onion, finely minced

3/8 teaspoon garlic powder

3/8 teaspoon black pepper

1/4 teaspoon salt

1. In a medium bowl, roughly mash the avocado with lime juice.

2. Add the remaining ingredients and stir until almost smooth (leaving a bit of avocado texture is optional, but nice).

**DARE TO COMPARE:** The Avocado Ranch Dressing at Taco Bell rings in at 80 calories and 8 grams of fat—for *a single* tablespoon!

**NUTRITION INFORMATION PER SERVING:** (2 tablespoons) Calories 50 | Carbohydrate 3g (Sugars 2g) | Total Fat 4g (Sat Fat 1g) | Protein 1g | Fiber 1g | Cholesterol 5mg | Sodium 90mg | Food Exchanges: 1 Fat | Carbohydrate Choices: 0 | Weight Watcher Smart Point Comparison: 2

# 5-Minute Shrimp Salsa

*ON A RECENT TRIP TO MY LOCAL MARKET* *the seafood department was sampling freshly made shrimp salsa. It was so good I found myself circling back several times just to grab another "taste." Upon inquiring how it was made, I was given these tasty tips: For the best quality, use fresh or thawed shrimp (not canned). To stretch your shrimp dollar and add some crunch, add another ½ cup of salsa and ½ cup chopped seeded cucumber. Knowing how quickly this disappears, I usually double the recipe!*

MAKES 1½ CUPS

1 cup prepared salsa

2 tablespoons chopped cilantro

2 tablespoons finely chopped green onion

1 tablespoon ketchup

Juice of ½ lime

½ cup cooked bay shrimp

1. In a medium bowl, combine all ingredients except shrimp, stirring well to combine.

2. Gently fold in the shrimp, and top with additional cilantro, if desired.

**Marlene Says:** *As the names large, jumbo, medium, or small shrimp often vary by packager or fish markets, it is best to buy shrimp based on the number per pound. For this recipe, extra small or a 100 to 125 shrimp-per-pound count works well.*

**NUTRITION INFORMATION PER SERVING:** (3 tablespoons) Calories 25 | Carbohydrate 3g (Sugars 1g) | Total Fat 0g (Sat Fat 0g) | Protein 2g | Fiber 0g | Cholesterol 20mg | Sodium 160mg | Food Exchanges: Free Food | Carbohydrate Choices: 0 | Weight Watcher Smart Point Comparison: 0

# Easy Pea-sy Bacon Topped Crostini

*THE FIRST TIME I TASTED CREAMY PURÉED PEAS ON A CRISPY CROSTINI was at an upscale restaurant in Philadelphia. I was amazed at what an incredible appetizer the peas made—especially when paired with bacon! I was doubly delighted when I discovered the recipe was made with ordinary frozen peas. I recently made these again and was reminded of how quickly this simple, inexpensive, yet elegant appetizer comes together. Don't be shy to try these easy colorful topped crostini. My guests loved them and I'm sure yours will, too!*

**MAKES 18 SERVINGS**

½ 8-ounce baguette

1 cup frozen peas, thawed

3 tablespoons light tub-style cream cheese

¼ teaspoon black pepper

⅛ teaspoon salt

3 tablespoons real bacon bits

2 tablespoons finely grated Parmesan

1. Preheat the oven to 400°F. At a slight angle, slice 18 half-inch bread slices from the baguette. Arrange slices on a baking sheet and spray tops with cooking spray. Bake for about 10 minutes, or until tops just begin to brown.

2. Place the peas, cream cheese, pepper, and salt in a blender and purée until smooth. Spread each crostini with about 2 teaspoons of pea mixture, sprinkle with bacon bits, and lightly dust with grated Parmesan. Bake for about 8 minutes, or until the cheese starts to melt. Serve immediately.

**Marlene Says:** *To quickly thaw frozen peas, simply place in a colander and pour very hot water over them. They will thaw almost immediately.*

**NUTRITION INFORMATION PER SERVING:** (2 crostinis) Calories 70 | Carbohydrate 9g (Sugars 1g) | Total Fat 2g (Sat Fat 0g) | Protein 4g | Fiber 1g | Cholesterol 10mg | Sodium 215mg | Food Exchanges: ½ Starch, ½ Fat | Carbohydrate Choices: ½ | Weight Watcher Smart Point Comparison: 1

# Chicken Nacho Dip

*LIKE THE BELOVED BUFFALO CHICKEN DIP in* Eat What You Love Everyday, *this hungry-man dip was a HUGE hit with my college-aged boys—and all their friends! Warm, creamy, cheesy, and loaded with flavor, no one will ever suspect this is "light" in any way. The inclusion of chicken and beans gives heft and packs plenty of protein and fiber into this hearty dip. Serve it with baby carrots, strips of red or green pepper, or the universal favorite of guys everywhere—tortilla chips and beer.*

**MAKES 10 SERVINGS**

¾ cup canned black beans, rinsed and drained

½ cup light tub-style cream cheese

½ cup light sour cream

1½ teaspoons Mexican hot sauce

1 cup shredded cooked chicken breast

¼ cup diced red bell pepper

3 tablespoons chopped green onion, divided

¼ cup shredded reduced-fat cheddar cheese

½ cup diced tomato

2 tablespoons chopped cilantro

1. Spread the black beans evenly in the bottom of a 1½ quart microwave-safe dish.

2. In a small bowl, combine the cream cheese, sour cream, and hot sauce, stirring well with a whisk or fork to combine. Add chicken, red pepper, and 2 tablespoons green onion, and stir gently to combine.

3. Spread the chicken mixture on top of beans and top with cheddar cheese. Microwave on high for 2 minutes. Garnish with tomato, cilantro, and remaining green onions.

**DARE TO COMPARE:** The traditional recipe for this dip had over 200 calories and 15 grams of fat per serving. With less than half the calories and 80% less fat, this enlightened dip is light done right!

**NUTRITION INFORMATION PER SERVING:** (¼ cup) Calories 75 | Carbohydrate 5g (Sugars 1g) | Total Fat 3g (Sat Fat 1g) | Protein 7g | Fiber 2g | Cholesterol 10mg | Sodium 150mg | Food Exchanges: 1 Lean Meat, ½ Fat | Carbohydrate Choices: 0 | Weight Watcher Smart Point Comparison: 1

# Tasty Homemade Taco Chips

*THESE ARE THE BEST BAKED TORTILLA CHIPS I HAVE EVER MADE. With some chips, "half-the-fat" means half of the flavor, but that is absolutely not the case here. Made with fresh lime juice and taco seasonings, these addictive chips are amped with flavor. Add Avocado Ranch Dip (page 80), Chicken Nacho Dip (page 85), or 5-Minute Shrimp Salsa (page 82) and let the party begin!*

MAKES 6 SERVINGS

Juice of 1 lime

4 teaspoons canola oil

1 teaspoon chili powder

1 teaspoon ground cumin

½ teaspoon garlic salt

12 thin corn tortillas
( I use Mission brand)

1. Preheat the oven to 350°F. Set out 2 baking sheets.

2. In a small bowl combine first 5 ingredients (lime juice through garlic salt).

3. Place the tortillas on a cutting board and lightly brush one side of each tortilla with the seasoning mix. Stack 6 tortillas, and using a sharp knife, cut each stack into 6 wedges. Repeat, and transfer pieces to the baking sheets. Bake for 15 minutes or until crisp. The tortillas will crisp up more upon cooling.

**Marlene Says:** *To air-fry these chips, preheat air-fryer to 360. Place ½ of the chips (or as many fit with some overlapping) into the air fryer and air-fry for 6 to 8 minutes, shaking once or twice, until lightly browned. Chips will crisp up further upon cooling.*

**NUTRITION INFORMATION PER SERVING:** (12 Chips) Calories 100 | Carbohydrate 17g (Sugars 0g) | Total Fat 4g (Sat Fat 0g) | Protein 2g | Fiber 2g | Cholesterol 0mg | Sodium 160 mg | Food Exchanges: 1 Carbohydrate, ½ Fat | Carbohydrate Choices: 1 | Weight Watcher Smart Point Comparison: 3

# Oven-Baked Buffalo Cauliflower Bites

**AIR FRY!**
SEE PAGE **325**

*THE GREAT TASTE OF BUFFALO WINGS COUPLED WITH THE CRUNCH OF FRIED CHICKEN send these better-for-you veggie bites flying off the serving plate. These were trickier than I expected to perfect, but I finally found the secret. A quick blanching of the cauliflower ensures it's perfectly tender in the same time it takes to cook up a crispy coating. These have plenty of flavor on their own, but you can add even more by serving them with blue cheese or Homemade Ranch Dressing (see page 308)!*

MAKE 6 SERVINGS

6 cups cauliflower florets (about 1 medium cauliflower)

1/4 cup nonfat Greek yogurt

2 tablespoons buffalo wing sauce (I prefer Frank's)

2 tablespoons light mayonnaise

2/3 cup Panko breadcrumbs

1/3 cup dry breadcrumbs

2 teaspoons canola oil

1/4 teaspoon garlic salt with parsley

1. Preheat the oven to 400°F. Line a baking sheet with foil and set aside. In a large skillet, place the cauliflower and 1 cup of water over medium high heat. Cover and steam for 5 minutes, then transfer the cauliflower onto a paper-towel-lined plate.

2. In a small bowl, whisk together the yogurt, wing sauce, mayonnaise, and 2 tablespoons water. In a separate shallow bowl or pie plate, combine remaining ingredients and toss to mix.

3. Hold a cauliflower floret by the stem, dip and twist the floret top through the Buffalo sauce, lightly wipe off excess sauce, roll into the crumbs, and place on the baking sheet. Repeat with remaining florets. Spray lightly with cooking spray.

4. Bake for 20 minutes, or until golden brown. If you would like your Buffalo Bites crispier or more browned, place them under the broiler for 1 minute before serving.

> **DARE TO COMPARE:** According to My Fitness Pal, an order of five Buffalo Chicken Bites from Applebee's has 360 calories and comes loaded with 24 grams of fat and over 1,000 milligrams of sodium!

**NUTRITION INFORMATION PER SERVING:** (3/4 cup or about 5 bites) Calories 90 | Carbohydrate 15g (Sugars 3g) | Total Fat 3g (Sat Fat 1g) | Protein 4g | Fiber 4g | Cholesterol 0mg | Sodium 280mg | Food Exchanges: 1/2 Starch, 1/2 Vegetable | Carbohydrate Choices: 1 | Weight Watcher Smart Point Comparison: 2

# "Fried" Macaroni & Cheese

SEE PAGE 325

*CREAMY, CHEESY, CRISPY, FRIED MACARONI AND CHEESE—could anything sound more decadent (or less healthy)? After many tries, I've come up with an amazingly creamy, cheesy, crispy "fried" restaurant-style mac and cheese appetizer with a mere fraction of the usual calories, sodium, and fat! Because the macaroni and cheese must chill before being cut and coated with breadcrumbs, I suggest you make it a day ahead of time. When you are ready to serve, simply cut it as directed, dust with breadcrumbs, bake (or freeze, then bake) and wait to hear the yums!*

**MAKES 8 SERVINGS**

1 recipe Easy Cheese Sauce (page 317)

1 (4-ounce) can fire-roasted diced green chiles

4 cups cooked elbow macaroni

½ cup shredded reduced-fat mozzarella cheese

1 cup Panko breadcrumbs

½ cup dry breadcrumbs

1 teaspoon garlic salt

¼ teaspoon black pepper

Everyday Marinara Sauce (page 315) (optional)

1. Make the cheese sauce according to recipe. Stir in green chiles and macaroni. Let cool slightly, and stir in the mozzarella. Spoon into an 8 x 8-inch square casserole dish or baking pan. Flatten, pressing firmly, and refrigerate at least 6 hours or overnight.

2. Preheat the oven to 400°F. With a sharp wet knife, cut the cold mac and cheese two times in each direction to form 9 squares. Cut squares in half diagonally to form 18 triangles. (Dip the knife in warm water between cuts as needed.)

3. In a medium bowl combine remaining ingredients (Panko through black pepper).

4. Place each triangle into the crumbs and carefully roll to coat, using a light spray of cooking spray on top if needed. (If desired, triangles can be frozen at this point.) Bake for 15 minutes (add 5 minutes if frozen), or until golden brown. Serve with marinara sauce, if desired.

> **DARE TO COMPARE:** At The Cheesecake Factory, an appetizer of four Fried Macaroni & Cheese balls has a staggering 1,530 calories, 1,760 milligrams of sodium, and over a day's worth of saturated fat.

**NUTRITION INFORMATION PER SERVING:** (Each) Calories 100 | Carbohydrate 14g (Sugars 2g) | Total Fat 3g (Sat Fat 1g) | Protein 6g | Fiber 1g | Cholesterol 5mg | Sodium 170mg | Food Exchanges: 1 Lean Meat, 1 Carbohydrate | Carbohydrate Choices: 1 | Weight Watcher Smart Point Comparison: 3

# Kettle-Style Kale Chips

*I HAVE TO ADMIT; I HAVE NEVER BEEN A BIG FAN OF KALE CHIPS—that is, until now. This recipe changed my mind (and that of my picky husband), and it might change yours, too. Unlike burnt or overly earthy tasting kale chips (of which I have had many), these sweet and salty "chips" have a taste reminiscent of kettle corn. The irresistible flavor keeps us munching, but knowing just how incredibly wholesome they are, it sure doesn't hurt!*

MAKES 3 SERVINGS

4 cups fresh curly kale, tightly packed

1½ teaspoons olive oil

1 teaspoon granulated sugar

⅛ teaspoon salt

1. Preheat the oven to 300°F. Line a baking sheet with parchment or a silicone baking sheet and set aside.

2. Wash the kale and dry it well using a salad spinner or paper towels. Tear out the center stalk, and tear the leaves into large "chips." Transfer kale to a large bowl, drizzle with olive oil, and sprinkle with the sugar and salt, tossing the leaves with your hands or tongs to distribute the ingredients.

3. Transfer kale to the baking pan and bake until leaves are dry and crispy, about 17 to 20 minutes, stirring after 10 minutes. Do not over-bake.

**Marlene Says:** *A single serving of these chips serves up several days' worth of vitamins A and K, a healthy helping of vitamin C, and 45 (yes, 45) disease-fighting flavonoids—all for less than ⅓ the calories and 85% less fat than a cup of potato chips.*

**NUTRITION INFORMATION PER SERVING:** (1 cup) Calories 40 | Carbohydrate 5g (Sugars 2g) | Total Fat 1.5g (Sat Fat 0g) | Protein 1g | Fiber 1g | Cholesterol 0mg | Sodium 110mg | Food Exchanges: 1 Vegetable | Carbohydrate Choices: 0 | Weight Watcher Smart Point Comparison: 1

# Chicken Caesar Lettuce Wraps

*I DEBATED FOR A LONG TIME ABOUT WHETHER TO ADD THIS RECIPE AND WHAT TO CALL IT. What required no debate was how much I love these wraps. Whenever I have leftover cooked chicken and romaine lettuce in the house, this is my go-to-recipe. In a flash, I have a low-cal, low-carb, high protein, handheld taco-shaped sensation, with the taste of chicken Caesar salad! Two wraps are a satisfying snack; double the recipe to create a light lunch for one. Want some more crunch? Top your wraps with a few croutons!*

**MAKES 1 SERVING**

2 medium Romaine lettuce leaves

4 teaspoons low-fat Creamy Caesar Dressing (page 310 or store-bought)

½ cup shredded cooked chicken breast

2 teaspoons grated Parmesan cheese

Fresh ground black pepper, to taste

1. Hold a romaine leaf in your hand and spoon 2 teaspoons dressing along ¾ of the length of the inner rib of the lettuce leaf. Sprinkle ¼ cup chicken on top of dressing.

2. Sprinkle chicken with 1 teaspoon Parmesan and black pepper to taste. Hold like a taco to eat. Repeat with remaining ingredients.

**NUTRITION INFORMATION PER SERVING: (2 wraps)** Calories 140 | Carbohydrate 2g (Sugars 0g) | Total Fat 7 g (Sat Fat 1.5g) | Protein 15g | Fiber 1g | Cholesterol 45mg | Sodium 320mg | Food Exchanges: 2 Lean Meat, 1 Fat | Carbohydrate Choices: 0 | Weight Watcher Smart Point Comparison: 2

# Muffin Tin Crab Cakes

*THESE ARE THE EASIEST CRAB CAKES EVER! No shaping and no frying—all you do is scoop 'em and bake 'em; the oven does the rest. The resulting "cakes" are crispy on the outside and moist and tender on the inside. I find these bake up nicely and release most easily from foil liners. (Plus, the liners make them easy to serve.) No foil liners? Simply spray your muffin tins well with cooking spray.*

**MAKES 6 SERVINGS**

8 ounces lump crabmeat

1/2 cup dry breadcrumbs

1/4 cup diced red pepper

1/4 cup diced green onion

2 tablespoons light mayonnaise

1 large egg white

1/4 teaspoon Old Bay seasoning

1. Preheat the oven to 425°F. Place foil cupcake liners in 6-cup muffin tin and spray the liners with cooking spray.

2. Combine all ingredients in a large bowl and gently mix together with a large spoon, taking care to keep as many large crab pieces as possible. Evenly divide the mixture among the muffin cups and bake for 20 to 25 minutes, or until crispy and cooked through. (If you do not use foil liners, while still warm, run a sharp knife around the crab cakes to ease removal.) Serve immediately.

**Marlene Says:** *Foil cupcake liners can be found with the other cupcake liners in most supermarkets. The foil liners come packaged with paper inserts. Use the foil alone and reserve the paper, if desired, for another use another time.*

**NUTRITION INFORMATION PER SERVING:** (1 crab cake) Calories 90 | Carbohydrate 7g (Sugars 1g) | Total Fat 2g (Sat Fat 0g) | Protein 9g | Fiber 0g | Cholesterol 50mg | Sodium 200mg | Food Exchanges: 1 Lean meat, 1/2 Starch | Carbohydrate Choices: 1/2 | Weight Watcher Smart Point Comparison: 1

# Pepperoni Pizzadilla

*THESE ARE REALLY GOOD, JUST ASK MY SON STEPHEN. When he came home from college for a holiday break, I asked him if he wanted to try one of my new recipes. One bite, and he was hooked. Crispy, saucy, cheesy and packed with pepperoni and pizza flavor, what's not to love? I love that they are also an excellent source of protein and fiber. It's a good health, great taste match made in heaven!*

MAKES 1 SERVING

1 (8-inch) reduced-carb high-fiber flour tortilla

1 tablespoon pizza sauce

5 slices turkey pepperoni

2 tablespoons shredded part-skim mozzarella cheese

1 pinch dried oregano

1 teaspoon grated Parmesan cheese

1. Spray a large nonstick skillet with cooking spray and place over medium heat. Place the tortilla in the skillet and spoon pizza sauce on one half of the tortilla. Top the sauce with pepperoni, and sprinkle the cheese and oregano over the pepperoni.

2. Fold tortilla in half over the filling and spray the top lightly with cooking spray. Sprinkle with Parmesan. Cook for 2 minutes, or until the cheese begins to melt and the bottom of the tortilla is golden brown. Carefully flip the quesadilla and cook for another 1 to 2 minutes until the cheese is fully melted and the Parmesan is golden brown.

**Marlene Says:** *Serve with additional pizza sauce on the side, if desired. To make 2 servings, use 2 tortillas. Lay one tortilla in the hot pan, top with double the sauce, pepperoni, cheese, and oregano. Top with the second tortilla, spray with cooking spray, and top with Parmesan. Cook according to directions, cut in half, and serve.*

**NUTRITION INFORMATION PER SERVING:** Calories 145 | Carbohydrate 18g (Sugars 2g) | Total Fat 4g (Sat Fat 2g) | Protein 12g | Fiber 6g | Cholesterol 20mg | Sodium 570mg | Food Exchanges: 1 Starch, 1 Lean Meat | Carbohydrate Choices: 1 | Weight Watcher Smart Point Comparison: 4

# Anytime Meatballs with Grape Jelly BBQ Sauce

*"GRAPE JELLY MEATBALLS" WERE POPULARIZED IN THE 1950S when hostesses across the country discovered that everyone loved the very easy, very tasty combination of grape jelly and cocktail sauce served over meatballs. Of course no one paid attention to sugar or fat back then. For this "do-over" I reduced the sugar content with an all-natural, low-sugar grape jelly, trimmed the fat with my tender turkey meatballs, and then kicked up the flavor! Still simple, and even more delicious, these clock in with 60% less sugar and 50% less fat than the traditional recipe. Cheers!*

**MAKES 16 SERVINGS**

1 recipe Anytime Turkey Meatballs (page 221)

²/₃ cup chili sauce

½ cup low-sugar grape jelly

2 tablespoons Worcestershire sauce

1 teaspoon liquid smoke

¼ teaspoon black pepper

1. Make and bake the meatballs as directed making 32-1-inch balls. This step can be done ahead of time.

2. Preheat the oven to 400°F. Place the remaining ingredients in a medium microwave-safe bowl (or in a small pot), and microwave on high (or over medium heat on stove) for 2 minutes, or until jelly melts.

3. Place the meatballs in a baking dish, pour sauce over meatballs, and bake for 15 to 20 minutes, or until hot and coated with sauce.

**Marlene Says:** *To make Crockpot Cocktail Meatballs, place 1 recipe of Any Day Turkey Meatballs in a slow cooker. In a quart (4-cup) measuring cup or bowl, combine 1 cup of chili sauce, ³/₄ cup grape jelly, 3 tablespoons Worcestershire sauce, 1½ teaspoons liquid smoke, and scant ½ teaspoon black pepper. Pour over meatballs and cook on low for 2 hours or until hot.*

**NUTRITION INFORMATION PER SERVING:** (2 meatballs coated with sauce) Calories 90 | Carbohydrate 9g (Sugars g) | Total Fat 3g (Sat Fat 1g) | Protein 7g | Fiber 0g | Cholesterol 25mg | Sodium 240mg | Food Exchanges: 1 Lean Meat, ½ Carbohydrate | Carbohydrate Choices: ½ | Weight Watcher Smart Point Comparison: 2

# Mini Corn Dog "Pup-Cakes"

*These are pure fun—for kids of all ages! To be honest, I left a plateful of these mini-corndog-like muffins on the counter thinking my husband would pass them by. But low and behold, when I returned the plate was empty and the grin on his face said it all. Made from scratch—in mere minutes—these are a super game-day or game-night snack. Yummy served plain, they are also mighty tasty when dipped in mustard or barbecue sauce. (Did I mention each is just 35 calories?)*

MAKES 12 SERVINGS

4 reduced-fat hot dogs

½ cup all-purpose flour

½ cup yellow cornmeal

2 tablespoons granulated sugar

2 teaspoons baking powder

¼ teaspoon baking soda

⅔ cup low-fat buttermilk

1 large egg

1½ tablespoons margarine or butter, melted

1. Preheat the oven to 400°F. Lightly coat 24 mini muffin cups with nonstick baking spray. Cut each hot dog into 6 pieces, and set aside.

2. In a large bowl, whisk together the flour, cornmeal, sugar, baking powder, and baking soda. In a medium bowl, whisk together buttermilk, egg, and margarine. Make a well in the center of the dry ingredients and pour in the buttermilk mixture. Mix with a spoon until all ingredients are combined.

3. Scoop a rounded tablespoon of the batter evenly into each muffin cup. Lightly press a hot dog piece into each cup. Spray the tops with cooking spray, and bake for 8 to 10 minutes, or until tops are lightly browned.

**Marlene Says:** *Run a knife around the edge of these muffins while they are still warm to make it easier to remove them from the pan. Leftovers (if there are any) should be stored in a sealed container in the refrigerator. They reheat well in the microwave.*

**NUTRITION INFORMATION PER SERVING:** (2 pup cakes) Calories 70 | Carbohydrate 11g (Sugars 4g) | Total Fat 1g (Sat Fat 0g) | Protein 4g | Fiber 1g | Cholesterol 25mg | Sodium 240 mg | Food Exchanges: 1 Starch | Carbohydrate Choices: 1 | Weight Watcher Smart Point Comparison: 2

# SOUPS & STEWS

## soups & stews

## *For the Love of*
## { FREEZING (and Eating!) }

Did you know that frozen produce can be even more nutritious than fresh? Today's fruit and veggies are flash frozen at their peak, ensuring the highest nutrient content (and for some, the best taste!). This means most fruits and vegetables are never out of season, offering unlimited options for making everything from beverages to dessert. Convenient, economical, and healthy, unadorned frozen produce helps put fabulous food on the table in a flash.

On the other hand, many prepared frozen foods are high in calories, fat, sugar, and sodium. Fortunately, you can make your own "prepared foods" by freezing many of the recipes in this book. And, as an added bonus, you can freeze individual servings to take the guesswork out of portion control and make mealtime a snap. To help you get started, here are some freezer-friendly hints:

**FREEZER FAVORITES:** Muffins, pancakes, burritos, soups and chilis, cookies, un-frosted cupcakes and cakes, meatballs, and slow-cooker dishes all freeze and reheat well.

**FREEZER FLOPS:** Cream sauces and dairy products tend to break when thawed, so are not freezer-friendly. I also find that prepared meat, poultry, and fish entrées, veggie sides, and many pasta dishes retain quality better if they are refrigerated, instead of frozen. Most hold well for up to 3 days.

**FREEZER FRESH:** The length of time that frozen home-prepared foods can retain their best quality varies, but a good rule of thumb is 1 to 2 months.

**UN-FREEZING:** While your grandmother may have defrosted the roast on the counter overnight, today we know that's not safe, as it increases the risk of food-borne illness. As a rule, food should go from the freezer to the fridge to defrost or to the oven to cook or reheat. (To thaw food quickly, place it in a sealed plastic bag and set the bag in cold water; replace the cold water every 30 minutes, or as it warms.)

**FOUR MORE FREEZING TIPS:**

1) Always cool foods first. Then wrap tightly in plastic wrap, foil, or freezer paper, and make sure airtight containers are filled to capacity (leave a bit of headspace with soups). Portioning food before freezing makes packages fit easier in the freezer and lessens defrosting time.

2) Space-saving freezer-safe plastic bags work great when freezing liquid foods like chili and soup. Simply fill, seal, and lay flat separately until frozen, then stack the bags.

3) For best quality, add toppings such as cheese, frosting, and garnishes after removing the dish from the freezer.

4) Always label food with the date and contents! This eliminates confusion and "mystery packages" in the freezer and ensures you eat the food while it's still at its best.

# Fast-Fix French Onion Soup

*MAKING FRENCH ONION SOUP IS NORMALLY A TIME-CONSUMING LABOR OF LOVE, but this quick recipe changes that. By taking advantage of your microwave to jumpstart the star ingredient, you'll love how fast you can get delicious bowlfuls of this fabulous soup on the table. Done in less than half the usual time, with the same delicious homemade quality.* Trés magnifique!

MAKES 4 SERVINGS

6 cups thinly sliced onions (about 2 large)

Pinch of salt

½ teaspoon dried thyme

1 teaspoon brown sugar

1 (14.5-ounce) can reduced-sodium beef broth

1 (14.5-ounce) can reduced-sodium chicken broth

2 teaspoons Worcestershire sauce

3 tablespoons sherry

2 thin slices Swiss cheese

2 slices sourdough bread

1. Place the onions in a microwave-safe bowl and cover with plastic wrap. Cook on high for 5 minutes.

2. Spray a medium soup pot with cooking spray and place over medium-high heat. Add onions and salt, cover, and cook for 10 minutes, stirring occasionally. Add thyme, brown sugar, and 2 tablespoons broth, and stir well.

3. Cook for 10 more minutes, or until onions are soft and well caramelized, stirring occasionally, and adding an additional tablespoon or two of broth, if needed, to keep the onions from sticking. Add remaining broth, Worcestershire and sherry, cover, and simmer on low for 15 minutes.

4. To serve, cut slices of bread and cheese in half. Turn on the broiler, place bread on a baking sheet, and lightly toast both sides. Top each piece with a slice of cheese and broil until cheese is melted. Ladle 1 generous cup of soup each into 4 bowls or crocks, and top with a piece of cheese toast.

> **DARE TO COMPARE:** A typical bowl of French onion soup at a sit-down restaurant delivers more than an entire day's worth of sodium.

**NUTRITION INFORMATION PER SERVING:** (1 generous cup + toast) Calories 150 | Carbohydrate 24g (Sugars 13g) | Total Fat 3g (Sat Fat 1g) | Protein 8g | Fiber 3g | Cholesterol 5mg | Sodium 520mg | Food Exchanges: 2 Vegetable, ¾ Carbohydrate, ½ Fat | Carbohydrate Choices: 1½ | Weight Watcher Smart Point Comparison: 3

# Tuscan Chicken Noodle Soup

*MEET MY NEW FAVORITE CHICKEN SOUP. Simply sensational and oh-so-nourishing, it combines a few of my favorite Italian ingredients—spinach, oregano, and bowtie pasta—with a classic chicken noodle soup broth. The sweet vermouth is optional (as I know not everyone keeps it on hand), but I love the slightly sweet taste and Italian flair it adds to this must-try 30-minute soup.*

**MAKES 4 SERVINGS**

1 teaspoon canola oil

1 medium onion, chopped

2 tablespoons sweet vermouth (optional)

2 medium carrots, cut into rounds

2 medium stalks celery, chopped

2 teaspoons garlic, minced

1 teaspoon dried oregano

2 (14.5-ounce) cans reduced-sodium chicken broth

1 cup dry bowtie pasta

1¾ cups cooked chicken breast, shredded

2 cups fresh spinach

Grated Parmesan cheese (optional)

1. Heat the oil in a large soup pot over medium-high heat. Add the onion and cook for 5 minutes or until it is translucent and begins to brown. Add the vermouth, if using, and stir to scrape the caramelized bits from the bottom of the pot. Add carrots, celery, garlic, and oregano, and cook for 2 minutes. Add chicken broth and ½ cup water.

2. Simmer for 5 minutes, add the pasta, and cook for 8 minutes. Gently stir in the chicken and spinach and simmer 2 to 3 minutes, or until chicken is warm and spinach wilted. Ladle into bowls and garnish with Parmesan, if desired.

**Marlene Says:** *Instead of cooked chicken, you can substitute 8 ounces of raw boneless, skinless chicken breast. Slice it very thinly across the grain and drop the slices into the hot soup as you would the shredded chicken.*

**NUTRITION INFORMATION PER SERVING: (1½ cups)** Calories 200 | Carbohydrate 20g (Sugars 7g) | Total Fat 3g (Sat Fat 0g) | Protein 16g | Fiber 3g | Cholesterol 30mg | Sodium 620mg | Food Exchanges: 1½ Lean Meat, 1 Starch, 1 Vegetable | Carbohydrate Choices: 1 | Weight Watcher Smart Point Comparison: 2

# Skinny Cheesy Cauliflower Soup

*WHAT'S NOT TO LOVE ABOUT A CREAMY, CHEESY, FLAVORFUL SOUP that can be whipped up in minutes and packs 50% of the daily requirement of vitamin A and 60% of the daily requirement for vitamin C in a skimpy 100 calories per serving? Pair it with the Tuna and Egg Salad Sandwich (page 122), Harvest Chicken Salad Sandwich (page 124), or Turkey Wrap with Pesto Mayo (page 126) for a super-satisfying, slimming soup-and-sandwich combo with less than 350 calories.*

MAKES 4 SERVINGS

2 (14.5-ounce) cans reduced-sodium chicken broth

10 ounces frozen cauliflower (or 3 cups)

1/2 cup onion, chopped

1/2 cup carrot, shredded

3/4 cup shredded reduced-fat cheddar cheese, divided

1 pinch cayenne pepper

2 tablespoons nonfat half-and-half

1. In a large soup pot, combine the first 4 ingredients (broth through carrot), place over medium heat, and bring to a boil. Reduce heat to medium-low and simmer for 15 minutes.

2. Transfer the hot soup to a blender (or use an immersion blender) and purée until smooth. If using a blender, return the puréed soup to the pot, add 1/2 cup of cheese, cayenne, and half-and-half, and simmer for 2 minutes. Serve each bowl garnished with 1 tablespoon of cheese.

**Marlene Says:** *Cauliflower is finally having its day. As a member of the* Brassica oleracea *(cancer-crushing cruciferous vegetable) family, cauliflower, along with its cousins cabbage, broccoli, and kale, is low in calories, high in protein, an excellent source of vitamin C, and a good source of sodium-negating potassium.*

**NUTRITION INFORMATION PER SERVING: (1¼ cups)** Calories 100 | Carbohydrate 8g (Sugars 4g) | Total Fat 4g (Sat Fat 2.5g) | Protein 11g | Fiber 2g | Cholesterol 10mg | Sodium 510mg | Food Exchanges: 1 Lean Meat, 1 Vegetable, 1/2 Fat | Carbohydrate Choices: 1/2 | Weight Watcher Smart Point Comparison: 1

# Cabbage Roll Soup

*THIS HEARTY MEAL-IN-A-BOWL IS A RIFF ON THE STUFFED CABBAGE ROLLS that my mother would make when I was a kid. What I love is that it has all the traditional Old World components and flavor of her cabbage rolls—without the considerable time and effort they took to make. The soup tastes great the next day, but may need a bit of water when reheating. A good dose of fresh black pepper adds the perfect finish.*

MAKES 4 SERVINGS

1 teaspoon canola oil

1 cup onion, chopped

2 teaspoons garlic, minced

½ pound lean ground beef

1 (14.5-ounce) can diced tomatoes

1 (8-ounce) can tomato sauce

1 (14-ounce) can reduced-sodium beef broth

2 tablespoons red wine vinegar

1 tablespoon brown sugar

¼ teaspoon salt

3 cups bag shredded coleslaw mix

¼ cup instant brown rice

1. Heat the oil in a large soup pot over medium heat. Add the onion and garlic, cover, and cook for 3 minutes, or until the onion begins to soften, stirring occasionally. Push the onions to one side of the pot, add beef to the empty side, and cook until it begins to brown, breaking it up with a wooden spoon. Stir the beef into the onions and cook another 3 minutes, or until the pink color is gone.

2. Add the next 6 ingredients to the pot (tomatoes through salt). Increase heat to high and bring to a boil. Stir in the coleslaw mix, reduce heat to medium-low, partially cover the pot, and simmer gently for 15 minutes.

3. Stir in the brown rice, cover, and cook until tender, about 10 minutes.

**NUTRITION INFORMATION PER SERVING:** (1½ cups) Calories 200 | Carbohydrate 21g (Sugars 10g) | Total Fat 6g (Sat Fat 2g) | Protein 16g | Fiber 4g | Cholesterol 25mg | Sodium 620mg | Food Exchanges: 2 Lean Beef, 1½ Vegetable, ½ Carbohydrate | Carbohydrate Choices: 1½ | Weight Watcher Smart Point Comparison: 4

# Fresh, Fast Cream of Zucchini Soup

*SHREDDING FRESH ZUCCHINI RIGHT INTO THE SOUP POT is the trick to making this fresh-from-the-garden 50-calorie soup in record time. As is, try it with My Favorite Caprese Sandwich (page 123) for lunch or a Steakhouse Steak Salad (page 158) for dinner, or, if you like, vary the flavor with any of the suggestions below. The possibilities with this perfect canvas of a soup are endless. For garnish, try Parmesan cheese (my favorite), light sour cream, and/or a drizzle of good olive oil.*

**MAKES 5 SERVINGS**

1 teaspoon olive oil

½ cup onion, chopped

2 teaspoons garlic, minced

1½ pounds medium zucchini, trimmed

1½ teaspoons dried dill

1 (14.5-ounce) can reduced-sodium chicken broth

1½ tablespoons instant flour (like Wondra)

½ teaspoon seasoned salt

Scant ¼ teaspoon black pepper

1. Heat the oil in a medium soup pot over medium heat. Add the onions and sauté for 3 to 4 minutes or until onions are soft. Add the garlic and sauté for 1 minute. Shred the zucchini into the pot, stir in the dill, and cook for 5 to 7 minutes, or until zucchini has softened.

2. Stir in the chicken broth plus 1¼ cups of water. Bring the soup to a boil, reduce heat to low, cover, and simmer for 10 minutes.

3. Transfer the hot soup to a blender, or use an immersion blender, and purée until smooth. If using a blender, return the puréed soup to the pot and bring to a low simmer. Whisk in the flour, salt, and pepper, bring to a low simmer and cook 2 minutes. Garnish as desired.

**Marlene Says:** *To vary the flavor, replace the dill with ½ teaspoon fresh, finely minced rosemary, 2 tablespoons fresh minced basil, or ½ teaspoon curry powder. To use all-purpose flour, mix it with a small amount of cold water, then add it to the soup.*

**NUTRITION INFORMATION PER SERVING:** (1 cup) Calories 50 | Carbohydrate 9g (Sugars 5g) | Total Fat 1g (Sat Fat 0g) | Protein 3g | Fiber 2g | Cholesterol 0mg | Sodium 430mg | Food Exchanges: 2 Vegetable | Carbohydrate Choices: ½ | Weight Watcher Smart Point Comparison: 0

# 5-Ingredient Black Bean Soup

*WHILE I STILL LOVE THE SPEEDY BLACK BEAN SOUP with Jalapeño Cream I created for my first* Eat What You Love *cookbook, it's hard not to say Olé! to a scrumptious soup with only 5 ingredients that takes only 15 minutes to make. Honestly, "homemade" just doesn't get much easier—or faster. I still use canned black beans for convenience, but here I combine them with prepared salsa, eliminating the need for several additional ingredients. (P.S. It's hard to beat a simple soup that delivers 12 grams of fiber!)*

MAKES 2 SERVINGS

1 (15-ounce) cans reduced-sodium black beans

3/4 cup reduced-sodium chicken broth

1/3 cup prepared salsa

1/2 teaspoon chili powder

1/4 teaspoon ground cumin

Reduced-fat shredded cheddar cheese (optional garnish)

Fresh cilantro (optional garnish)

1. Pour the beans (and their juice) into a medium pot. Add broth, salsa, and spices and roughly purée with an immersion blender. (Alternately, place all of the ingredients in a blender, purée, and transfer puréed ingredients to the pot.)

2. Place the pot over medium-high heat, and bring to a simmer. Reduce heat to medium low and simmer, partially covered, stirring occasionally to blend flavors and thicken, for 10 to 12 minutes. Garnish, if desired, with cheese and chopped cilantro.

**Marlene Says:** *To keep sodium in check, use only reduced-sodium products and salsa that has no more than 200 milligrams of sodium per serving. For extra flavor, try using fire-roasted salsa or add a dash of your favorite hot sauce.*

**NUTRITION INFORMATION PER SERVING:** (1¼ cups) Calories 195 | Carbohydrate 37g (Sugars 3g) | Total Fat 1g (Sat Fat 0g) | Protein 12g | Fiber 12g | Cholesterol 0mg | Sodium 690mg | Food Exchanges: 1½ Starch, 1½ Lean Meat, ¼ Vegetable | Carbohydrate Choices: 2½ | Weight Watcher Smart Point Comparison: 0

# Smokey Slow-Cooker Split Pea Soup

*THE SIGN ON THE FREEWAY READS, "Only 112 miles to Pea Soup Anderson's." People travel far and wide to dine at this 90-year-old pea soup institution in Buellton, California, and it was here that I first appreciated pea soup. It has been my standard for pea soup ever since, so I used its beloved taste as a guide when I fashioned this slow-cooker soup. At the end of a long day, this soup is worth a visit.*

**MAKES 7 SERVINGS**

1 pound dry green split peas

1 medium onion, chopped

2 medium carrots, chopped

2 medium stalks celery, chopped

3 cloves (or 1 tablespoon) garlic, minced

3/4 teaspoon dried thyme

1 teaspoon seasoned salt

1/4 teaspoon black pepper

1 bay leaf

7 ounces turkey kielbasa sausage, thinly sliced

1¼ teaspoons liquid smoke, or to taste

Black pepper, to taste

1. Place the split peas in a 4- to 6-quart slow cooker. Add the next 8 ingredients (onion through bay leaf) plus 7 cups water. Stir, then cook for 8 to 10 hours on low or 4 to 6 hours on high, or until the peas are soft.

2. Remove and discard the bay leaf. Using an immersion blender, purée the soup in the slow cooker. (Or, purée the soup in batches in a blender, being careful to leave the lid ajar to keep the hot soup from spurting out. Return the puréed soup to the slow cooker.)

3. Stir in the sliced kielbasa and liquid smoke. Cover and cook on high for 30 minutes or until the kielbasa is heated through. Serve with additional black pepper to taste.

**NUTRITION INFORMATION PER SERVING:** (1⅓ cups) Calories 275 | Carbohydrate 44g (Sugars 8g) | Total Fat 3g (Sat Fat 1g) | Protein 22g | Fiber 11g | Cholesterol 30mg | Sodium 500mg | Food Exchanges: 2 Starch, 2 Lean Meat, 1 Vegetable | Carbohydrate Choices: 2½ | Weight Watcher Smart Point Comparison: 1

# Quickie Chicken and Shrimp Gumbo

*SPICY STICK-TO-THE-RIBS GUMBO MAY HAVE ORIGINATED IN THE "BIG EASY," but the time and effort required to make this stew is anything but—especially on a weeknight when you need to get dinner on the table in a hurry. Using pre-cooked chicken and quick-thaw frozen shrimp for convenience, zesty Cajun seasoning for that familiar flavor, and a dusting of flour as a thickener (instead time-consuming, fat-laden roux), brings this satisfyingly slimmed-down version of New Orleans' signature dish to the table in record time.*

MAKES 4 SERVINGS

1 tablespoon butter

3 stalks celery, chopped

1 medium onion, chopped

1 medium green pepper, chopped

2 teaspoons Cajun seasoning

3 tablespoons instant flour (like Wondra)

1 (14.5-ounce) can reduced-sodium chicken broth

1 (14.5-ounce) can no-salt-added diced tomatoes

1½ cups chopped cooked chicken breast

½ pound large frozen shrimp, thawed

1. Heat the butter in a large soup pot over medium heat. Add the next 4 ingredients (celery through Cajun seasoning) and cook, stirring occasionally, for 7 to 8 minutes, or until the onions are soft. The seasoning will brown; do not let it burn. Sprinkle vegetables with flour and stir to coat.

2. Stir in chicken broth, tomatoes, chicken, and ½ cup of water to the pot, and simmer for 5 minutes, or until thickened. Add the shrimp and simmer for an additional 2 minutes, or until shrimp is cooked.

**NUTRITION INFORMATION PER SERVING:** (1½ cups) Calories 180 | Carbohydrate 13g (Sugars 6g) | Total Fat 4g (Sat Fat 2g) | Protein 21g | Fiber 3g | Cholesterol 120mg | Sodium 570mg | Food Exchanges: 2½ Lean Meat, 2 Vegetable | Carbohydrate Choices: 1 | Weight Watcher Smart Point Comparison: 2

# At-Home Asian Chicken Noodle Soup Bowls

*AS SOMEONE WHO LOVES EATING BIG ASIAN NOODLE SOUP BOWLS, words can't possibly describe how happy I am with how this soup turned out. Quick cooking vermicelli instead of ramen brought down the fat and sodium content, but what really excites me about this soup, in addition to its intoxicating aromatic broth, is how quickly the chicken cooks (in just 2 minutes!)—and how remarkably tender it stays. Fresh jalapeño pepper, bean sprouts, and cilantro add the crowning touches.*

**MAKES 4 SERVINGS**

1 medium carrot

4 ounces dried vermicelli pasta (or 2 cups cooked)

2 (14.5-ounce) cans reduced-sodium chicken broth

1 teaspoon jarred minced ginger

1 teaspoon minced garlic

2 teaspoons reduced-sodium soy sauce

1 teaspoon granulated sugar

8 ounces boneless skinless chicken breast, thinly sliced

1 jalapeño pepper, thinly sliced

2 cups fresh bean sprouts

½ cup lightly chopped cilantro

1. Peel the carrot, trimming the ends. Using the vegetable peeler, continue peeling down the length of the carrot to form wide, thin ribbons. Cut the ribbons in half (horizontally) and set aside. Cook the pasta according to package directions. Drain and set aside.

2. While the pasta is cooking, in a medium saucepan, over medium heat, combine the next 5 ingredients (chicken broth though sugar) plus 1 cup water, and simmer for 5 minutes. Add carrot, chicken, and half of the jalapeño slices, and simmer for 2 minutes, or until chicken is cooked.

3. To serve soup, place ½ cup cooked vermicelli in each bowl. Pour 1¼ cups of the soup mixture over the noodles and top with ½ cup bean sprouts and 2 tablespoons cilantro. Garnish with remaining jalapeño slices.

**NUTRITION INFORMATION PER SERVING:** (1¾ cups plus toppings) Calories 215 | Carbohydrate 30g (Sugars 5g) | Total Fat 2g (Sat Fat 0g) | Protein 21g | Fiber 4g | Cholesterol 35mg | Sodium 630mg | Food Exchanges: 2 Lean Meat, 1½ Starch, 1 Vegetable | Carbohydrate Choices: 2 | Weight Watcher Smart Point Comparison: 4

# Very Veggie Chickpea Chili

*I GUARANTEE THAT NO ONE WILL BE MISSING THE MEAT in this tasty 20-minute chili. A splash of barbecue sauce and pinch of cayenne pleases carnivores and veggie lovers alike by kicking in just enough "sweet and heat," and with the hefty 7 grams of fiber this is no wimpy veggie chili! Make it on a meatless Monday and you can enjoy the leftovers throughout the week. (Traditional chili toppers welcomed!)*

MAKES 4 SERVINGS

1 teaspoon canola oil

1/2 medium onion, chopped

1 medium red bell pepper, chopped

1 medium zucchini, chopped (about 1 1/3 cups)

2 teaspoons chili powder

1 teaspoon cumin

1/2 teaspoon minced garlic

1 pinch cayenne pepper

1 (15-ounce) can garbanzo beans, rinsed and drained

1 (14.5-ounce) can diced fire-roasted tomatoes

1 tablespoon barbecue sauce

1. Heat the oil in a medium soup pot over medium heat. Add the onion, bell pepper, and zucchini, and cook for 5 minutes, or until onions are slightly softened.

2. Stir in the chili powder, cumin, garlic, and cayenne, and cook for 2 minutes. Add garbanzos, tomatoes, barbecue sauce, and 1 cup water. Bring to a simmer and cook for 10 to 15 minutes.

**Marlene says:** *Go easy when cooking with cayenne pepper because a pinch goes a long way. Remember, you can always add more, but you can't take it out! A garnish of sour cream is a great way to cool the heat.*

**NUTRITION INFORMATION PER SERVING:** (1 cup) Calories 160 | Carbohydrate 27g (Sugars 7g) | Total Fat 3g (Sat Fat 0g) | Protein 8g | Fiber 7g | Cholesterol 0mg | Sodium 330mg | Food Exchanges: 1 Starch, 1 Vegetable, 1/2 Lean Meat | Carbohydrate Choices: 2 | Weight Watcher Smart Point Comparison: 0

# Good & Easy Turkey Chili

*EVERY COOK HAS HIS OR HER FAVORITE GO-TO RECIPES for busy weeknights and this chili is one of mine. With ingredients from a well-stocked pantry and a few fresh additions from the fridge, you've got a great supper that's as easy as 1, 2, 3. As with my Very Veggie Chickpea Chili (page 113), my secret flavor booster is a touch of barbecue sauce that delivers a rich depth of flavor in a flash. With this recipe in hand and a package of lean ground turkey in the freezer, you'll never be caught empty-handed at dinnertime again!*

**MAKES 6 SERVINGS**

1 teaspoon canola oil

1 medium onion, chopped

1 medium red or green pepper, chopped

1 pound lean ground turkey

2 tablespoons chili powder

2 teaspoons cumin

1 (28-ounce) can crushed tomatoes

2 tablespoons barbecue sauce

1 (15-ounce) can reduced-sodium kidney beans, rinsed and drained

Pinch of cayenne pepper

1. Heat the oil in a large saucepan over medium-high heat. Add the onion and bell pepper and sauté for 3 to 4 minutes, or until slightly softened.

2. Add the turkey and cook, turning to break up the meat, until it begins to brown. Add the chili powder and cumin and cook for 1 minute.

3. Add remaining 4 ingredients along with ½ cup of water. Stir well and simmer for 15 minutes.

**NUTRITION INFORMATION PER SERVING: (1 cup)** Calories 220 | Carbohydrate 22g (Sugars 4g) | Total Fat 7g (Sat Fat 2g) | Protein 18g | Fiber 7g | Cholesterol 60mg | Sodium 340mg | Food Exchanges: 2 Lean Meat, 2 Vegetable, 1 Starch | Carbohydrate Choices: 1½ | Weight Watcher Smart Point Comparison: 2

# Slow Cooker Texas Beef and Black Bean Chili

*THERE ARE AS MANY RECIPES FOR TEXAS CHILI as there are cooks in Texas. Cooks wrangle about adding tomatoes or, heaven forbid, beans in chili, but at the end of the day, it's all about what tastes good to you. This fix-it-and-forget-about-it chili is made—as they do it in Texas—with chopped (not ground) beef and smoky chipotle chilies. To round it out, I elect to add both tomatoes and fiber-rich beans, and then cook it low and slow for fork-tender meat and one mighty tasty chili. "Enjoy, y'all!"*

MAKES 10 SERVINGS

2¼ pounds lean beef stew meat

1 teaspoon canola oil

1 large onion, chopped

2 large bell peppers (preferably 1 red, 1 green)

1 tablespoon minced garlic

1 tablespoon ground cumin

½ teaspoon salt

½ teaspoon black pepper

1 (28-ounce) can chopped tomatoes in juice

1 (6-ounce) can tomato paste

2 (15-ounce) cans black beans, rinsed and drained

2 to 3 canned chipotle peppers in adobo, finely chopped

1. Spray a large nonstick skillet with cooking spray and place over high heat. In two batches, add the beef and cook, turning occasionally, until beef is lightly browned. (You can leave this step out, but browning the beef enhances the flavor.) Transfer the beef to a 5- to 7- quart slow cooker.

2. Add the remaining ingredients and ½ cup of water and stir well. Cover and cook on low for 8 to 9 hours or on high for 4 to 5 hours or until the meat is fork tender. If the chili is not thick enough for you, uncover and cook on high for the last 30 minutes.

**Marlene Says:** *Canned chipotle peppers in adobo can be found in the Mexican food section of the grocery store. Two medium peppers make a slightly spicy chili. If preferred, you can substitute 2 tablespoons of regular chili powder. The chili will still be delicious, but will lack the chipotle pepper's smokey flavor.*

**NUTRITION INFORMATION PER SERVING:** (1 cup) Calories 280 | Carbohydrate 25g (Sugars 6g) | Total Fat 8g (Sat Fat 3g) | Protein 26g | Fiber 9g | Cholesterol 95mg | Sodium 500mg | Food Exchanges: 3 Lean Meat, 1 Starch, 2 Vegetables | Carbohydrate Choices: 1½ | Weight Watcher Smart Point Comparison: 5

# SANDWICHES, BURGERS & TACOS

## sandwiches, burgers, & tacos

*For the Love of*
# { GLUTEN-FREE RECIPES! }

If you or someone you love is on a gluten-free diet or has a sensitivity to gluten you'll be happy to know that many of Mother Nature's finest and healthiest foods are naturally gluten-free, including fruits, vegetables, meats, seafood, beans, nuts and eggs—along with nutrient-rich dairy products and oil. While foods made with wheat based flour (or barley or rye), like bread, cakes, and cookies still fill the shelves, today's vast array of gluten-free varieties makes it easier than ever to cook and eat gluten-free! Here's how to eat G-free quickly and easily from morning till night (including desserts!) with the recipes in this book:

## MORNING

+ Indulge in an Almond Joy (page 41) or Oatmeal Cookie Breakfast Smoothie (page 44)!

+ For the delectable One-Bowl Double Chocolate Pancakes (page 60), or Cinnamon Swirl Quick Cake (page 53), simply substitute Gluten-Free Bisquick®.

+ For other breakfast fare such as French toast and breakfast pizzas, use your favorite gluten-free breads or tortillas. The 5-Ingredient Banana-Oat Pancakes for One (page 70) recipe is gluten-free!

## NOON

+ All of the sandwiches can be made gluten-free by simply swapping in gluten-free bread. Or go "bunless" by wrapping sandwich fillings in lettuce leaves. Made with corn tortillas, the Chicken Enchilada Tacos (page 130) and the 15-minute Crispy Tacos (page 331) are already G-free, as are the Korean-style BBQ Tacos (page 131) when Tamari sauce is swapped for soy.

+ In the Soup and Chili chapter, the soups on pages 104, 105, 108, and 109—are gluten-free when made with gluten-free broth, as are all of the chili recipes (most barbecue sauces are G-free). Each of the other nine recipes takes just one common gluten-free ingredient swap to make them gluten-free (such as gluten-free bread for the Fast-Fix French Onion Soup or gluten-free pasta for the noodle soups). For thickening, substitute half as much cornstarch mixed with a little water.

+ Ten of the fourteen salad recipes in the Salads chapter including the Whole Grain Mediterranean Salad (page 145) are already gluten-free! To make the rest gluten-free, simply use gluten-free bread for the croutons in the Chicken BLT Salad with Ranch Dressing (page 153), gluten-free pasta for Creamy Potato Mac Potluck Salad (page 149), gluten-free pretzels to top the Upside-Down Strawberry-Pretzel Salad (page 150), and gluten-free Teriyaki (like Kikkoman's) when making the Teriyaki Salmon and Spinach Salad (page 156).

## NIGHT

✦ Indulge freely in the vegetable dishes (without incorporated grains) in the Sensationally Easy Sides or Air Fryer chapter. As a side starch, try the Instant Brown Rice Pilaf (page 199). Use gluten-free pasta to make Better-than-Ever Stovetop Mac & Cheese (page 197) or One-Pot Spaghetti and Spinach (page 195). Note: Couscous contains gluten.

✦ For pasta dishes, use your favorite gluten-free pasta or pour pasta sauces over cooked rice, spaghetti squash, or even baked potatoes halves.

✦ Chicken, beef, pork and fish entrées like 2-Minute Greek Lemon Chicken (page 215), Chinese Pepper Steak (page 233), or 5-Ingredient Spinach-Stuffed Salmon (page 250), can be made so easily by using a dusting of cornstarch or gluten-free flour for coating and thickening and gluten-free breadcrumbs for coating. When replacing flour with cornstarch or tapioca flour for thickening, use half as much.

## DESSERTS

✦ For baked goods, store-bought gluten-free "flour" is the easy way to go. There are many brands to choose from, but Cup 4 Cup gluten-free "flour" is the best replacement for all-purpose flour I have found. Use in any of the muffin, cookie, or cake recipes.

✦ Chocolate Hazelnut (Nutella®) Mousse (page 284), 2-Minute Microwave Pumpkin Pie (page 273), 3-Ingredient Shortcut Strawberry Soufflés (page 292), No-Churn Fruity Frozen Yogurt (page 277), and the Chocolate-Covered, Crispy Peanut Butter Bon Bons (page 280) and the Chocolate Soufflés for Two (page 344) are gluten-free recipes. Purchase ready-made gluten-free graham cracker crusts for the no-bake pies, or make your own with gluten-free graham crackers or cookie crumbs, and the recipes on pages 268-270, 272, 275, 290, 297, and 341 will also be gluten-free.

✦ Sugar-free pudding, Jello®, ice cream, whipped topping, jam, cream cheese, coconut, and sucralose, and stevia-based sweeteners are all G-free.

*Note: Experts agree that there is no need to avoid wheat if you do not have celiac disease or gluten sensitivity. A gluten-free diet does not guarantee weight loss or better health. Many gluten-free foods are higher in sugar, fat, and calories, as well as lower in nutrients such as fiber, B vitamins, and iron. Consult a physician or registered dietitian before starting a gluten-free diet. Gluten Free Diet: A Comprehensive Resource Guide by Shelley Case RD is an excellent resource.*

# Tuna 'n Egg Salad Sandwich

*THIS SLIMMED DOWN SANDWICH MARRIES MY TWO FAVORITE SANDWICH FILLINGS. After sampling this sandwich on different types of bread, I found perfection with a toasted English muffin. The warm crunchiness is picture-perfect with the cool, creamy filling. To take the edge off the sharpness of the red onion, soak the diced onion in a bowl of ice water for 5 to 10 minutes (and pat dry) before adding to the salad mixture. To make the perfect hardboiled egg, see below.*

MAKES 2 SERVINGS

2 hardboiled eggs

1 (5-ounce) can white albacore tuna, drained well and flaked

2 tablespoons light mayonnaise

1 tablespoon diced red onion

2 teaspoons sweet pickle relish

2 light multi-grain English muffins

4 red leaf lettuce leaves

2 thick tomato slices

1. Peel the eggs and cut in half lengthwise. Remove and discard one of the egg yolks. Coarsely chop eggs and egg whites and place in a medium bowl. Add the tuna, mayonnaise, onion, and relish, and stir gently to combine.

2. To assemble the sandwiches, split and toast 2 English muffins. Place a lettuce leaf on 2 of the halves. Top with a slice of tomato, then add the tuna salad (about ½ cup), another lettuce leaf, and the remaining muffin half.

**Marlene Says:** *For perfect hardboiled eggs, place eggs in a saucepan in a single layer and cover with cold water. Bring water to a boil; remove from heat, cover pan, and let sit for 12 minutes. Drain hot water from eggs and replace with cold water. Drain and then give the pan a hard shake to crack the shells. Add cold water and let sit for 5 minutes. Eggs should peel easily.*

**NUTRITION INFORMATION PER SERVING: (1 sandwich)** Calories 250 | Carbohydrate 31g (Sugars 3g) | Total Fat 8g (Sat Fat 1.5g) | Protein 23g | Fiber 9g | Cholesterol 90mg | Sodium 510mg | Food Exchanges: 2½ Lean Meat, 1½ Starch, ½ Vegetable | Carbohydrate Choices: 2 | Weight Watcher Smart Point Comparison: 4

# My Favorite Caprese Sandwich

*THE CULINARY TERM "CAPRESE" ORIGINATED ON THE ISLAND OF CAPRI to describe a salad with the same colors as the Italian flag, made from fresh mozzarella, tomatoes, and basil. Layer this colorful trio on toasty garlicky bread and top with a drizzle of reduced balsamic vinegar, and you've created one of my favorite sandwiches. For this open-faced delight, the fresher the ingredients, the tastier the sandwich!*

MAKES 2 SERVINGS

¼ cup balsamic vinegar

¼ of an ounce baguette (or 2 1-ounce slices of bread)

1 garlic clove, peeled

4 slices fresh mozzarella cheese (about 3 ounces total)

1 large tomato, sliced

Salt and black pepper, to taste

1 tablespoon thinly sliced fresh basil

1. Place the vinegar in a small saucepan and simmer over medium heat for 4 to 6 minutes, or until thickened and reduced by about half (watch carefully at the end of the reduction time as it will burn quickly). Remove from heat and set aside.

2. Turn on the broiler. Cut a 6-inch-long piece from the baguette and slice it open lengthwise. Open and toast both halves under the broiler until lightly browned. Slice the garlic clove in half and rub the cut sides over the bread.

3. Layer each piece of the warm bread with one half of the cheese and tomatoes. Sprinkle lightly with salt and pepper, drizzle each with 1½ teaspoons balsamic glaze. and top with fresh basil.

**Marlene Says:** *Did you know that fresh mozzarella cheese has 40% less fat and calories than regular Monterey jack or cheddar? For a fabulous farm-fresh meal at less than 300 calories, serve this sandwich with a cup of Fresh, Fast Cream of Zucchini Soup (page 107).*

**NUTRITION INFORMATION PER SERVING:** (1 sandwich) Calories 220 | Carbohydrate 24g (Sugars 8g) | Total Fat 8g (Sat Fat 5g) | Protein 14g | Fiber 2g | Cholesterol 20mg | Sodium 450mg | Food Exchanges: 1½ Lean Meat, 1 Starch, ½ Vegetable | Carbohydrate Choices: 1½ | Weight Watcher Smart Point Comparison: 8

# Harvest Chicken Salad Sandwich

*DICED APPLE, CIDER VINEGAR, AND CRANBERRIES give this deliciously satisfying chicken salad its autumn accent, but there is no need to wait until fall to enjoy it. I've added celery for crunch, but if calories are less of a concern for you, a handful of toasted pecans is another option. When served on a bed of lettuce, this creamy and deceptively slim chicken salad has only 110 calories, 4 grams of fat, and 9 grams of carbohydrate per serving.*

MAKES 4 SERVINGS

3 tablespoons light mayonnaise

3 tablespoons nonfat Greek yogurt

2 teaspoons cider vinegar

2 teaspoons sugar

1½ cups diced cooked chicken breast

½ cup diced celery

½ cup chopped apple

3 tablespoons reduced-sugar dried cranberries

4 large red lettuce leaves

4 slices light wheat or white bread

1. In a medium bowl, mix together the mayonnaise, yogurt, vinegar, and sugar. Add the next 4 ingredients (chicken through cranberries), and stir well to combine.

2. To assemble the sandwiches, take 2 slices of bread and place a lettuce leaf on each. Top with ⅔ cup of chicken salad, and a remaining slice of bread.

**Marlene Says:** *I used Ocean Spray Reduced Sugar Craisins in this recipe. They have 50% less sugar and three times the fiber of the original Craisins dried cranberries.*

**NUTRITION INFORMATION PER SERVING:** (1 sandwich) Calories 200 | Carbohydrate 28g (Sugars 9g) | Total Fat 5g (Sat Fat 0.5g) | Protein 16g | Fiber 6g | Cholesterol 30mg | Sodium 380mg | Food Exchanges: 1½ Lean Meat, 1 Starch, ½ Fruit | Carbohydrate Choices: 2 | Weight Watcher Smart Point Comparison: 4

# Turkey Wrap with Pesto Mayo

*TAKEOUT CAN'T COMPETE WITH THE HOMEMADE GOODNESS of this zesty deli-style wrap. It's got it all: A creamy basil pesto sauce slathered underneath America's number-one sandwich meat, turkey, along with lettuce, tomato, and onion, all wrapped in a soft, fiber-rich tortilla. Roll one together and roll out the door in no time! Customize it with avocado or a piece of low-fat cheese if you wish—but I find this sandwich so flavorful, it's not required.*

MAKES 2 SERVINGS

2 tablespoons light mayonnaise

1 tablespoon reduced-fat basil pesto

2 (8-inch) light high-fiber flour tortillas

4 ounces reduced-sodium deli-style turkey breast

1 cup shredded Romaine lettuce

1 Roma tomato, thinly sliced

1/4 cup slivered red onion

1. In a small bowl, combine mayonnaise and pesto. Spread 1½ tablespoons of pesto mayo on one half of one of the tortillas, and top with one half each of turkey, lettuce, tomato, and onion.

2. Fold the empty part of the tortilla upward to cover filling, and then fold in the sides and roll up. Place a toothpick in the center of the wrap to hold it shut. Repeat procedure with remaining ingredients.

**DARE TO COMPARE:** Watch out, restaurant-made turkey wraps can have as many as 1,000 calories! A small Turkey Wrap at Schlotzsky's deli clocks in with 679 calories, with 35 grams of fat and 2,280 milligrams of sodium.

**NUTRITION INFORMATION PER SERVING: (1 wrap)** Calories 200 | Carbohydrate 21g (Sugars 2g) | Total Fat 9g (Sat Fat 2g) | Protein 16g | Fiber 6g | Cholesterol 15mg | Sodium 675mg | Food Exchanges: 2 Lean Meat, 1 Starch, ½ Vegetable, 1 Fat | Carbohydrate Choices: 1 | Weight Watcher Smart Point Comparison: 4

# Chicken and Blue Buffalo Wrap

*WHILE TOURING WASHINGTON, DC, last year we grabbed a quick lunch at a spot known for their freshly made sandwiches and salads. My son James was particularly happy with his choice of a warm chicken and blue cheese buffalo wrap. I had to agree, it was downright delicious. So, of course, I had to create my own! My additions of shredded carrot and lettuce give this sandwich an even fresher taste, and using a higher-fiber tortilla along with my low-fat Ranch dressing makes it healthier. James gives it two thumbs-up!*

**MAKES 1 SERVING**

½ cup shredded chicken

2 teaspoons hot wing sauce (like Frank's)

1 (8-inch) reduced-carb high-fiber tortilla

1 tablespoon crumbled blue cheese

2 tablespoons shredded carrot

1 tablespoon thinly sliced green onion

⅔ cup shredded romaine lettuce

2 tablespoons low-fat ranch dressing (page 308 or store-bought)

1. Place the chicken in a small bowl, drizzle with wing sauce, and gently toss to coat.

2. Place the tortilla in a medium nonstick skillet over medium-low heat. Sprinkle blue cheese along the center of the tortilla, top with chicken, and heat for 2 minutes, or until the cheese starts to melt.

3. Remove from pan and top the chicken with shredded carrot, green onion, and lettuce. Drizzle with ranch dressing. Fold the bottom 1½ inches of the tortilla upward to cover filling and then fold in sides to create wrap.

**DARE TO COMPARE:** This wrap has 50% less sodium, 60% less calories, and 70% less fat than the one we ordered at the sandwich shop!

**NUTRITION INFORMATION PER SERVING: (1 wrap)** Calories 210 | Carbohydrate 20g (Sugars 4g) | Total Fat 7g (Sat Fat 2g) | Protein 19g | Fiber 7g | Cholesterol 45mg | Sodium 680mg | Food Exchanges: 2 Lean Meat, 1 Starch, ½ Vegetable | Carbohydrate Choices: 1 | Weight Watcher Smart Point Comparison: 5

# Quesadilla Burger

*COMBINE A JUICY BURGER WITH A CHEESY QUESADILLA and what do you get? Well, if it's Applebee's Quesadilla Burger, you get a cheesy, Southwestern-inspired, crave-worthy entrée—along with one of the Top 10 Worst (for You) Fast Foods! What you get here instead is a minimal-effort, mouthwatering burger-stuffed-quesadilla that satisfies your taste buds while saving you more than 1,000 calories. Am I excited to share this marvelous makeover with you? Bet your better burger I am!*

MAKES 2 SERVINGS

2 tablespoons salsa

2 tablespoons low-fat ranch dressing (page 308 or store-bought)

8 ounces lean ground beef

1½ teaspoons taco seasoning (page 312 or store-bought)

2 (8-inch) reduced-carb high fiber tortillas

2 slices reduced-fat American cheese, sliced in half

½ cup shredded iceberg lettuce

½ cup chopped tomato

¼ cup chopped red onion

1. In a small bowl, whisk together the salsa and ranch dressing. Set aside. In a medium bowl, mix together beef and taco seasoning. Pat the meat into a circle 1 inch smaller than the tortilla and cut it in half (to make two half-moon-shaped patties).

2. Spray a medium nonstick skillet with cooking spray and place over medium heat. Cook the burgers for about 3 minutes per side, or until just cooked through. Remove patties from pan and wipe the pan clean with a paper towel.

3. Return skillet to heat, place 1 tortilla in the pan, and top one side of tortilla with half of the cheese. Place a burger on top of the cheese, and top with half of the lettuce, followed by the red onion and tomato. Spread half of the dressing mixture on the empty side of the tortilla, lift it over the burger, pressing to close the tortilla, and remove it from pan (the cheese should be melted). Repeat with remaining ingredients.

> **DARE TO COMPARE:** The Quesadilla Burger at Applebee's has a stunning 1,430 calories, including 108 grams of fat, 45 grams (over 2 days' worth) of saturated fat, and 3,230 milligrams of sodium.

**NUTRITION INFORMATION PER SERVING:** (1 burger) Calories 320 | Carbohydrate 25g (Sugars 6g) | Total Fat 13g (Sat Fat 6g) | Protein 30g | Fiber 7g | Cholesterol 60mg | Sodium 590mg | Food Exchanges: 3½ Lean Beef, 1 Starch, 1 Vegetable, ½ Fat | Carbohydrate Choices: 1½ | Weight Watcher Smart Point Comparison: 8

# Chicken Enchilada Tacos

*MESSY AND OH-SO-GOOD, this ultra-fast recipe combines chicken tacos and saucy enchiladas. While store-bought enchilada sauce is fine in a pinch, I highly recommend making these with my richer-tasting, less expensive (and lower sodium) Easy Red Enchilada Sauce (page 316). I like to serve these with a simple green salad topped with thinned Avocado Ranch Dip (page 80) and Grilled Mexican Corn on the Cob (page 189). Be sure to have plenty of napkins on hand!*

MAKES 4 SERVINGS

1½ cups shredded cooked chicken breast

1 cup store-bought or Easy Red Enchilada Sauce (page 316)

8 (6-inch) corn tortillas

½ cup reduced-fat shredded Mexican blend cheese

1 cup shredded iceberg lettuce

1. In a small saucepan, heat the chicken in the enchilada sauce for 2 to 3 minutes, or until hot.

2. Lightly wet the tortillas and wrap them in either a clean dish-towel or paper towel and microwave 1 minute, or until warmed. Spoon about ¼ cup of chicken mixture into each tortilla, sprinkle with 1 tablespoon cheese, and top with 2 tablespoons shredded lettuce. Repeat with remaining ingredients.

**Marlene Says:** *You will use half of the sauce with this recipe. The remainder will keep for up to a week in the refrigerator. Try it spooned on to a cheese omelet or as a dipping sauce for grilled chicken.*

**NUTRITION INFORMATION PER SERVING:** (2 tacos) Calories 200 | Carbohydrate 24g (Sugars 3g) | Total Fat 5g (Sat Fat 2g) | Protein 15g | Fiber 4g | Cholesterol 40mg | Sodium 510mg | Food Exchanges: 2 Lean Meat, 1 Starch | Carbohydrate Choices: 1½ | Weight Watcher Smart Point Comparison: 4

# Korean-Style BBQ Tacos

*ORIGINATING FROM A HUMBLE TACO TRUCK IN LOS ANGELES IN 2008, tantalizing Korean-style tacos have taken the food world by storm. Either beef, or in this case pork, is marinated in a sweet and spicy Asian marinade, grilled or stir-fried, stuffed into a corn tortilla, and then topped with a tangy cabbage slaw. The result is an intoxicating mix of east-meets-southwest textures and flavors that has folks lining up. If you love Asian flavors, these are a must-try.*

**MAKES 4 SERVINGS**

3 tablespoons reduced-sodium soy sauce

2 teaspoons sesame oil

1 teaspoon minced garlic

1 teaspoon minced fresh ginger

1/8 teaspoon red pepper flakes

3 tablespoons rice vinegar, divided

1 1/2 tablespoons plus 2 teaspoons brown sugar, divided

12 ounces pork tenderloin, chopped

2 cups bagged coleslaw mix

2 green onions, thinly sliced

2 tablespoons chopped cilantro

8 (6-inch) corn tortillas

1. In a medium bowl, whisk together the first 5 ingredients (soy sauce through pepper flakes) with 1 tablespoon rice vinegar and 1 1/2 tablespoons brown sugar. Add the pork, stir, and let marinate for 10 to 15 minutes.

2. In another medium bowl, combine the coleslaw mix, green onions, cilantro, remaining 2 tablespoons vinegar, and remaining 2 teaspoons brown sugar. Set aside.

3. Place a large nonstick skillet over medium-high heat, add half the pork (not crowding it in the pan browns it much better), and cook for 4 to 5 minutes, or until nicely browned, stirring occasionally. Set aside and repeat with remaining pork.

4. Lightly wet the tortillas and wrap them in a dishtowel or paper towel and microwave for 1 minute, or until warm. Spoon about 1/4 cup pork into each tortilla and top with 1/4 cup slaw.

**Marlene Says:** *To chop the pork tenderloin, cut the loin into half-inch-thick slices. Place slices on a cutting board and pound lightly to flatten. With a sharp knife, chop into bite-sized pieces.*

**NUTRITION INFORMATION PER SERVING: (2 tacos)** Calories 265 | Carbohydrate 31g (Sugars 11g) | Total Fat 7g (Sat Fat 2g) | Protein 22g | Fiber 3g | Cholesterol 50mg | Sodium 550mg | Food Exchanges: 3 Lean Meat, 2 Starch, 1/2 Vegetable | Carbohydrate Choices: 2 | Weight Watcher Smart Point Comparison: 7

# Blackened Tilapia Po'Boys

*WHEN MADE WITH DEEP FRIED FISH AND RICH REMOULADE SAUCE, a traditional po'boy (Southern-style sub sandwich) can easily break the bank when it comes to both fat and calories. When creating this better 'boy, I made sure to include all the classic ingredients, including the crusty bread and a zesty remoulade-style sauce. I must have gotten it right because when I asked my husband to taste it, the only response I got was "Mmm. . . ."*

MAKES 4 SERVINGS

3 tablespoons light mayonnaise

3 tablespoons plain low-fat Greek yogurt

2 tablespoons dill pickle relish

1½ teaspoons cider vinegar

1 green onion, minced

A few drops of hot sauce

4 (4- to 5-ounce) tilapia fillets

2 teaspoons Cajun seasoning

4 pieces crusty baguette (2 ounces each)*

2 cups shredded iceberg lettuce

1 tomato, thinly sliced

1. To make the sauce, in a small bowl, whisk together first 6 ingredients (mayonnaise through hot sauce) and set aside.

2. To make the sandwich, sprinkle each side of the tilapia fillets with ½ teaspoon of Cajun seasoning. Spray a large nonstick skillet with cooking spray and place over medium-high heat. When the skillet is hot, add tilapia, seasoned side down, and cook for 2 minutes. Flip and continue to cook for 3 more minutes, or until cooked through.

3. Split the baguette pieces horizontally and spread the bottom half of each with 2 tablespoons of the sauce. Top with fish, lettuce, and tomato slices and close the top half of the baguette.

**Marlene Says:** *To keep flavor at a maximum and sodium in check, select a Cajun seasoning where salt is not the first ingredient. McCormick Gourmet Cajun seasoning is one I like, but feel free to use your favorite Cajun mix.*

\* One-fourth of an 8-ounce baguette works great for each roll, or use a crusty French roll of your choice.

**NUTRITION INFORMATION PER SERVING:** (1 sandwich) Calories 300 | Carbohydrate 34g (Sugars 4g) | Total Fat 5g (Sat Fat 1g) | Protein 29g | Fiber 3g | Cholesterol 55mg | Sodium 680mg | Food Exchanges: 3 Lean Meat, 2 Starch, ½ Vegetable | Carbohydrate Choices: 2 | Weight Watcher Smart Point Comparison: 6

# Loaded Philly Cheesesteak

*WHEN ORDERING A CHEESECAKE IN PHILLY, you say "wit" if you want onions and "wit whiz" if you want onions and cheese whiz (an ooey gooey combo that is hard to beat). If you really want to go for it, you can add sautéed mushrooms, and that is what I have done here. Loaded to the hilt with caramelized veggies, flavorful beef, and melted American cheese, this is what I call a scrumptious sandwich (oh, and it's a better-for-you sandwich too!).*

MAKES 2 SERVINGS

2 pieces of crusty baguette (2 ounces each)*

5 ounces sirloin steak

¼ teaspoon garlic salt, divided

½ large onion, sliced

1 small green pepper, sliced

1½ cups thinly sliced mushrooms

1½ teaspoons Worcestershire sauce, divided

½ teaspoon dried oregano

2 slices reduced-fat American cheese

1. Slice pieces of baguette in half lengthwise. Set aside. Slice the steak across the grain as thinly as possible. Spray a nonstick skillet with cooking spray and place over medium-high heat. When the skillet is hot, add the beef, sprinkle with ⅛ teaspoon garlic salt, and sauté, turning for 1 to 2 minutes, or until just no longer pink. Remove from pan.

2. Spray the skillet with cooking spray and add onions and peppers. Cook for 3 to 4 minutes, or until slightly softened and starting to brown. Add mushrooms, sprinkle with 1 teaspoon Worcestershire sauce, oregano, and remaining ⅛ teaspoon garlic salt. Add 1 tablespoon water and sauté vegetables, stirring often, until the onions start to caramelize and the vegetables are soft.

3. Return the steak to the skillet, sprinkle with remaining ½ teaspoon Worcestershire sauce, and stir. Separate mixture in half and place 1 slice of cheese over each half. Add 1 tablespoon water, cover skillet, and cook for 30 seconds or until cheese is melted. Scoop one half of filling into each roll.

**DARE TO COMPARE:** According to the University of Pennsylvania Health System, a Philadelphia cheesesteak packs 900 calories, 40 grams of fat, and over 1,500 milligrams of sodium.

* One-fourth of an 8-ounce baguette works great for each roll, or use a crusty French roll of your choice.

**NUTRITION INFORMATION PER SERVING: (1 sandwich)** Calories 345 | Carbohydrate 42g (Sugars 7g) | Total Fat 8g (Sat Fat 4g) | Protein 31g | Fiber 4g | Cholesterol 65mg | Sodium 750mg | Food Exchanges: Starch, 1½ Vegetable, 3 Lean Meat | Carbohydrate Choices: 3 | Weight Watcher Smart Point Comparison: 8

# Southwest Beef & Bean Burgers

*IF YOU'RE LOOKING FOR AN EASIER, FASTER, BETTER BURGER, this one has it all! With a 50/50 blend of healthy, fiber-rich beans and Southwest-seasoned lean beef, these flavor-packed patties take only a few minutes to create and just eight minutes under the broiler to cook (without a messy pan or grill to clean). And if the great flavor weren't enough, these economical ⅓-pound burgers pack a whopping 13 grams of fiber. That's something you can't say about many burgers!*

MAKES 4 SERVINGS

1 (15-ounce) can black beans, rinsed and drained

12 ounces lean ground beef

¼ cup prepared salsa

1 tablespoon DIY Taco Seasoning mix (page 312 or store-bought)

¼ cup minced fresh cilantro

4 whole-grain hamburger buns

1 cup shredded iceberg lettuce

¼ cup light sour cream

Extra salsa and cilantro (optional)

1. Heat the broiler and line a baking sheet with foil.

2. Place the beans in a medium bowl. Mash them with a potato masher or large fork, leaving about one-fourth of the beans whole. Add the beef, salsa, taco seasoning, and cilantro, and mix gently to combine.

3. Divide the beef mixture into 4 portions and flatten to form four 4-inch patties. Place on prepared baking sheet and broil for 4 to 5 minutes, or until a light crust forms. Turn and broil for 4 minutes, or until a light crust forms on second side, and the burgers are warmed through.

4. Warm the hamburger buns. On the bottom of each bun, place a burger and top with ¼ cup lettuce and 1 tablespoon sour cream. Garnish with additional salsa and cilantro, if desired, and add top half of the bun.

**Marlene Says:** *Once the patties are made, they can be wrapped tightly and refrigerated for up to 2 days or frozen for several weeks. Cook them on a grill sheet or rack.*

**NUTRITION INFORMATION PER SERVING: (1 burger)** Calories 320| Carbohydrate 39g (Sugars 5g) | Total Fat 7g (Sat Fat 4g) | Protein 27g | Fiber 13g | Cholesterol 45mg | Sodium 540mg | Food Exchanges: 3 Lean Meat, 2 Starch | Carbohydrate Choices: 2½ | Weight Watcher Smart Point Comparison: 6

# Double Mushroom Swiss Burger

*MY HUSBAND IS A BIG FAN OF MUSHROOM SWISS BURGERS—and he's got plenty of company! In this big, beefy classic burger, mushrooms do double duty; finely minced mushrooms add extra flavor and moisture, and sliced, seasoned shrooms adorn the melty, cheesy top. Once you enjoy this burger at home you may agree with my husband: There's no reason to ever order it out again.*

**MAKES 4 SERVINGS**

1 (8-ounce) package whole mushrooms, divided

3 tablespoons dry breadcrumbs

1 large egg white

¼ teaspoon salt

1 pound lean ground beef

4 teaspoons Worcestershire sauce, divided

½ teaspoon plus a pinch black pepper, divided

4 slices reduced-fat Swiss cheese

4 whole grain hamburger buns

Red onion and lettuce (optional)

1. Remove the stems from the mushrooms. Slice mushroom caps into ¼-inch slices. Combine stems and enough slices to make ¾ cup. Mince only measured mushrooms and transfer to a large bowl. Add next 4 ingredients (breadcrumbs through beef), along with 1 tablespoon of Worcestershire and ½ teaspoon black pepper. Mix gently to combine. Divide the mixture into 4 portions and flatten to form patties.

2. Coat a large nonstick skillet with cooking spray and place over medium-high heat. Add remaining sliced mushrooms and cook for 4 minutes, or until mushrooms begin to brown. Add 2 tablespoons water, remaining teaspoon of Worcestershire sauce, and a pinch of black pepper, stirring to coat mushrooms. Cook until most the liquid is gone, and transfer to a plate.

3. Wipe the skillet clean, coat with cooking spray, and place over medium heat. Add the patties and cook for 3 to 4 minutes on each side, or until barely cooked though. Top each with a slice of cheese and cover skillet for 2 minutes. Warm buns, top with lettuce and onion, if desired. Add beef patties, top with mushrooms, add second half of buns, and serve.

**DARE TO COMPARE:** Eating the restaurant version of a mushroom Swiss burger, without sides, averages 900 calories, 50 grams of fat, and over 1,000 milligrams of sodium.

**NUTRITION INFORMATION PER SERVING:** (1 burger) Calories 330 | Carbohydrate 28g (Sugars 3g) | Total Fat 12g (Sat Fat 5g) | Protein 32g | Fiber 7g | Cholesterol 60mg | Sodium 380mg | Food Exchanges: 1½ Starch, ½ Vegetable, 4 Lean Meat | Carbohydrate Choices: 1½ | Weight Watcher Smart Point Comparison: 8

# SIMPLE SIDE & ENTRÉE SALADS

## simple side & easy entrée salads

# Mixed Greens with Tomato Balsamic Vinaigrette

*ONE OF THE HEALTHIEST (AND TASTIEST) TRICKS to reduce fat in salad dressings is to replace some of the fat with a vegetable or fruit purée. For this dressing I've added a juicy ripe tomato, which not only adds fantastic flavor, but also banishes over 700 calories of unwanted fat! This versatile vinaigrette keeps well in the fridge for several days, so feel free to double it. It's terrific with spinach greens.*

**MAKES 4 SERVINGS**

Dressing

1 medium tomato

3 tablespoons balsamic vinegar

2 tablespoons minced shallot or red onion

1½ tablespoons extra-virgin olive oil

¼ teaspoon salt

¼ teaspoon black pepper

Salad

5 cups mixed greens

¾ cup garbanzo beans, drained and rinsed

2 medium tomatoes, sliced

1 small cucumber, seeded and sliced

½ cup thinly sliced red onion (optional)

1. To make the dressing, seed and chop the tomato (you should have about ¾ cup). Add the remaining dressing ingredients in a blender and blend until smooth.

2. For the salad, in a large bowl, combine the mixed greens, garbanzos, tomatoes, cucumber, and onion, if desired. Pour the dressing over the salad and toss lightly.

**DARE TO COMPARE:** A 2-tablespoon serving of this dressing has 40 calories, 3.5 grams fat, 100 milligrams of sodium, and 3 grams of carbohydrates. In comparison, a single tablespoon of oil has 120 calories and 14 grams of fat.

**NUTRITION INFORMATION PER SERVING:** (1 ¾ cups) Calories 135 | Carbohydrate 17g (Sugars 5g) | Total Fat 6g (Sat Fat 1g) | Protein 5g | Fiber 5g | Cholesterol 0mg | Sodium 180mg | Food Exchanges: 1½ Vegetable, ½ Starch, 1 Fat | Carbohydrate Choices: 1 | Weight Watcher Smart Point Comparison: 2

# Anytime Tomato Salad

*AS FAR AS I AM CONCERNED, YOU CAN NEVER HAVE TOO MANY SIMPLE SALADS or sides in your recipe repertoire—and this salad is one of my favorites. The quick-to-make sweet and sour dressing takes the humble tomato, cucumber, and red onion to new heights in a hurry. It's a versatile salad that pairs perfectly with a sandwich, grilled chicken, steak, or fish. It's also easy to throw together for a last-minute potluck.*

MAKES 4 SERVINGS

¼ cup apple cider vinegar

1 tablespoon brown sugar

1 tablespoon canola oil

½ teaspoon salt

¾ cup red onion, thinly sliced

3 medium tomatoes (about 1 pound)

1 small cucumber

Fresh ground black pepper, to taste

1. In a medium bowl, whisk together the vinegar, sugar, oil, and salt. Add the onions and let stand for 10 minutes.

2. Cut the tomatoes into wedges and the cucumber into thin slices (I leave on the peel), and add them to the onion mixture. Stir gently to combine. Serve with fresh ground pepper to taste.

**Marlene Says:** *Try this with Turkey Wrap with Pesto Mayo (page 126), 2-Minute Greek Lemon Chicken (page 215), Everyday Marinated Steak (page 229), or Grilled Steak-Style Portobellos (page 265).*

**NUTRITION INFORMATION PER SERVING:** (¾ cup) Calories 65 | Carbohydrate 11g (Sugars 8g) | Total Fat 3g (Sat Fat 0g) | Protein 2g | Fiber 2g | Cholesterol 5mg | Sodium 120mg | Food Exchanges: 1½ Vegetable, ½ Fat | Carbohydrate Choices: 1 | Weight Watcher Smart Point Comparison: 1

# Bibb and Blue Salad

*SWEET, SALTY, CREAMY, AND CRUNCHY—this winning (and slimming) makeover of the popular Bibb & Bleu Salad at Romano's Macaroni Grill offers the great taste of the original, only now with a fraction of the calories, fat, and sodium. I swapped out the pricy prosciutto bits for gorgeous green apple slices, but other than that all of the same elements are here—including the wonderfully sweet and tangy pickled red onions. Weeknight-easy, this salad is also special-occasion worthy.*

MAKES 4 SERVINGS

1 medium red onion, thinly sliced

¼ cup cider vinegar

2 teaspoons sugar

¼ teaspoon salt

1 recipe Buttermilk Scallion Dressing (page 309)

1½ to 2 heads bibb lettuce, torn into individual leaves

1 Granny Smith apple, cored and thinly sliced

¼ cup reduced-fat blue cheese

¼ cup coarsely chopped walnuts

1. In a small bowl, toss the red onion, vinegar, sugar, and salt together. Let stand at least 20 minutes, and up to 2 hours. Just before using, drain off the liquid. Make the dressing and set aside.

2. To make each salad, portion the lettuce leaves among 4 plates, stacking the leaves on each other. Top each with a quarter of the green apple slices, drizzle with 2 rounded tablespoons dressing, and top with a quarter of the red onions. Garnish each salad with 1 tablespoon each blue cheese and walnuts.

**DARE TO COMPARE:** As stated on the menu, the Bibb & Bleu Salad at Romano's Macaroni Grill has a stunning 680 calories, 56 grams of fat, including 14 grams of saturated fat, and 2,020 milligrams of sodium.

**NUTRITION INFORMATION PER SERVING: (1 salad)** Calories 120 | Carbohydrate 8g (Sugars 6g) | Total Fat 7g (Sat Fat 1.5g) | Protein 6g | Fiber 2g | Cholesterol 5mg | Sodium 160mg | Food Exchanges: 1 Vegetable, 1 Fat | Carbohydrate Choices: ½ | Weight Watcher Smart Point Comparison: 3

# Tender Kale and Bacon Salad with Strawberry Vinaigrette

*MY HUSBAND HAS EATEN PLENTY OF KALE SALADS. So I listened keenly when he fessed up that he never really liked any of them. He said that he ate them because he figured they were good for him. But after one bite of this kale salad, he declared that he would happily eat it every day! The scrumptious taste comes from the combination of sweet dressing, fresh strawberries, and smoky bacon, but what really sets this salad apart is the simple technique of massaging the kale to soften it. Prepare to be amazed at the difference it makes.*

MAKES 4 SERVINGS

Dressing

2 tablespoons balsamic vinegar

2 tablespoons reduced-sugar strawberry jam

1 teaspoon Dijon mustard

1/8 teaspoon black pepper

1 tablespoon olive oil

Salad

1 bunch curly or dinosaur kale

1 teaspoon olive oil

1/8 teaspoon salt

1 large carrot, peeled and sliced into ribbons

2/3 cup fresh sliced strawberries

2 tablespoons real bacon bits

1. In a small bowl, whisk together the vinegar, jam, mustard, and pepper. Drizzle in the oil and whisk until combined. Set aside.

2. Remove the ribs from the kale and roughly chop into 3/4-inch strips. Place the kale in a large bowl, drizzle with oil, and sprinkle with salt. Gently rub (massage) the kale between your fingers for 30 to 35 seconds, or until it wilts slightly and the leaves smooth. Add the strawberries and carrots and gently toss the salad with the dressing. Sprinkle bacon bits on top and serve.

**NUTRITION INFORMATION PER SERVING:** (1½ cups) Calories 140 | Carbohydrate 14g (Sugars 7g) | Total Fat 7g (Sat Fat 2g) | Protein 7g | Fiber 2g | Cholesterol 10mg | Sodium 420mg | Food Exchanges: 1 Vegetable, 1 Fat, ½ Fruit | Carbohydrate Choices: 1 | Weight Watcher Smart Point Comparison: 2

# Whole Grain Mediterranean Salad

*THIS TWIST ON A CLASSIC TABBOULEH SALAD swaps out whole grain bulgur wheat for superfood whole grain quinoa. Tremendously fresh tasting as well as tremendously good for you, this salad packs a solid nutritional punch, delivering healthy doses of vitamins C, E, and K, in addition to minerals like magnesium, manganese, and iron. I like to keep a bit of the cucumber skin on for color, but how much you keep is up to you. Fresh chopped basil or mint leaves are delicious herbaceous additions.*

MAKES 4 SERVINGS

⅓ cup uncooked quinoa

2 tablespoons fresh lemon juice

1 tablespoon olive oil

¼ teaspoon salt

¼ teaspoon black pepper

1 medium tomato, chopped

½ cucumber, peeled, seeded and chopped

¼ cup chopped parsley

¼ cup chopped green onion

1. Place the quinoa in a strainer, rinse well, and prepare according to package directions. When cooked, transfer to a medium bowl to cool (this can be done ahead of time).

2. In a small bowl, whisk together lemon juice, olive oil, salt, and pepper.

3. When the quinoa is cool, add the next 4 ingredients (tomato through green onion) and the dressing, and toss to combine. Refrigerate until served.

**NUTRITION INFORMATION PER SERVING:** (¾ cup) Calories 85 | Carbohydrate 11g (Sugars 2g) | Total Fat 4g (Sat Fat 0g) | Protein 2g | Fiber 2g | Cholesterol 0mg | Sodium 150mg | Food Exchanges: ½ Starch, ½ Vegetable | Carbohydrate Choices: 1 | Weight Watcher Smart Point Comparison: 2

# Watermelon Feta "Pizza" Salad

*COLD, JUICY, SWEET WATERMELON, paired with creamy, salty feta and fresh mint is a spectacular combination of tastes and textures. It's also visually gorgeous. It's no wonder this has become a summer salad sensation for foodies and food bloggers alike. Inspired by one of my favorite food bloggers, Brokeass Gourmet, I serve this salad pizza-style! There's no need to cube the watermelon, and no forks are required. Sticking to the theme, I've also added a sweet and tangy balsamic drizzle as the "sauce." So fun, so fresh, so fantastic!*

MAKES 4 SERVINGS

¼ cup balsamic vinegar

1 teaspoon honey

¾- to 1½-inch slice of watermelon

¼ cup slivered red onion

2 tablespoons crumbled feta cheese

1 tablespoon fresh mint leaves, thinly sliced

1. To make the balsamic syrup, stir the vinegar and honey together in a small pot, and simmer over medium heat for 4 to 6 minutes, or until thick and syrupy and reduced by one half. (Watch carefully near the end of cooking—once reduced, the syrup can burn quickly.)

2. Cut the watermelon round into 4 wedges, keeping pieces together. Top watermelon evenly with onion slivers, followed by the feta and mint. Drizzle 2 teaspoons of balsamic syrup over the entire watermelon round immediately before serving (there will be leftover syrup).

**NUTRITION INFORMATION PER SERVING: (1 wedge)** Calories 50 | Carbohydrate 9g (Sugars 8g) | Total Fat 1g (Sat Fat .5g) | Protein 1g | Fiber 0g | Cholesterol 10 g | Sodium 70mg | Food Exchanges: ½ Fruit | Carbohydrate Choices: ½ | Weight Watcher Smart Point Comparison: 1

# Creamy Crunchy Pea Salad

*TERRIFIC FOR POTLUCKS, SPECIAL OCCASIONS, AND SUNDAY SUPPERS, cool, creamy pea salads—made with plenty of cheese, mayonnaise, and bacon—are a beloved Southern tradition. I am pleased to say that while I have lightened up this salad, I have still done the South proud. All the delectable must-have essentials are still here, plus water chestnuts for extra crunch and green onions for extra flavor. Quick tip: Run hot water over frozen peas and they thaw almost immediately!*

MAKES 6 SERVINGS

1 (12-ounce) bag frozen peas, thawed

1 (8-ounce) can sliced water chestnuts, drained and chopped

1/4 cup light mayonnaise

3 tablespoons plain nonfat yogurt

4 green onions, sliced diagonally, divided

1/4 teaspoon salt

6 tablespoons shredded reduced-fat sharp cheddar cheese

1 tablespoon real bacon bits

1. In a medium bowl, gently mix together peas, water chestnuts, mayonnaise, yogurt, 3/4 of the green onions, and salt.

2. To serve, top with cheese, remaining green onions, and bacon bits.

**Marlene Says:** *When compared to classic pea and cheddar salad, this recipe has just 1/3 of the calories and 90% less fat! To keep at its creamiest best, mix the salad within 1 to 2 hours of serving.*

**NUTRITION INFORMATION PER SERVING:** (2/3 cup) Calories 100 | Carbohydrate 11g (Sugars 4g) | Total Fat 3g (Sat Fat 0.5g) | Protein 6g | Fiber 5g | Cholesterol 0mg | Sodium 230mg | Food Exchanges: 1/2 Starch, 1/2 Fat | Carbohydrate Choices: 1/2 | Weight Watcher Smart Point Comparison: 1

# Creamy Potato Mac Potluck Salad

*IF YOU THINK YOU HAVE TO CHOOSE BETWEEN THE POTLUCK FAVORITES of potato salad and macaroni salad, think no more. Based on a side dish that you might find at one of Hawaii's popular plate lunch restaurants, this creamy, potluck-sized salad combines the two, with fresh broccoli to boot! To streamline the preparation, a single pot of boiling water cooks the potatoes, macaroni, and broccoli.*

**MAKES 10 SERVINGS**

¼ cup light mayonnaise

¼ cup plain nonfat Greek yogurt

2 tablespoons low-fat milk

½ teaspoon salt, divided

¼ teaspoon fresh ground black pepper

1 pound small red potatoes

1 cup dry large tube-shaped pasta, such as large elbows or ziti

4 cups broccoli florets

2 tablespoons rice vinegar

2 medium carrots, coarsely grated

2 medium stalks celery, thinly sliced

¼ cup sliced green onion

1. In a small bowl, whisk together the mayonnaise, yogurt, milk, ¼ teaspoon salt, and pepper.

2. Place the potatoes in a pot of cold water and bring to a boil over medium-high heat. Cook potatoes 15 to 20 minutes, or until fork-tender but not mushy. Using a slotted spoon, lift potatoes out of the water and transfer to a large bowl, leaving the water boiling.

3. Add the macaroni to the boiling water and cook for 6 minutes. Add the broccoli and cook for 3 more minutes. Strain the pasta and broccoli and rinse with cold water.

4. While the pasta cooks, peel and cube the warm potatoes, return to bowl, and sprinkle with the vinegar and remaining ¼ teaspoon salt. Add the drained pasta mixture, carrots, celery, and green onion. Within 1 hour of serving, add the dressing and gently stir until mixed. Garnish with additional green onion, if desired. (Dressing the salad sooner will make it less creamy.)

**NUTRITION INFORMATION PER SERVING:** (¾ cup) Calories 110 | Carbohydrate 20g (Sugars 3g) | Total Fat 2g (Sat Fat 0g) | Protein 4g | Fiber 3g | Cholesterol 0mg | Sodium 190mg | Food Exchanges: 1 Starch, ½ Vegetable | Carbohydrate Choices: 1 | Weight Watcher Smart Point Comparison: 3

# Upside-Down Strawberry Pretzel Salad

*I HAVE TAKEN THIS BELOVED DESSERT-STYLE SALAD and its irresistible tastes and textures and turned it upside down! Tasting fresher than ever, with no pretzel crust required, I guarantee there will be plenty of oohs and ahhs when you bring this to the table. It can be prepped a day ahead of time, and is the perfect addition to your next buffet or holiday gathering. (Psst . . . there's no need to share that is has just 1/3 of the usual calories and carbs and 80% less fat!)*

MAKES 12 SERVINGS

1 large package (8-serving size) sugar-free strawberry gelatin

3 cups sliced strawberries

3/4 cup low-fat cottage cheese

3/4 cup light tub-style cream cheese

1/4 cup granulated no-calorie sweetener*

1 1/4 cups light whipped topping, thawed

1 teaspoon lemon zest

3/4 cup roughly crushed pretzels

1. Place the gelatin and 1 1/2 cups boiling water in a medium bowl and whisk for 2 minutes or until gelatin is dissolved. Stir in 1 1/2 cups ice water. Refrigerate until mixture is slightly thickened, about 30 minutes. Stir in the strawberries, transfer to a 2-quart rectangular casserole dish, and refrigerate.

2. Place the cottage cheese in a food processor or blender and process until completely smooth. Add cream cheese and pulse until blended. Transfer mixture into a medium bowl, and fold in sweetener, whipped topping, and lemon zest. Cover and refrigerate.

3. When gelatin has set, spread with the cream cheese mixture. Just before serving, top with crushed pretzels.

**DARE TO COMPARE:** A credit-card-sized serving of the classic pretzel-crusted strawberry cream cheese salad has 310 calories and 20 grams of fat—and 9 Weight Watcher Plus Points. You would have to walk 3 miles to burn off one meager-sized piece.

*See page 36 for sweetener options.

**NUTRITION INFORMATION PER SERVING:** (2/3 cup) Calories 105 | Carbohydrate 10g (Sugars 5g) | Total Fat 4g (Sat Fat 3g) | Protein 5g | Fiber 1g | Cholesterol 10mg | Sodium 250mg | Food Exchanges: 1/2 Fruit, 1/2 Carbohydrate, 1/2 Fat | Carbohydrate Choices: 1 | Weight Watcher Smart Point Comparison: 3

# Chicken BLT Salad with Ranch Dressing

*MIRRORING THE DOWN HOME GOODNESS OF A BLT SANDWICH, this better-for-you, man-loving, kid-friendly salad only tastes sin-sational. Creamy ranch dressing adorns fresh greens plump with ripe tomatoes, tender shredded chicken, and mayonnaise-laced croutons. Then comes the bacon and, of course, only the real thing will do. To keep it quick, I use Rotisserie chicken and when time is extra tight I top the salad with pre-cooked bacon bits (1 tablespoon = 1 slice of lean cooked bacon).*

MAKES 4 SERVINGS

4 slices sourdough or French bread

2 tablespoons light mayonnaise

6 slices center-cut bacon

8 cups chopped green leaf lettuce

2 medium tomatoes, chopped

2 cups coarsely shredded cooked chicken breast

3/4 cup Homemade Ranch Dressing (page 308 or store-bought)

1/4 cup chopped green onion

1. Preheat the oven to 425°F. Spread one side of each slice of bread with 1½ teaspoons mayonnaise. Place directly on rack in oven (mayo-side up) and bake for 8 minutes, or until bottoms are golden brown. Remove and cut into 1-inch croutons. Set aside.

2. Cook the bacon until crisp. Roughly crumble and set aside.

3. To assemble salad, place 2 cups lettuce onto each of four plates. Tuck equal amounts of tomato and croutons into lettuce, and top each salad with ½ cup shredded chicken. Drizzle 3 table-spoons dressing over each, sprinkle with 1 tablespoon green onion, and top with equal amounts of bacon.

**DARE TO COMPARE:** There are 639 calories in a Burger King Garden Fresh BLT Salad with Chicken, including a whopping 45 grams of fat.

**NUTRITION INFORMATION PER SERVING:** (1 salad) Calories 255 | Carbohydrate 21g (Sugars 4g) | Total Fat 10g (Sat Fat 1.5g) | Protein 24g | Fiber 3g | Cholesterol 50mg | Sodium 620mg | Food Exchanges: 2 Lean Meat, 1 Starch, 1 Vegetable, 1 Fat | Carbohydrate Choices: 1 | Weight Watcher Smart Point Comparison: 4

# Creamy Shrimp and Dill Wedge

*FOR ME, A SEAFOOD SALAD IS A PERFECT LUNCH. Luckily, I can make this lovely, slim shrimp salad for my husband and myself in just 15 minutes. I buy cooked shrimp from the seafood case, but frozen will also work. "Bay" shrimp size, or a 50 to 60 per-pound count, are just right. To thaw shrimp quickly, place them in a bowl of cold water for about 15 minutes. A freshly boiled warm egg is a delicious complement to this cool, creamy salad.*

MAKES 2 SERVINGS

**Dressing**

¼ cup low-fat milk

2 tablespoons light mayonnaise

2 tablespoons plain nonfat Greek yogurt

½ teaspoon dried dill weed

½ teaspoon lemon zest

⅛ teaspoon salt

**Salad**

½ head iceberg lettuce

8 ounces small cooked shrimp

½ cup thinly sliced cucumber

1 large hard-boiled egg, quartered

Lemon wedges, for garnish

1. In a small bowl, whisk together the dressing ingredients. Set aside.

2. Cut lettuce into 2 wedges and place each onto a plate. Top each wedge with half the shrimp and half the dressing (about ¼ cup). Arrange half of the cucumber slices and 2 egg quarters on the plate around each wedge. Serve with lemon wedges for squeezing over any bare lettuce or shrimp.

**Marlene Says:** *This recipe is easily doubled for a dinner party. Here's a shortcut: Instead of individually plating the salads, place the lettuce wedges on a long tray, top them with the shrimp and dressing, and use the eggs, cucumber slices, and lemon wedges to decorate the tray. Beautiful.*

**NUTRITION INFORMATION PER SERVING: (1 salad)** Calories 220 | Carbohydrate 7g (Sugars 5g) | Total Fat 8g (Sat Fat 1.5g) | Protein 32g | Fiber 2g | Cholesterol 315mg | Sodium 580mg | Food Exchanges: 4 Lean Meat, 1 Vegetable | Carbohydrate Choices: ½ | Weight Watcher Smart Point Comparison: 2

# Nacho Chip Taco Salad

*IN 2012, TACO BELL INTRODUCED THE DORITOS LOCOS TACO—seasoned ground beef topped with lettuce, cheese, and sour cream tucked into a nacho-flavored taco shell. Within a year they sold 500 million of them! This speedy salad, tossed in a sweet and tangy dressing, has the same delicious flavors. I could eat this salad every day, and I truly believe if it were on the menu, it would be a runaway bestseller (my son James and his friends tore through the sample bowl in no time flat!). If you need a great party dish, double the recipe to serve up to 12 as part of a buffet.*

MAKES 4 SERVINGS

8 ounces lean ground beef

1 tablespoon DIY Taco Seasoning (page 312 or packaged)

6 cups chopped iceberg lettuce

1 large tomato, diced

1/2 cup shredded reduced-fat cheddar cheese

1/2 cup light French or Catalina dressing

2 ounces crumbled nacho cheese tortilla chips, like Doritos

Light sour cream (optional)

1. Spray a large nonstick skillet with cooking spray and place over medium high heat. Add the beef and taco seasoning, and cook for 5 to 7 minutes, or until beef is browned.

2. For the salad, in a large bowl, place the lettuce, tomato, cheese, and cooked beef. Pour the dressing over the salad and toss gently to combine. Add the crumbled tortilla chips and toss lightly. Garnish with light sour cream, if desired.

**Marlene Says:** *I prefer regular, not baked chips, for this salad. To keep myself from eating an entire large bag, I simply buy a couple of the small lunch-sized ones to make the salad.*

**NUTRITION INFORMATION PER SERVING:** (2 cups) Calories 290 | Carbohydrate 24g (Sugars 11g) | Total Fat 12g (Sat Fat 5g) | Protein 22g | Fiber 3g | Cholesterol 40mg | Sodium 740mg | Food Exchanges: 2½ Lean Meat, 1 Vegetable, 1½ Carbohydrate | Carbohydrate Choices: 1½ | Weight Watcher Smart Point Comparison: 8

# Teriyaki Salmon and Spinach Salad

*A FRESH ORANGE DOES TRIPLE DUTY in this 20-minute, dinner-worthy, heart-healthy salad. The zest and juice go into the citrusy dressing and juicy slices adorn the finished salad. For the teriyaki sauce, I recommend Kikkoman Less Sodium Teriyaki Marinade and Sauce. For restaurant flair, try sprinkling on some sesame seeds or sliced almonds as a garnish.*

MAKES 2 SERVINGS

Dressing

1 medium orange

2 tablespoons seasoned rice vinegar

1/2 teaspoon toasted sesame oil

1/4 teaspoon yellow mustard

Salad

4 cups spinach leaves

1/4 cup shredded carrot

1/2 cucumber, peeled and sliced into rounds

1/2 cup sliced water chestnuts

2 tablespoons reduced-sodium Teriyaki sauce

2 teaspoons brown sugar

2 (5-ounce) salmon fillets, rinsed and patted dry

Fresh ground black pepper

1. Cut the orange in half. Zest one of the halves and place 1/2 teaspoon zest in a small bowl. Squeeze in the juice from the zested half, add the remaining dressing ingredients, and whisk. Divide the spinach leaves between two plates. Top equally with the carrots, cucumber, and water chestnuts. Cut remaining orange half into slices, garnish the salad plates, and set aside.

2. In a small bowl, combine teriyaki sauce and brown sugar. Coat a large nonstick skillet with cooking spray and place over medium-high heat. Add the salmon, brush the top with the teriyaki sauce, and cook for 4 minutes, or until bottoms are browned. Add 1 tablespoon of water to the pan, turn the salmon, reduce heat to medium, cover the skillet, and cook for 2 to 3 minutes or until pieces are well glazed. Flip salmon back over and cook just until the fish flakes when teased with a fork.

3. Dress each salad with half of the dressing, top with salmon, and garnish with freshly ground pepper.

**NUTRITION INFORMATION PER SERVING: (1 salad)** Calories 270 | Carbohydrate 22g (Sugars 16g) | Total Fat 6g (Sat Fat 1g) | Protein 31g | Fiber 4g | Cholesterol 75mg | Sodium 780mg | Food Exchanges: 4 Medium Fat Meat, 2 Vegetables, 1 Carbohydrate, 1/4 Fruit | Carbohydrate Choices: 1 1/2 | Weight Watcher Smart Point Comparison: 2

# Steakhouse Steak Salad

*STEAKHOUSES OFTEN LIST STEAK SALADS ON THEIR MENUS in an effort to appeal to health-conscious diners, but with more than 1,000 calories in a typical steak salad, they're not nearly as healthy as they appear. With tender lean beef, warm, savory mushrooms, ripe tomato wedges, and a creamy horseradish-tinged dressing—all for a mere 250 calories—this manly steak salad shows how tasty and healthy one can be. I serve it family-style, but it can also be individually plated.*

**MAKES 4 SERVINGS**

¾ cup Buttermilk Scallion Dressing (page 309)

2 teaspoons prepared horseradish

6 cups chopped romaine lettuce

2 medium tomatoes, cored and cut into wedges

1 pound well-trimmed sirloin steak, ¾" thick

¼ teaspoon salt

¼ teaspoon black pepper

1 (8-ounce) package sliced mushrooms

¼ cup reduced-fat blue cheese

½ small red onion, thinly sliced

1. In a small bowl, whisk together the dressing and horseradish. On a large serving platter, heap the romaine in the center. Arrange the tomatoes around the edge of the lettuce.

2. Spray a large nonstick skillet with nonstick cooking spray and place over medium-high heat. Sprinkle the steak with salt and pepper and place in the skillet. Cook until browned, about 5 minutes on each side for medium-rare. Transfer to a carving board, cover, and let rest.

3. Add the mushrooms to the skillet and cook until they begin to brown, about 2 minutes. Add one tablespoon water, and stir, scraping up browned bits with a spoon. Cook another 3 to 4 minutes, or until mushrooms are tender. Remove from heat.

4. Cut the steak across the grain into thin slices. Pour dressing over lettuce and arrange the steak on top, and drizzle with the slicing juices. Spoon the mushrooms over the steak, sprinkle with the blue cheese and garnish with red onion. Serve immediately.

**DARE TO COMPARE:** With 1,022 calories, 72 grams of fat, and 1,435 milligrams of sodium, the Steak Salad at Outback Steakhouse is no better-for-you bargain.

**NUTRITION INFORMATION PER SERVING:** (¼ salad) Calories 250 | Carbohydrate 10g (Sugars 4g) | Total Fat 8g (Sat Fat 4g) | Protein 30g | Fiber 3g | Cholesterol 105mg | Sodium 320mg | Food Exchanges: 4 Lean Meat, 2 Vegetables | Carbohydrate Choices: ½ | Weight Watcher Smart Point Comparison: 4

# PASTA & PIZZA

## pasta & pizza

# For the Love of
## { PIZZA PIE }

How much do I love pizza? Let me count the ways: One pepperoni, two pepperoni. . . . Clearly, I'm not alone. Americans eat approximately 100 acres of pizza every day —that's 76 football fields worth of dough, sauce, and cheese!

Unfortunately, no matter how you slice it, most traditional pizzas are loaded with calories and sky-high levels of saturated fat and sodium. With a variety of meats and cheeses, heavy hitters can easily top out at an astounding 600 calories, with over 1,000 milligrams of sodium—in a single slice! The good news is that homemade pizza is healthy, easy to make, and tasty—and can be on the table as fast as takeout. Here are my favorite tricks for thinking outside the (pizza) box:

### FAST AND FIT TIPS, TRICKS, AND SWAPS FOR FABULOUS PIZZA

1) **THE CRUST:** To get dinner (or breakfast!) on the table pronto, try high-fiber tortillas, English muffins, flatbread, or thin pre-made pizza crust paired with your favorite healthy toppings. Many of these fun "crusts" make a perfect single-serving pizza, which is great for portion control.
   **Tip:** Lightly pre-bake or toast the crust to ensure they cook up nice and crispy before adding toppings.

2) **THE SAUCE:** For a traditional pizza, grab a jar of pizza sauce. Low in fat and calories, it's also rich in lycopene, a powerful antioxidant linked to preventing stroke, cancer, and heart disease. My other favorite "sauces" include reduced-fat pesto, BBQ sauce, salsa, and for a creamy topper, light mayonnaise mixed with herbs.
   **Tip:** With stronger-flavored sauces like pesto or BBQ sauce, remember, a little goes a long way!

3) **THE CHEESE:** Think Italian! Instead of smothering the pizza with cheese, sprinkle on the cheese with a light hand to allow all of the toppings to shine. Fresh reduced-fat mozzarella, reduced-fat cheddar and feta, and aged Parmesan are healthy choices.
   **Tip:** Pre-shredded cheeses are often dusted with anti-caking agents which can inhibit melting. Grate it yourself to guarantee a gooey, melty, cheesy pizza.

4) **THE TOPPINGS:** Pile on the veggies and herbs. These "freebies" are packed with flavor, color, and texture, and add heft, fiber, and minimal calories. For a "salad-style" pizza (like the BLT Chicken Pizza), add lettuce, spinach, fresh tomatoes, and other salad toppers immediately after taking your pizza out of the oven.
   **Tip:** To avoid a wet pizza, microwave raw mushroom slices on a paper towel for one minute before placing them on your unbaked pizza.

# Penne Pasta with Sausage and Kale

*THIS NUTRITIONAL POWERHOUSE OF A PASTA DISH is not only quick to prepare, it can easily be prepared as a one-pot meal. Simply cook the pasta first and use the same pot to cook the vegetables and sausage. It takes a few more minutes up front but will leave you with just one pot to clean when dinner is done!*

MAKES 6 SERVINGS

8 ounces dry penne pasta

1 (14.5-ounce) can reduced-sodium chicken broth

1 tablespoon cornstarch

12 ounces Italian turkey sausage

1 medium onion, chopped

1 (8-ounce) package sliced mushrooms

1 bunch kale, stemmed and chopped (about 8 cups)

1 medium red bell pepper, chopped

1/2 teaspoon crushed red pepper flakes

1/3 cup shredded Parmesan cheese

1. Cook the pasta according to package directions. While pasta cooks, in a medium bowl, whisk together chicken broth and cornstarch. Set aside.

2. Spray a large skillet (or the pasta pot after the pasta is cooked and drained) with cooking spray and place over medium-high heat. Add sausage and cook for 5 minutes, or until it is no longer pink, breaking up the meat as it cooks. Add the onion and mushrooms and cook for 4 minutes, stirring constantly.

3. Transfer the sausage mixture to the pot, if needed, and stir in the kale and red bell pepper. Reduce heat to medium, add broth mixture, and simmer for 3 to 4 minutes, or until sauce thickens and kale wilts. Add the cooked pasta, stir in red pepper flakes, and cook for 3 minutes to heat all ingredients. Transfer to a serving dish, and top with Parmesan cheese.

> **Marlene Says:** *To help keep pasta dishes warm, drain the hot pasta water into your serving dish, empty it, and add the finished pasta dish to it.*

**NUTRITION INFORMATION PER SERVING (1½ cups):** Calories 305 | Carbohydrate 42g (Sugars 7g) | Total Fat 8g (Sat Fat 2.5g) | Protein 21g | Fiber 7g | Cholesterol 35mg | Sodium 650mg | Food Exchanges: 2 Vegetable, 1½ Starch, 2 Lean Meat | Carbohydrate Choices: 2½ | Weight Watcher Smart Point Comparison: 7

# Chili's-Style Creamy Cajun Chicken Pasta

*INSPIRED BY THE EVER-POPULAR CAJUN PASTA at Chili's Bar and Grill, this scintillating pasta creation also features penne pasta tossed in a cream sauce flavored with just a hint of lemon and topped with spicy Cajun-coated chicken, fresh tomatoes, and Parmesan. Adding fresh green beans is my personal touch—as is eliminating 75% of the calories, 80% of the fat, and 90% of the sodium!*

**MAKES 4 SERVINGS**

1¾ cups dry penne pasta

1½ cups fresh green beans, cut in half

4 boneless, skinless, chicken breasts (about 1 pound)

4 teaspoons Cajun seasoning

2 teaspoons butter

½ cup nonfat half-and-half

1 tablespoon cornstarch

1 cup low-fat milk

¼ teaspoon salt

¼ teaspoon black pepper

¼ teaspoon garlic powder

¼ teaspoon lemon zest

¾ cup chopped tomatoes

¼ cup shredded Parmesan cheese

1. Cook the pasta according to package directions, adding the green beans during the final 3 minutes of cooking; drain, and set aside. While pasta is cooking, gently pound breasts to ¼-inch thickness and sprinkle both sides with Cajun seasoning.

2. Add the butter to a large nonstick skillet and place over medium-high heat. Add chicken and brown well on both sides (about 2 minutes per side). Add 1 tablespoon water to pan, cover, and cook for 1 minute. Remove lid, and cook chicken until done. Transfer to a cutting board and cover.

3. In a small bowl, whisk together the half-and-half and cornstarch until smooth. Add mixture to pan, and place over medium heat. Stir in next 5 ingredients (milk through lemon zest) and cook for 2 minutes, stirring, until sauce thickens. Add pasta and beans and continue to cook, stirring, for about 2 minutes, until mixture is hot and coated. Transfer to a serving platter or individual plates; slice chicken breasts and place on top. Top chicken with tomatoes and Parmesan.

**DARE TO COMPARE:** An order of Cajun Pasta with Grilled Chicken at Chili's has 1,290 calories (550 from fat!), 115 grams of carbs, and 4,680 milligrams of sodium.

**NUTRITION INFORMATION PER SERVING:** (1½ cups plus chicken breast) Calories 330 | Carbohydrate 43g (Sugars 7g) | Total Fat 7g (Sat Fat 3.5g) | Protein 26g | Fiber 6g | Cholesterol 50mg | Sodium 750mg | Food Exchanges: 3 Lean Meat, 2 Starch, 1 Vegetable | Carbohydrate Choices: 2½ | Weight Watcher Smart Point Comparison: 7

# Weeknight Lasagna Roll-Ups

*UNFORTUNATELY FOR LASAGNA LOVERS (LIKE ME!), homemade lasagna is as time-consuming as it is beloved. Enter the lasagna roll-up! Lasagna roll-ups have all the cheesy goodness of lasagna and are quicker to make (and bake). Even better, you can refrigerate individual portions—before or after baking—for three to four days or freeze them for even longer. Eat some, refrigerate some, and freeze some! Disposable foil mini loaf pans fit 2 rolls perfectly.*

MAKES 8 SERVINGS

8 lasagna noodles

1 (15-ounce) container low-fat ricotta cheese

1 (10-ounce) package chopped spinach, thawed and squeezed dry

1 cup low-fat cottage cheese

1 teaspoon dried oregano

1/2 teaspoon garlic salt

1/8 teaspoon black pepper

3/4 cup shredded reduced-fat mozzarella cheese, divided

1 cup Everyday Marinara Sauce (page 315 or store-bought)

1. Preheat the oven to 425°F. Spray a baking sheet with cooking spray and set aside. Cook the lasagna noodles according to package directions. Drain noodles well, and transfer to baking sheet.

2. While noodles are cooking, in a medium bowl, combine next 6 ingredients (ricotta through black pepper) plus 1/2 cup mozzarella, and stir well to combine. Spread a scant 1/2 cup of the cheese mixture along the length of each lasagna noodle, leaving a 1/2-inch border at both ends, and roll them up.

3. Spray a casserole dish with cooking spray and transfer roll-ups, seam-side down, to the dish. Top with marinara sauce, sprinkle with remaining cheese, and bake for 15 to 20 minutes, or until cheese melts and filling is hot. Let set for 5 minutes before serving.

**NUTRITION INFORMATION PER SERVING: (1 piece)** Calories 190 | Carbohydrate 23g (Sugars 5g) | Total Fat 4g (Sat Fat 2.5g) | Protein 17g | Fiber 2g | Cholesterol 20mg | Sodium 380mg | Food Exchanges: 1 Starch, 2 Lean Meat, 1 Vegetable | Carbohydrate Choices: 1 1/2 | Weight Watcher Smart Point Comparison: 5

# One-Pot BBQ Chicken Pasta

*THIS EASY, CHEESY ONE-POT MEAL IS A KEEPER! Simply cook bacon, onions, and garlic for a few minutes, add the rest of the ingredients (with the exception of the melty, cheesy top), and you're done. While this hands-off, no-fuss family favorite is cooking, you've even got time to make a fresh green salad and Homemade Ranch Dressing (see page 308). It pairs perfectly with the pasta.*

MAKES 4 SERVINGS

2 slices center-cut bacon, diced

1 medium onion, chopped

2 teaspoons minced garlic

1 medium red bell pepper, chopped

1 (14.5-ounce) can fire-roasted diced tomatoes

1 (14.5-ounce) can reduced-sodium beef broth

1/4 cup barbecue sauce

1 1/2 cups dry rotini pasta

2 cups shredded cooked chicken breast

2/3 cup shredded reduced-fat Mexican blend cheese

1. In a large nonstick skillet over medium heat, cook the bacon until crisp. Add the onion and cook for 3 minutes, or until onion begins to soften. Add garlic and cook for 1 more minute.

2. Add the next 5 ingredients (bell pepper through pasta) and bring to a simmer. Reduce heat to medium low, cover, and simmer for 15 minutes, or until the pasta is nearly cooked through. Stir in the chicken, top with cheese, cover, and cook for 5 more minutes. Serve.

**NUTRITION INFORMATION PER SERVING:** (1 1/2 cups) Calories 300 | Carbohydrate 33g (Sugars 9g) | Total Fat 7g (Sat Fat 3.5g) | Protein 24g | Fiber 3g | Cholesterol 55mg | Sodium 690mg | Food Exchanges: 2 1/2 Lean Meat, 1 1/2 Carbohydrate, 1 Vegetable | Carbohydrate Choices: 2 | Weight Watcher Smart Point Comparison: 6

# Buttons, Bowties, and Blue Cheese Chicken Pasta

*FEELING BLUE? THIS SIMPLY DELICIOUS DISH FOR TWO IS SURE TO PICK YOU UP. Elegant and rich-tasting, this pasta is akin to something you would find on the menu of a fancy bistro. The silky blue cheese-tinged sauce melds gorgeously with the spinach and peas, and shredded chicken breast adds a welcome protein boost. If you really want to take this over the top, garnish with a few additional crumbles of blue cheese and chopped toasted walnuts, and serve it on your best china.*

MAKES 2 SERVINGS

1¼ cups dry bowtie pasta

3 cups fresh spinach

½ cup frozen peas

¾ cup reduced-sodium chicken broth

¼ cup nonfat half-and-half

2 teaspoons cornstarch

4 tablespoons blue cheese, divided

1 cup shredded cooked chicken breast

Fresh ground black pepper, to taste

Salt, to taste

1. Cook the pasta according to package directions. While the pasta cooks, place spinach and peas in a colander and place in the sink.

2. In a large nonstick skillet over medium heat, heat the chicken broth. In a small bowl, whisk together half-and-half and cornstarch and add to the skillet. Cook for one minute, or until mixture thickens. Add 2 tablespoons blue cheese and stir.

3. Drain the pasta in the colander over the peas and spinach. Shake to remove excess water, and transfer pasta mixture to the skillet, along with chicken. Cook for 3 to 4 minutes, using tongs to mix and coat pasta. Season with ground pepper and salt to taste, and top with remaining blue cheese. Serve immediately.

**Marlene Says:** *Blue cheese is not low in fat, but its strong flavor gives it a big bang for its calorie buck. Use any leftovers to make the side Bibb and Blue Salad on page 142, or the entrée Steakhouse Steak Salad on page 158.*

**NUTRITION INFORMATION PER SERVING:** (1½ cups) Calories 330 | Carbohydrate 40g (Sugars 6g) | Total Fat 6g (Sat Fat 3g) | Protein 28g | Fiber 6g | Cholesterol 60mg | Sodium 670mg | Food Exchanges: 2½ Starch, 2½ Lean Meat | Carbohydrate Choices: 2½ | Weight Watcher Smart Point Comparison: 6

# 15-Minute Shrimp and Penne Pasta with Marsala Marinara

*I'M ALWAYS ON THE LOOKOUT FOR WAYS TO ADD FRESH FLAVOR to premade ingredients for fix-it-fast meals, and after preparing this one night on a whim, I can't help but share it. Just start with store-bought marinara sauce (or Everyday Marinara Sauce, page 315), pump it up with fresh bell peppers, oregano, plump, juicy shrimp, and Marsala wine, and you've got a dish that tastes like it came straight from an Italian Trattoria. To make this ultra-fast, use frozen mixed bell pepper strips.*

**MAKES 4 SERVINGS**

6 ounces dry penne pasta (about 1¾ cups)

1 teaspoon olive oil

½ medium red bell pepper, julienned

½ medium yellow bell pepper, julienned

½ teaspoon dried oregano

2 cups Everyday Marinara Sauce (page 315 or store-bought)

1 pound large shrimp, peeled and deveined

⅓ cup Marsala wine

1. While preparing the sauce, cook the pasta according to the package directions.

2. Heat the olive oil in a large nonstick sauté pan over medium heat. Add the red and yellow bell pepper and oregano and sauté for 5 minutes, or until peppers begin to soften. Add the marinara and shrimp and bring to a simmer. Cover and cook for 4 minutes.

3. Uncover the pan, add the Marsala, and let simmer for 1 more minute. Drain the pasta, add to the sauce, toss to coat, and serve.

**NUTRITION INFORMATION PER SERVING:** (1½ cups) Calories 350 | Carbohydrate 44g (Sugars 10g) | Total Fat 7g (Sat Fat 2.5g) | Protein 27g | Fiber 7g | Cholesterol 145mg | Sodium 650mg | Food Exchanges: 2 Starch, 2 Vegetable, 3 Lean Meat | Carbohydrate Choices: 2½ | Weight Watcher Smart Point Comparison: 6

# Super-Fast Fresh Tomato and Zucchini Pasta

*IT'S HARD TO BEAT A FRESH-OFF-THE-VINE TOMATO AND FRAGRANT BASIL SAUCE—especially when it's lightning fast to make! Instead of roasting the tomatoes, which can take an hour or more, simply pop them under the broiler for 10 short minutes, then toss them in the food processor for a quick whirl. Add a touch of seasoning and basil, and you have a versatile sauce that soars with fresh flavor. Zucchini couples well here, but so would grilled chicken or fish.*

MAKES 4 SERVINGS

1¾ pounds Roma tomatoes, halved lengthwise

2 large garlic cloves, peeled

1 tablespoon extra-virgin olive oil

⅓ cup packed fresh basil leaves, plus more for garnish

½ teaspoon salt

¼ teaspoon hot red pepper flakes

6 ounces spaghetti

2 large zucchini, cut into long thin strips

¼ cup grated Parmesan cheese

1. Preheat the broiler on high with the rack 4 to 6 inches from the heat source.

2. Spray a metal baking pan with nonstick cooking spray. Place tomatoes, cut-side up, in the pan. Tuck garlic between tomatoes so garlic is just peeking out (this protects it from burning). Brush tomatoes with oil and broil for 10 minutes, or until tomatoes are tinged with charred spots and garlic is lightly browned. Transfer garlic and 2 tomatoes to a food processor and process to mince the garlic. Add basil, remaining tomatoes, salt, and red pepper flakes, and pulse until almost smooth.

3. Meanwhile, cook the pasta according to the package directions, adding zucchini to the water during the last minute of cooking. Drain well and return to the cooking pot. Add 2 cups of sauce and toss. Place pasta in a shallow bowl or deep platter and top with remaining sauce and Parmesan cheese.

**Marlene Says:** *To quickly cut the zucchini into thin strips, first cut it lengthwise into ¼-inch-thick slabs. Stack the slabs a couple at a time, and cut into long strips.*

**NUTRITION INFORMATION PER SERVING: (1½ cups)** Calories 250 | Carbohydrate 40g (Sugars 8g) | Total Fat 6g (Sat Fat 2g) | Protein 13g | Fiber 7g | Cholesterol 10mg | Sodium 410mg | Food Exchanges: 2 Starch, 2 Vegetable, 1 Lean Meat | Carbohydrate Choices: 1½ | Weight Watcher Smart Point Comparison: 6

# Shortcut Veggie Lasagna

*I HAVE ALWAYS LOVED VEGGIE LASAGNA, but all the dicing, slicing, cooking, and layering of the vegetables, cheese, sauce, and noodles . . . well, it's enough to send even me to the freezer case. This remarkable recipe took me by surprise. While hopeful, I did not expect the refrigerated ravioli to coalesce with the veggie-loaded marinara sauce so well that it would actually look (and cut) just like lasagna. And the taste, yum! Finally, here's a simple-to-make, healthy, and oh-so-good veggie lasagna.*

MAKES 4 SERVINGS

1 (9-ounce) package refrigerated cheese ravioli

1 (10-ounce) package frozen chopped spinach

2 teaspoons olive oil, divided

1 (8-ounce) package sliced mushrooms

1 medium zucchini

2½ cups Everyday Marinara Sauce (page 315 or store-bought), divided

½ teaspoon garlic powder

1 teaspoon dried oregano

½ teaspoon black pepper

⅔ cup shredded reduced-fat mozzarella cheese

1. Preheat the oven to 375°F. Spray a 7 x 11-inch casserole dish with cooking spray. Boil the ravioli according to package directions (until barely cooked), about 3 minutes. Drain ravioli, transfer to prepared casserole dish, and drizzle with 1 teaspoon oil to keep them from sticking.

2. While the pasta cooks, microwave the spinach according to package directions. Drain it, and gently squeeze to remove moisture. In a large nonstick skillet, add remaining oil and place over medium heat. Add mushrooms and cook for 3 minutes, or until they begin to soften. Grate zucchini into the pan, and cook for 3 more minutes, stirring often.

3. Stir in 2 cups of the marinara, the spinach, the garlic powder, oregano, and black pepper, and cook for 5 minutes. Top ravioli with the sauce, mixing it in to combine, and then smooth the top. Spread remaining ½ cup of marinara over top, sprinkle with cheese, and cover with foil. Bake for 15 to 20 minutes, or until "lasagna" is bubbling at the edges and cheese is melted.

**NUTRITION INFORMATION PER SERVING:** (1½ cups) Calories 320 | Carbohydrate 39g (Sugars 10g) | Total Fat 9g (Sat Fat 5g) | Protein 18g | Fiber 8g | Cholesterol 35mg | Sodium 750mg | Food Exchanges: 3 Vegetable, 1½ Starch, 1½ Lean Meat, 1 Fat | Carbohydrate Choices: 2½ | Weight Watcher Smart Point Comparison: 7

# Asian Pork and Noodles

*IF YOU LIKE ASIAN NOODLE DISHES, YOU ARE GOING TO LOVE THIS ADDICTIVE TWIST! It combines the gingery, garlicky, sweet-and-salty flavors of a traditional Shanghai pork noodle dish with the comfort and convenience of home-cooked noodles and bagged cabbage slaw. I literally couldn't stop eating it, and my husband, Chuck, coined it "Asian comfort food" after only one bite. You'll be racing for the leftovers (if you have any) the next day! (Jarred minced ginger works fine.)*

**MAKES 4 SERVINGS**

3 cups dry broad noodles

1/2 cup reduced-sodium chicken broth

2 tablespoons reduced-sodium soy sauce

2 tablespoons oyster sauce

2 teaspoons sesame oil

1½ teaspoons cornstarch

1 teaspoon granulated sugar

8 ounces lean ground pork

2 teaspoons minced garlic

1½ teaspoons minced ginger

1 (14-ounce) bag cabbage slaw

Black pepper, to taste

1. Cook the noodles according to the package directions, reserving 1/3 cup of the cooking water, and set aside. While the noodles cook, in a large measuring cup, whisk together the next six ingredients (chicken broth through sugar).

2. Heat a large nonstick skillet over medium-high heat. Add the pork and cook for 2 to 3 minutes, or until just browned, breaking up the meat as it cooks. Stir in garlic and ginger, and then add slaw mix. Add the noodle water to the pan, and cover. Let steam for 2 minutes, uncover, and toss lightly.

3. Add the chicken broth mixture and noodles to the pan and cook for 2 minutes, tossing with tongs, until the sauce thickens and noodles are well coated.

**Marlene Says:** *Oyster sauce is slightly sweet and deeply savory. It can be found in Asian noodle dishes, stir-fries, and fried rice (like mine!). Look for it in the Asian section of your market.*

**NUTRITION INFORMATION PER SERVING:** (1½ cups) Calories 260 | Carbohydrate 33g (Sugars 5g) | Total Fat 6g (Sat Fat 1.5g) | Protein 19g | Fiber 4g | Cholesterol 33mg | Sodium 730mg | Food Exchanges: 2 Lean Meat, 1½ Starch, 1 Vegetable | Carbohydrate Choices: 2 | Weight Watcher Smart Point Comparison: 7

# Taco Stuffed Shells

*MY BOYS LOVED THIS SOUTH-OF-THE-BORDER TWIST ON AN ITALIAN CLASSIC. Cream cheese in the meat may seem odd, but it creates a luscious filling reminiscent of the creamy meat filling you may find in classic Italian stuffed shells. Scintillating salsa steps in for traditional marinara, and melty cheese tops them off. I say Mucho bellisimo! Finely chopped green onions make a nice garnish.*

**MAKES 4 SERVINGS**

12 jumbo pasta shells

12 ounces lean ground turkey

1½ teaspoons chili powder

½ teaspoon ground cumin

¼ cup light cream cheese

1¾ cups jarred mild salsa,* divided

⅔ cup shredded reduced-fat Mexican blend cheese

1. Preheat the oven to 350°F. Boil pasta shells according to package directions and drain well.

2. In a medium nonstick skillet over medium heat, add the turkey, chili powder, and cumin, and cook for 6 to 8 minutes, or until browned, breaking up the meat as it cooks. Remove from heat and stir in the cream cheese and ½ cup salsa.

3. Arrange the shells in a baking dish and spoon about 3 tablespoons filling into each shell. Cover the shells with the remaining salsa, and sprinkle shells with cheese. Cover with foil (tent if necessary), and bake for 20 minutes, or until heated through and the cheese is melted.

**Marlene Says:** *Jarred salsas vary considerably. If the brand you use is very thick, add 1 to 2 tablespoons water to make it easier to spread over the shells. The brand used for testing was Newman's Own and its mild saucy tomato base was perfect for this dish.*

**NUTRITION INFORMATION PER SERVING: (3 stuffed shells)** Calories 280 | Carbohydrate 32g (Sugars 4g) | Total Fat 9g (Sat Fat 5g) | Protein 15g | Fiber 1g | Cholesterol 40mg | Sodium 390mg | Food Exchanges: 2 Lean Meat, 1½ Starch, 1 Vegetable, 1 Fat | Carbohydrate Choices: 2 | Weight Watcher Smart Point Comparison: 8

# Deep-Dish Skillet Pizza

*WHILE SOME PIZZA AFICIONADOS SAY THE BEST PIZZAS HAVE "THIN" CRUST, others claim "thick" is the ticket. But ask a Chicagoan, and they'll tell you the best pizza on the planet is "deep-dish"! This style of pizza is usually cooked in a cake-type pan able to hold the heavily layered (and usually heavily-caloried) "upside-down" toppings to the crust: cheese first, toppings next, and sauce last. In the time it takes for delivery, you can have this deeply satisfying deep-dish-style pepperoni-topped pizza on your table.*

**MAKES 6 SERVINGS**

1 (8-ounce) package sliced mushrooms

1 tablespoon cornmeal

1 (14-ounce) can pizza dough (like Pillsbury)

1 cup shredded mozzarella cheese

½ medium green pepper, diced

⅓ cup finely sliced red onion

¾ cup diced tomatoes

1 cup pizza sauce

12 slices turkey pepperoni

½ teaspoon Italian seasoning

1. Preheat the oven to 425° F. Spread mushrooms onto a paper towel–lined plate and microwave on high for 3 minutes. Pat off extra water and set aside.

2. Spray a 9-inch ovenproof skillet with cooking spray, and sprinkle with 2 teaspoons cornmeal. Press the dough into the bottom and all the way up the sides, looping it over the rim of the skillet. Sprinkle remaining cornmeal onto top edges of crust. Prick dough well cooked with a fork, place skillet in oven, and bake for 5 minutes, or until dough starts to puff. Remove from oven.

3. Top crust with cheese, then mushrooms, green pepper, onion, and tomatoes. Spread pizza sauce across the top, top with pepperoni, and sprinkle with Italian seasoning. Place skillet in oven and bake for 15 to 20 minutes or until crust is browned and tomato sauce is hot.

**DARE TO COMPARE:** An individual deep-dish Prima Pepperoni pizza at Pizzeria Uno has 2,160 calories, 148 grams of fat, and 4,490 milligrams of sodium. A single slice of the deep-dish cheese pizza has 640 calories and 1,200 milligrams of sodium.

**NUTRITION INFORMATION PER SERVING:** (⅙ pizza) Calories 240 | Carbohydrate 35g (Sugars 7g) | Total Fat 5g (Sat Fat 2g) | Protein 13g | Fiber 5g | Cholesterol 5mg | Sodium 600 mg | Food Exchanges: 2 Starch, 1 Vegetable, 1 Lean Meat| Carbohydrate Choices: 2 | Weight Watcher Smart Point Comparison: 6

# BLT Chicken Pizzas

*WITH THEIR AMAZINGLY CRISPY CRUSTS AND CREAMY GARLIC MAYO "SAUCE,"—these bacon-laced personal pizzas are a BLT lover's dream. What I love best is the post-oven addition of cool, crispy lettuce and ripe cherry tomatoes (and the fact the entire pizza delivers less calories than a typical slice!). To kick up the flavor and texture another notch, try topping your pizza with a drizzle of Homemade Ranch Dressing (page 308).*

MAKES 2 SERVINGS

2 high fiber tortillas (like Mission Carb Balance)

3 tablespoons light mayonnaise

¼ teaspoon garlic powder

¼ teaspoon dried basil

½ cup shredded cooked chicken breast

6 tablespoons shredded reduced-fat cheddar

1 cup shredded romaine lettuce

½ cup cherry tomatoes, halved

4 teaspoons real bacon bits

1. Preheat the oven to 425°F. Place the tortillas on a baking pan and spray lightly with cooking spray. Bake for 4 minutes or until lightly crisped. In a small bowl, whisk together the mayonnaise, garlic powder, and basil.

2. Remove tortillas from oven and spread each with 1½ teaspoons of the creamy garlic spread. Top each with ¼ cup chicken and 3 tablespoons cheese. Return to the oven and bake for 4 minutes, or until cheese is melted and crust is crispy.

3. Top each pizza with half the lettuce and tomatoes, and sprinkle each with 2 teaspoons bacon bits.

**DARE TO COMPARE:** A single slice of Domino's California Chicken Bacon Ranch Pizza has 670 calories, 42 grams of carbohydrate, 15 grams of saturated fat, and 1,480 milligrams of sodium.

**NUTRITION INFORMATION PER SERVING: (1 pizza)** Calories 250 | Carbohydrate 20 g (Sugars 2g) | Total Fat 10g (Sat Fat 4g) | Protein 20g | Fiber 7g | Cholesterol 35mg | Sodium 450 mg | Food Exchanges: 2 Lean Meat, 1 Starch, ½ Vegetable, 1 Fat | Carbohydrate Choices: 1 | Weight Watcher Smart Point Comparison: 7

# Greek Flatbread Pizza

*WHILE THE INGREDIENT LIST FOR THIS RECIPE IS A BIT LONGER THAN MOST in this book, this tasty flatbread pizza can be made and ready to eat in just 15 minutes. Just warm fresh spinach and mix it with wholesome yogurt and garlic to yield a creamy spread with classic Greek flavor, then top it with veggies and cheese, and you've got a wonderful vegetarian pizza packed with tons of flavor—along with a hefty serving of fiber, vitamins, calcium, and iron.*

**MAKES 2 SERVINGS**

2 light flatbread wraps

4 cups fresh spinach, chopped

1/4 teaspoon garlic salt with parsley

1/4 teaspoon onion powder

1/3 cup plain nonfat Greek yogurt

2 tablespoons grated Parmesan cheese

2/3 cup drained quartered artichoke hearts, chopped

2/3 cup cherry tomatoes, halved

1/4 cup red onion, thinly sliced

6 tablespoons shredded low-fat mozzarella

1/4 teaspoon dried oregano

1. Preheat the oven to 425°F. Place the flatbreads on a baking sheet and spray lightly with cooking spray. Bake for 3 to 4 minutes or until lightly crisped.

2. Put spinach in a small bowl and microwave on high for 1 minute. Gently press water out. Stir in the garlic salt, onion powder, yogurt, and Parmesan.

3. Spread each flatbread with half of the spinach topping. Divide the artichoke hearts, tomatoes, and red onion between each flatbread. Sprinkle each pizza with 3 tablespoons mozzarella and 1/8 teaspoon oregano. Bake for 5 to 7 minutes, or until cheese melts and crust is crispy.

**NUTRITION INFORMATION PER SERVING: (1 pizza)** Calories 260 | Carbohydrate 32g (Sugars 5g) | Total Fat 8g (Sat Fat 3g) | Protein 27g | Fiber 16g | Cholesterol 20mg | Sodium 650mg | Food Exchanges: 3 Lean Meat, 1 Starch, 2 Vegetable | Carbohydrate Choices: 1 1/2 | Weight Watcher Smart Point Comparison: 4

# SENSATIONALLY EASY SIDES

# *sensationally easy sides*

# { ORGANIC *or* CONVENTIONAL LOVE }

Whether you buy produce at a traditional grocery store or a farmer's market, you've probably noticed how the availability of organic produce has grown over the past few years—and you've probably noted its cost. Simply stated, organic produce is grown without synthetic pesticides or fertilizers, and natural is better, right?

The truth is that while I love the natural goodness and increased availability of organic produce, not all organic fruits and vegetables are better for you than their conventional cousins, and from a health perspective, it's good to know many are not worth the extra cost. As this book features lots of recipes brimming with healthy, good-for-you fruits and veggies, here is some information to help you shop for them with both your health and budget in mind.

**NUTRITION:** Major studies by Stanford University and the UK Food Standards Agency found that organic and conventional produce are the same in terms of nutritional content. Both are packed with disease-fighting vitamins, minerals, antioxidants, phytochemicals, and fiber.
**THE BOTTOM LINE:** The most nutritious thing you can do is to eat an abundance of fruits and vegetables, whether organic or conventional, or whether they are fresh, frozen, or even canned. Shop local and in season for the freshest nutrient-rich produce.

**SAFETY:** When it comes to bacteria that can cause food-borne illness, organic and conventional foods carry the same risks. Washing all produce reduces the risk (and can lower pesticides).
**THE BOTTOM LINE:** Thoroughly wash all fruits and vegetables with water before cooking or eating.

**PESTICIDES:** Conventionally grown produce has higher levels of pesticide residue, but that doesn't mean it's unsafe to eat. The Environmental Protection Agency monitors how much pesticide remains on food and only allows levels that are not considered a risk to human health.
**THE BOTTOM LINE:** While there is debate as to the risks from pesticide residue, there is no debate that the incredible nutrition benefits offered by consuming a variety of fruits and vegetables outweigh them. When in doubt (or preferred), use the information below and buy organic.

**COST:** The biggest obstacle to buying organic is often price. Thankfully, various agencies have measured residues on the most commonly eaten fruits and vegetables to help you know what to pick, and what you can skip.
**BOTTOM LINE:** Not everything needs to be organic. The listings below will help you get the biggest bang for your produce buck. More important, fill your cart liberally with fruits and vegetables!

| Buy Organic | | | Buy Conventional | | |
|---|---|---|---|---|---|
| • Apples | • Kale | • Sweet Bell | • Avocados | • Corn | • Mushrooms |
| • Celery | • Peaches | Peppers | • Bananas | • Frozen Peas | • Onions |
| • Cherry | • Potatoes | | • Blueberries | • Frozen | • Oranges |
| Tomatoes | • Spinach | | • Broccoli | Strawberries | • Watermelon |
| • Cucumbers | • Strawberries | | • Cabbage | • Green Onions | |
| • Green Beans | | | • Cauliflower | • Kiwi | |

# Easiest-Ever Glazed Carrots

SEE PAGE **325**

*MY NEWEST KITCHEN ASSISTANT, TRICIA, GRADUATED FROM THE RENOWNED Le Cordon Bleu cooking school where she learned the art of creating perfectly glazed carrots. She told me that learning to make them was a several step process that demanded her full attention, and a fair share of butter and sugar! In contrast, this ridiculously easy recipe produces gorgeously glazed carrots with little effort, minimal sugar, and not a trace of butter. Tricia found this recipe "bleu ribbon" worthy, and I hope you do too.*

**MAKES 4 SERVINGS**

1 pound carrots, baby or regular

1½ teaspoons canola oil

¼ teaspoon dried thyme

¼ teaspoon salt

2 tablespoons low-sugar orange marmalade

Black pepper, to taste

1. Preheat the oven to 425°F. In a medium bowl, add the first 4 ingredients (carrots through salt, crushing tyme in with your fingers), and toss to combine. Transfer to a sheet pan, set the bowl aside, and roast carrots for 10 minutes.

2. Open the oven and give the pan a good shake or two. Bake the carrots 10 to 15 minutes longer, or until some of the carrots have brown spots, and they are tender to the bite.

3. Transfer the carrots back to the bowl and toss with the marmalade. Add black pepper and additional salt to taste, and serve.

> **Marlene Says:** *To use regular-sized carrots, peel and quarter them by cutting in half crossways and then lengthwise. For thicker carrots, cut the thick end in half again lengthwise so all the pieces are of uniform thickness.*

**NUTRITION INFORMATION PER SERVING:** (¾ cup) Calories 70 | Carbohydrate 14g (Sugars 7g) | Total Fat 2g (Sat Fat 0g) | Protein 1g | Fiber 2g | Cholesterol 0mg | Sodium 200mg | Food Exchanges: 1 Vegetable, ½ Fat | Carbohydrate Choices: 1 | Weight Watcher Smart Point Comparison: 1

# Green Beans with Tomatoes and Bacon

*I REALLY WANTED TO CALL THIS RECIPE* "best ever green beans with sweet, buttery tomatoes, fragrant basil, and smoky bits of bacon," *but it was too long. Instead I'll hope you'll take my word when I tell you these are some of the best green beans I have ever made. When served as a side dish, this recipe comfortably serves six. As a testament to how good they are, my husband and I have come mighty close to devouring the entire platter ourselves!*

MAKES 6 SERVINGS

1 pound green beans, trimmed

3/8 teaspoon salt, divided

1 1/2 tablespoons butter

1 1/2 teaspoons granulated sugar

1 1/2 teaspoons minced garlic

1 1/2 cups cherry tomatoes, halved

2 tablespoons fresh basil, stemmed and chopped

1 rounded tablespoon real bacon bits

Black pepper, to taste

1. To a large skillet, add the green beans, 3/4 cup water, and 1/8 teaspoon salt and place over medium-high heat. Bring to a boil, cover, reduce heat to medium, and simmer for 6 to 7 minutes, or until beans are crisp-tender. Uncover beans and cook off any remaining water.

2. While the beans are cooking, in a small skillet over medium heat, combine next 4 ingredients (butter through tomatoes) and remaining salt. Cook for 2 to 3 minutes, or until tomatoes just begin to soften. Remove from heat and stir in the basil.

3. Place the green beans on a serving platter and pour the tomatoes over the beans. Use tongs or a fork to gently combine the tomato mixture with the green beans. Sprinkle evenly with bacon bits and add black pepper to taste, and serve.

> **DARE TO COMPARE:** Garnishing the beans with cooked bacon rather than cooking them *with* the bacon, as other recipes do, saves over 100 calories and 11 grams of fat per serving—and also enhances the bacon flavor!

**NUTRITION INFORMATION PER SERVING:** (~ 2/3 cup) Calories 70 | Carbohydrate 9g (Sugars 3g) | Total Fat 4g (Sat Fat 2g) | Protein 2g | Fiber 3g | Cholesterol 10mg | Sodium 245mg | Food Exchanges: 1 Vegetable, 1/2 Saturated Fat | Carbohydrate Choices: 1/2 | Weight Watcher Smart Point Comparison: 2

# 10-Minute Broccoli Gratin

*STEAMED BROCCOLI IS A NO-BRAINER AS A GO-TO SIDE DISH, but let's face it, it gets old. Here's a way to make it new again by sprucing it up gratin-style—in under 10 minutes! Under the heat of the broiler, mayonnaise, lemon juice, and mustard form a perfect, tangy, creamy sauce while Panko breadcrumbs and Parmesan cheese create the customary crispy topping. I like to blanch my broccoli in the microwave, but you can also do so on the stovetop.*

MAKES 5 SERVINGS

5 cups broccoli florets, with stems

1/4 cup light mayonnaise

1 tablespoon fresh lemon juice

2 teaspoons Dijon mustard

Dash of hot sauce (optional)

2 tablespoons Panko bread-crumbs

2 tablespoons grated Parmesan cheese

1. Preheat the broiler with the rack about 8 inches from the broiler. Spray a shallow flameproof, microwave-safe 1½-quart dish with cooking spray.

2. Spread the florets in the dish, add ½ cup water, cover tightly with plastic wrap, and cook on high for 2½ to 3 minutes, or until crisp-tender. Drain the water off, and set aside.

3. In a small bowl, whisk the mayonnaise, lemon juice, and mustard until smooth and spread it over the broccoli. Combine the Panko and Parmesan and sprinkle evenly over the spread. Place the dish under the broiler and broil, watching carefully, for about 2 minutes, or until the topping is golden brown and bubbly.

**NUTRITION INFORMATION PER SERVING:** (~3/4 cup) Calories 70 | Carbohydrate 7g (Sugars 2g) | Total Fat 4g (Sat Fat 1g) | Protein 4g | Fiber 3g | Cholesterol 0mg | Sodium 210mg | Food Exchanges: 1 Vegetable, 1 Fat | Carbohydrate Choices: 1/2 | Weight Watcher Smart Point Comparison: 2

# Cheesy Cauliflower Bake

*IT'S GREAT TO SEE A VEGETABLE AS HEALTHY AS CAULIFLOWER back in the spotlight. Low in calories, fat, and carbs, it's an excellent source of vitamins C and K, and as a member of the cabbage family, a proven cancer fighter. It may surprise you, but in England "cauliflower cheese" or creamy baked cauliflower is as popular as macaroni and cheese in America. Quick stints in both the microwave and the oven bring this creamy, cheesy, comforting cauliflower casserole to the table in double-time.*

**MAKES 5 SERVINGS**

5 cups cauliflower florets (about 1 medium head cauliflower)

²/₃ cup fat-free or light sour cream

²/₃ cup grated reduced-fat cheddar cheese, divided

2 tablespoons light mayonnaise

¼ teaspoon paprika (smoked preferred)

¼ teaspoon salt

Pinch of red pepper flakes (optional)

1. Preheat the oven to 375°F. Spray a shallow 2-quart microwave-safe baking dish with cooking spray. Place the cauliflower in dish, add ½ cup water, and tightly cover with plastic wrap. Microwave on high for 8 minutes. Remove from microwave; carefully remove plastic wrap, and drain well.

2. While cauliflower is cooking, in a medium bowl, combine sour cream, ⅓ cup cheese, mayonnaise, paprika, salt, and red pepper flakes, if desired. With a spatula, spread the mixture on top of the cauliflower, and sprinkle the remaining cheese over the top.

3. Place in the oven and bake for 15 minutes, or until the cheese is melted. Serve immediately.

> **DARE TO COMPARE:** Lightening up the cheese, sour cream, and salt in this recipe brings it to the table with all the healthy goodness and 60% less calories, 65% less sodium, and 75% less fat than a classic cauliflower gratin recipe.

**NUTRITION INFORMATION PER SERVING:** (³/4 cup) Calories 100 | Carbohydrate 10g (Sugars 3g) | Total Fat 4g (Sat Fat 2g) | Protein 8g | Fiber 3g | Cholesterol 10mg | Sodium 220mg | Food Exchanges: 1 Vegetable, ½ Lean Meat, ½ Fat | Carbohydrate Choices: ½ | Weight Watcher Smart Point Comparison: 2

# Easiest-Ever Corn on the Cob

*HERE'S A DROP-DEAD EASY AND DELICIOUS WAY TO COOK FRESH CORN ON THE COB. Just trim the stem end and throw corn, husk and all, into the microwave. After five minutes, simply pull on the silk end and the husk and silk threads will slip right off! Enjoy the corn as is, or check the Marlene Says below for Mexican-style grilled corn. The tasty topping combo provides tons of flavor and clocks in with about the same calories (and less saturated fat) than one-half of a tablespoon of butter. I say Ole!*

MAKES 2 SERVINGS

**2 medium ears of corn, unshucked**

1. Trim the stem (or shank) ends of the corncobs, cutting just to where the corn kernels start, and place ears in the microwave. Cook on high power for 5 minutes. Let corn cool slightly, then, with a pot holder or towel, grab the husk at the silk end and squeeze the corn out of the husks. (If you double the recipe, four ears of corn will take 8 minutes.)

**Marlene Says:** *To make* **Grilled Mexican Corn:** *Heat an indoor or outdoor grill. Cook corn as directed above. While corn is cooking, in a small bowl combine 2 tablespoons light mayonnaise, ½ teaspoon minced garlic, 1 dash Tabasco sauce (a drop or two). Set aside. As soon as husks are removed, move the corn to the grill, and cook for 3 to 4 minutes, or until ears are lightly charred. Remove from heat and brush corn with the mayonnaise mixture, then dust with 1 tablespoon grated Parmesan. (This variation adds 55 calories, 1 gram of carbohydrates, 5 grams of fat, and 2 points to each ear.)*

**NUTRITION INFORMATION PER SERVING: (1 ear)** Calories 75 | Carbohydrate 17g (Sugars 3g) | Total Fat 1 g (Sat Fat 0.5g) | Protein 5g | Fiber 3g | Cholesterol 0mg | Sodium 55mg | Food Exchanges: 1 Starch | Carbohydrate Choices: 1 | Weight Watcher Smart Point Comparison: 0

# Warm Cabbage Slaw

*EVERY TIME I MAKE THIS 10-MINUTE SLAW, I am reminded of how very tasty a simple side dish can be. Practically, it makes perfect use of that leftover half a head of cabbage that's sitting in the fridge, and literally, well, it can make the meal, especially when served with pork, like the Autumn Apple Pork Chop Skillet (page 243), or a simple dinner of reduced-fat sausage and potatoes.*

MAKES 4 SERVINGS

1 teaspoon canola oil

1/2 medium head of cabbage, shredded (about 5 cups)

1/2 tablespoon butter

Scant 1/2 teaspoon dried dill

1/4 teaspoon salt, or to taste

1/8 teaspoon celery seed

1. Heat the oil in a large nonstick skillet over medium heat. Add the cabbage and toss with tongs to coat. Cook for 3 to 4 minutes, or until cabbage starts to soften. Reduce heat to medium, add 1 tablespoon water, cover skillet, and cook for 1 minute.

2. Uncover skillet and add the remaining ingredients. Continue to toss and cook for 3 to 4 more minutes, or until cabbage is softened and slightly translucent.

**Marlene Says:** *To shred cabbage, core it, lay cut side down, and slice thinly with a chef's knife.*

**NUTRITION INFORMATION PER SERVING:** (2/3 cup) Calories 70 | Carbohydrate 5g (Sugars 1) | Total Fat 5g (Sat Fat 1g) | Protein 1g | Fiber 2g | Cholesterol 5mg | Sodium 210 mg | Food Exchanges: 1 Vegetable, 1 Fat | Carbohydrate Choices: 0 | Weight Watcher Smart Point Comparison: 1

# Classic Creamed Peas & Onions

*WITH THE EASE AND CONVENIENCE of keeping frozen vegetables on hand for last-minute cooking, it's nice to know that frozen can be as good as fresh. Peas and pearl onions are great examples. It turns out that flash-freezing them preserves their flavor, texture, and nutrients perfectly, making them ideal for this luscious, fuss-free lighter take on classic creamed peas and onions. Believe me, no one will ever think this is a "light" recipe!*

MAKES 4 SERVINGS

1 cup frozen pearl onions

2 teaspoons butter

1 tablespoon instant flour (like Wondra)

1 1/2 cups frozen peas

1/4 cup nonfat half-and-half

2/3 cup reduced-sodium chicken broth

1/4 teaspoon salt

1/8 teaspoon black pepper

1. In a medium skillet, add the onions and 1 cup water, and simmer for 3 to 4 minutes, or until onions soften. Drain water from pan, add butter, and cook over medium heat for 3 minutes, or until onions are lightly browned, stirring occasionally. Add the flour and stir to coat onions.

2. Add the remaining ingredients and cook over medium-low heat for 2 to 3 minutes, or until sauce thickens.

**Marlene Says:** *Creamed peas and onions are often reserved for holidays, but there is no need to do so with this easy recipe. Serve these with a grilled steak and any day will feel special.*

**NUTRITION INFORMATION PER SERVING:** (1/2 cup) Calories 90 | Carbohydrate 13g (Sugars 4g) | Total Fat 2g (Sat Fat 1g) | Protein 4g | Fiber 3g | Cholesterol 5mg | Sodium 260mg | Food Exchanges: 1/2 Starch, 1 Vegetable | Carbohydrate Choices: 1 | Weight Watcher Smart Point Comparison: 1

# Last-Minute Roasted Red Potatoes

*CRISPY ON THE OUTSIDE, CREAMY ON THE INSIDE, and dusted with a savory ranch-style seasoning, these are not only some the quickest potatoes I have ever made, but they rank with the best! I can't count the times I thought that if I only had a bit more time I would be able to make roasted potatoes. This weeknight-friendly side makes use of the microwave to jump-start the cooking in order to produce flavorful roasted potatoes in only 20 minutes. Even shorter than the time you'll spend cooking these potatoes is the time you'll spend devouring them.*

**MAKES 4 SERVINGS**

1 pound small red potatoes, halved

1 tablespoon olive oil

1/2 teaspoon salt

1/2 teaspoon black pepper

1/2 teaspoon garlic powder

1/2 teaspoon onion powder

1 teaspoon dried parsley

1. Preheat the oven to 450°F. Place the potatoes, cut-side down, on a large microwave-safe plate. Microwave on high for 4 to 5 minutes, or until potatoes are tender enough to pierce with a fork, but not mushy.

2. Remove potatoes from microwave and transfer to a baking sheet. Top with olive oil, sprinkle with seasonings (salt through onion powder) and toss to coat. Turn potatoes so that flat sides are down. Bake for 15 minutes, or until potato skins are fully tender and flesh side (bottom) is well browned.

**NUTRITION INFORMATION PER SERVING:** (1/4 pan) Calories 120 | Carbohydrate 23g (Sugars 1g) | Total Fat 3g (Sat Fat 0g) | Protein 2g | Fiber 2g | Cholesterol 0mg | Sodium 250mg | Food Exchanges: 1 1/2 Starch | Carbohydrate Choices: 1 1/2 | Weight Watcher Smart Point Comparison: 4

# Pan-Roasted Broccolini

*IF YOU HAVE NEVER ENJOYED THE PLEASURE OF COOKING (OR EATING) BROCCOLINI, let me introduce you to this super vegetable. Sometimes called baby broccoli, it's actually a cross between regular broccoli and Chinese broccoli. When compared to regular broccoli, its florets are smaller and leafier and its stalks are thinner, sweeter, and more tender (which shortens cooking time). It can be steamed like regular broccoli, but pan roasting is my favorite way to cook it. When seasoned simply with olive oil and garlic salt, it's absolutely delicious.*

MAKES 4 SERVINGS

1 pound broccolini

1 tablespoon olive oil

1/2 teaspoon garlic salt

Black pepper, to taste

1. Wash broccolini and pull apart any pieces with stalks thicker than 1 inch to create fairly uniform pieces. Place the broccolini in a large nonstick skillet, add 1/3 cup water, bring to a simmer, cover, turn down the heat to medium, and cook for 4 minutes.

2. Remove the lid, cook off any remaining water, and drizzle olive oil into the pan. Using tongs, turn the broccolini spears to coat evenly with the oil, sprinkle with garlic salt, and continue to turn and cook over medium-high heat for about 4 to 5 minutes, or until tender and lightly browned. (When finished, leaves should be slightly charred.) Season with pepper to taste.

**DARE TO COMPARE:** How much sodium? The Bonefish Grill serves delicious wood-fired broccolini, but sadly each order has 242 calories (206 of them from fat), and 2,222 milligrams of sodium!

**NUTRITION INFORMATION PER SERVING :** (1/4 of pan) Calories 60 | Carbohydrate 6g (Sugars 2g) | Total Fat 3.5g (Sat Fat 0.5g) | Protein 3g | Fiber 3g | Cholesterol 0mg | Sodium 140mg | Food Exchanges: 1 Vegetable, 1/2 Fat | Carbohydrate Choices: 0 | Weight Watcher Smart Point Comparison: 1

# One-Pot Spaghetti and Spinach

*HERE'S A GREAT SIDE DISH THAT DOES DOUBLE DUTY. A single portion serves up one serving of fiber-rich whole grains and also one of nutrient-rich greens, and you'll be delighted at how quickly the two come together! Since most thin spaghetti takes only six minutes to cook, and spinach wilts almost instantly, you're never more than a few minutes away from having this tasty side on the table. My secret seasoning trick is using Lawry's Garlic Salt with Parsley. It adds the perfect garlic flavor without excess salt.*

**MAKES 4 SERVINGS**

4 ounces whole grain thin spaghetti

2 teaspoons olive oil

½ teaspoon garlic salt with parsley

4 cups thinly sliced fresh baby spinach

Fresh ground black pepper, to taste

1. Boil the pasta for one minute less than the package directions. Drain the pasta, reserving ¼ cup of the pasta cooking water.

2. Return the pasta to the saucepan, toss with oil and salt, and place the pan over low heat. Add the spinach, cover, and let set 1 minute.

3. Uncover, and use tongs to toss the ingredients together. Add a small amount of pasta water to moisten if the pasta seems dry. Season with black pepper to taste.

**Marlene Says:** *One of my favorite pairings is Tilapia Piccata (page 248) served on a bed of this spaghetti.*

**NUTRITION INFORMATION PER SERVING:** (3/4 cup) Calories 115 | Carbohydrate 19g (Sugars 1g) | Total Fat 3g (Sat Fat 0g) | Protein 5g | Fiber 4g | Cholesterol 5mg | Sodium 135mg | Food Exchanges: 1 Starch, 1 Vegetable | Carbohydrate Choices: 1 | Weight Watcher Smart Point Comparison: 3

# Better-than-Ever Stovetop Mac & Cheese

*THIS RECIPE IS AN UPDATED VARIATION OF THE EASY STOVETOP MACARONI I created for my first* Eat What You Love Cookbook, *and dare I say I like it even better? In this version, I have added diced green chilies, and while the chili taste is subtle in the finished dish, they add an extra layer of flavor that is delectable. I also use this quick-fix creamy mac to make the "Fried" Macaroni and Cheese on page 88!*

MAKES 6 SERVINGS

8 ounces dry large macaroni shells

3/4 cup low-fat evaporated milk

1/2 cup reduced-sodium chicken broth

1 tablespoon cornstarch

3/4 teaspoon dry mustard

1/2 teaspoon garlic salt with parsley

1 1/2 cups reduced-fat shredded sharp cheddar cheese, divided

1 (4-ounce) can diced green chiles

1. Cook the pasta according to package directions. Be careful not to overcook.

2. While the pasta is cooking, in a small saucepan over medium heat, combine the next five ingredients (evaporated milk through garlic salt). Whisk and cook for 2 minutes, or until the mixture comes to a low boil and thickens. Turn off the heat, and stir in 1 cup of cheese. When smooth, stir in the green chiles.

3. Drain the cooked pasta, leaving it just slightly wet, and add it back to the pot. Immediately stir in the cheese sauce and last 1/2 cup cheese, and stir well until the pasta is creamy and well coated.

**NUTRITION INFORMATION PER SERVING:** (3/4 cup) Calories 220 | Carbohydrate 33g (Sugars 4g) | Total Fat 5g (Sat Fat 2.5g) | Protein 15g | Fiber 2g | Cholesterol 10mg | Sodium 280mg | Food Exchanges: 2 Starch, 1 Lean Meat | Carbohydrate Choices: 2 | Weight Watcher Smart Point Comparison: 6

# 10-Minute Broccoli and Parmesan Couscous

*TAKING A MERE FIVE MINUTES TO PREPARE, couscos is a go-to side dish in my home—and apparently I am not alone. A quick peek at the grocery shelf reveals over a dozen different flavors of quick-cooking couscous, including several that include vegetables such as broccoli. Unfortunately, the amount of "vegetables" they add is miniscule, and the amount of sodium vast. Instead, you'll find this side dish brimming with fresh broccoli and slimmed down in sodium. If that weren't enough, there's no comparison in how much better it tastes!*

MAKES 5 SERVINGS

1 cup reduced-sodium chicken broth

2 cups finely chopped broccoli florets

3/4 cup plain uncooked couscous

1/3 cup grated Parmesan cheese

2 teaspoons extra-virgin olive oil

Black pepper, to taste

1. In a medium saucepan, place chicken broth, 2 tablespoons water, and broccoli. Place over medium-high heat, cover, and bring to a boil.

2. Stir in couscous, re-cover, remove from heat, and let sit 5 minutes. Uncover, and stir in Parmesan and olive oil. Add black pepper to taste and serve.

**DARE TO COMPARE:** When compared to boxed Near East Broccoli and Cheese Couscous, this recipe has half the sodium, 25% less carbs, and three times the vitamin C!

**NUTRITION INFORMATION PER SERVING:** (2/3 cup) Calories 160 | Carbohydrate 23g (Sugars 2g) | Total Fat 4g (Sat Fat 1.5g) | Protein 8g | Fiber 2g | Cholesterol 5mg | Sodium 230mg | Food Exchanges: 1 Starch, 1 Vegetable, 1 Fat | Carbohydrate Choices: 1½ | Weight Watcher Smart Point Comparison: 4

# Instant Brown Rice Pilaf

*WHEN CREATING THIS VERSATILE SIDE DISH I DISCOVERED SOMETHING. Unlike regular brown rice, the amount of liquid required and the final yield for 10-minute instant brown rice differs by brand, even when the amount of dry rice remains the same. My go-to is fluffy Uncle Ben's brand, as it is the lightest in taste, calories, and carbs. If you want to use another brand to make this easy veggie-laced pilaf, it's easy: Just use the tips that follow the recipe.*

MAKES 4 SERVINGS

1 teaspoon canola oil

2 green onions, sliced

2/3 cup instant brown rice*
(I use Uncle Ben's)

1¼ cups reduced-sodium
chicken broth

⅛ teaspoon salt

3 cups thinly sliced fresh baby
spinach leaves

Black pepper, to taste

1. In a medium saucepan, heat the oil over medium-high heat. Add white part of onion and sauté for 2 minutes, or until it begins to soften. Add brown rice and stir for 1 minute, or until lightly toasted.

2. Add the broth and salt and bring to a boil. Cover, reduce heat to low, and simmer for 8 minutes. Stir in spinach and remaining green onion, cover, and cook for 2 to 3 minutes, or until rice is done. Fluff rice with a fork, add black pepper to taste, and serve.

**Marlene Says:** *For this recipe note the package directions for a yield of the rice of about 2 cups. Minute is another common brand of quick-cooking brown rice. If you use it, measure 1½ cups of dry rice and 1½ cups of broth.*

**NUTRITION INFORMATION PER SERVING:** (½ cup) Calories 140 | Carbohydrate 26g (Sugars 1g) | Total Fat 2g (Sat Fat 0g) | Protein 4g | Fiber 2g | Cholesterol 0mg | Sodium 240mg | Food Exchanges: 1½ Starch, 1 Vegetable | Carbohydrate Choices: 1½ | Weight Watcher Smart Point Comparison: 4

# Presto Pizza Bread

*IMAGINE BEING ABLE TO MAKE HOMEMADE BREAD from start to finish in 30 minutes. Yes, just 30 little minutes. The bread mixture for this recipe has just five basic ingredients. And the most unexpected is beer. That's right, beer! If you don't like the taste of beer (like me), don't worry, the yeasty, hoppy quality of the beer adds the flavor of yeast, not beer, to the bread. Its bubbles also help the bread rise. Cheers!*

MAKES 9 SERVINGS

1 teaspoon olive oil

1½ cups all-purpose flour

1¾ teaspoons baking powder

¼ teaspoon salt

¾ cup light-colored beer (regular or non-alcoholic)

½ cup jarred pizza sauce

¾ teaspoon dried oregano

⅓ cup grated Parmesan cheese

1. Preheat the oven to 400°F. Coat the bottom of an 8-inch square (preferably metal) baking pan with olive oil, and set aside.

2. In a large bowl, whisk together the flour, baking powder, and salt. Make a well, and pour in the beer. Mix batter with a spoon until all the flour is moistened (batter will be stiff and sticky).

3. Spread the dough in the prepared pan. (It helps to lightly coat finger tips with oil to press dough into corners.) Spread dough with pizza sauce and sprinkle with oregano.

4. Bake for 15 minutes, top with cheese, and bake another 5 minutes, or until edges are brown, and a toothpick inserted in the center comes out clean.

**Marlene Says:** *Mozzarella cheese and turkey pepperoni also make great toppers for this bread.*

**NUTRITION INFORMATION PER SERVING:** Calories 100 | Carbohydrate 17g (Sugars 2g) | Total Fat 2g (Sat Fat 0.5g) | Protein 3g | Fiber 0g | Cholesterol 20mg | Sodium 260mg | Food Exchanges: 1 Starch | Carbohydrate Choices: 1 | Weight Watcher Smart Point Comparison: 3

# Amazing Zucchini "Butter"

*BEFORE TESTING THIS RECIPE I WOULD NEVER HAVE IMAGINED that zucchini could be rendered into such a creamy, buttery texture. Or so easily. When cooked down quickly with a bit of stirring and a smidgen of real butter, finely grated squash transforms into a versatile and luscious side/spread/ topping that compliments almost anything. Moreover, a satisfying quarter cup contains the same amount of fat as half a tablespoon of butter. Amazing.*

MAKES 4 SERVINGS

½ pound zucchini

½ pound yellow squash

¼ plus ⅛ teaspoon salt, divided

1½ tablespoons butter

1 medium shallot, minced

Black pepper, to taste

1. Coarsely grate the zucchini and squash into a colander. Sprinkle with ¼ teaspoon salt and toss to coat. Let sit for 3 to 4 minutes, place in a colander, and press firmly with a small pot lid to remove excess liquid.

2. Place a large skillet over medium heat and add the butter. Add shallots and sauté for 3 minutes, or until translucent. Add the grated squash and cook for 15 to 18 minutes, or until the squash is a creamy, buttery consistency, stirring occasionally. (If the mixture begins to scorch, add a teaspoon of water to deglaze the pan and turn down the heat slightly). Add remaining salt and pepper to taste. Serve immediately or refrigerate for up to a week.

**Marlene Says:** *You can use only zucchini, but I find the combo of yellow and green squash most appealing.*

**NUTRITION INFORMATION PER SERVING:** (¼ cup) Calories 70 | Carbohydrate 5g (Sugars 2g) | Total Fat 5g (Sat Fat 3g) | Protein 3g | Fiber 1g | Cholesterol 10mg | Sodium 190mg | Food Exchanges: 1 Vegetable, ½ Fat | Carbohydrate Choices: 0 | Weight Watcher Smart Point Comparison: 2 (1 point with 1 tbsp. of butter)

# CHICKEN & TURKEY

# chicken & turkey

# Coconut Coconut Chicken

**AIR FRY!**
SEE PAGE **325**

*THIS RECIPE IS FOR THOSE WHO ASKED IF MY COCONUT COCONUT SHRIMP RECIPE could be made with chicken. After a few rounds in the kitchen—to ensure it would turn out equally great—I found that not only was a longer baking time required, but that egg white worked much better in getting the coating to stick to chicken. So here you have it, Coconut Coconut Chicken! (The honey mustard topping is optional, but just a drizzle makes this recipe dazzle.)*

MAKES 4 SERVINGS

4 boneless, skinless chicken breasts (about 1 pound)

1 large egg white

1/8 teaspoon coconut extract

1/4 cup Panko breadcrumbs

1/4 cup plain breadcrumbs

1/4 cup unsweetened or sweetened shredded coconut

1/4 teaspoon salt

1/4 teaspoon black pepper

1 teaspoon canola oil

Honey mustard (optional, see Marlene Says)

1. Preheat the oven to 425°F. Cover the chicken breasts in plastic wrap and gently pound to 1/4-inch thickness. Set aside.

2. In a medium shallow bowl, whisk together the egg white and coconut extract. In another medium shallow bowl mix together the breadcrumbs, coconut, salt, pepper, and oil.

3. Dip each breast into the egg mixture, allowing the excess to drip off, roll in coconut crumbs, and place on a baking sheet. Spray chicken breasts with cooking spray and bake for 18 to 20 minutes, or until coating is golden brown and chicken is cooked through. Serve with honey mustard, if desired.

**Marlene Says:** *To make the honey mustard, whisk together 1 tablespoon each Dijon mustard and light mayonnaise, with 2 teaspoons each honey and vinegar. Drizzle scant tablespoon onto each breast. Adds 25 calories and 1 gram of fat per serving.*

**NUTRITION INFORMATION PER SERVING (1 chicken breast):** Calories 190 | Carbohydrate 7g (Sugars 1g) | Total Fat 6g (Sat Fat 3.5g) | Protein 24g | Fiber 1g | Cholesterol 55mg | Sodium 370mg | Food Exchanges: 3 1/2 Lean Meat, 1/2 Starch | Carbohydrate Choices: | Weight Watcher Smart Point Comparison: 3

# Amazing Smashed Garlic Butter Chicken

*THIS 10-MINUTE, THREE-INGREDIENT RECIPE IS SIMPLY AMAZING!* Simply microwave a head of garlic for forty-five seconds and voilà—the raw cloves not only slip right out of their skins but are magically transformed into a mild-tasting, nutty, buttery, soft pulp. A quick few minutes under the broiler cooks the chicken in record time and turns the softened garlic into the best garlic butter chicken topping you've ever tasted. It's so easy, so fast, and so good!

**MAKES 2 SERVINGS**

1 whole head garlic

1 tablespoon butter, softened

Pinch of salt

2 (5-ounce) boneless, skinless chicken breasts

Fresh ground black pepper

1. Place the whole (unpeeled) head of garlic in the microwave and cook on high for 20 seconds. Turn head upside down and cook for another 20 to 25 seconds. Let stand for 1 minute. Squeeze cloves out of the papery skin, place on cutting board, and use the broad side of a knife to smash them. Transfer garlic paste to a small bowl, add butter and salt, and stir to combine.

2. Position oven rack about 6 inches below broiler, and turn on the broiler. Wrap chicken breasts in plastic wrap and pound to 1/4-inch thickness. Line a baking sheet with foil, place chicken on foil, and spray with cooking spray. Broil chicken for 4 minutes. Turn, and broil for 2 more minutes.

3. Remove pan from oven, blot any excess juice off top of chicken, and smear half the garlic butter onto each breast. Top with freshly ground pepper and broil for an additional 1 to 2 minutes, or until browned and bubbly.

**Marlene Says:** *Please don't be deterred because of the amount of garlic. Cooking it the microwave takes out the bite and leaves you with a delicious, mild-tasting garlicky flavor.*

**NUTRITION INFORMATION PER SERVING (1 chicken breast):** Calories 210 | Carbohydrate 4g (Sugars 0g) | Total Fat 7g (Sat Fat 3g) | Protein 31g | Fiber 0g | Cholesterol 100mg | Sodium 230mg | Food Exchanges: 4 1/2 Lean Meat, 1/2 Fat | Carbohydrate Choices: 0 | Weight Watcher Smart Point Comparison: 3

# Cheesy Bacon Chicken with Honey Mustard Drizzle

*ONE OF THE MOST POPULAR ENTRÉES AT OUTBACK STEAKHOUSE is their Alice Springs Chicken. Seriously, what's not to like about a juicy chicken breast topped with tender cooked mushrooms, melty cheese, and crumbled bacon served with a honey mustard sauce? My version is a quick, easy, and ridiculously tasty variation of this famous dish. By keeping the same marvelous taste and losing 75% of the fat, I'll spring for this one any day.*

MAKES 4 SERVINGS

4 boneless, skinless chicken breasts (about 1 pound)

1 tablespoon Dijon mustard

1 tablespoon light mayonnaise

1 tablespoon honey

2 teaspoons vinegar

2 teaspoons butter

1 (8-ounce) package sliced mushrooms

Black pepper, to taste

3/4 cup shredded reduced-fat cheddar cheese

8 teaspoons real bacon bits

1/4 cup sliced green onions tops

1. Cover the chicken breasts in plastic wrap and gently pound to 1/4-inch thickness. For the honey mustard, in a small bowl, whisk together next 4 ingredients (mustard through vinegar). Set aside.

2. Melt the butter in a large nonstick skillet over medium heat; add the mushrooms and cook for 7 to 10 minutes, or until they are tender and browned. Remove from pan and set aside.

3. Coat the skillet with nonstick cooking spray and turn heat to medium-high. Add chicken to the pan and cook for 3 minutes, or until underside is golden brown. Turn, and top each breast with 1/4 cup mushrooms. Add black pepper to taste, and sprinkle each breast with 3 tablespoons cheese and 2 teaspoons bacon. Add 2 tablespoons of water to the pan and immediately cover. Cook for 2 minutes, or until cheese is melted and chicken is cooked through.

4. To serve, top each breast with 1 tablespoon green onions, and drizzle with a scant tablespoon of the honey mustard sauce.

**DARE TO COMPARE:** An order of Alice Springs Chicken at Outback Steakhouse (without sides) will set you back 750 calories, 44 grams of fat, and 1,550 milligrams of sodium.

**NUTRITION INFORMATION PER SERVING:** (1 chicken breast) Calories 265 | Carbohydrate 8g (Sugars 5g) | Total Fat 10g (Sat Fat 5g) | Protein 35g | Fiber 1g | Cholesterol 85mg | Sodium 650mg | Food Exchanges: 4 1/2 Lean Meat | Carbohydrate Choices: 1/2 | Weight Watcher Smart Point Comparison: 4

# Chicken Paprikash

*THIS POPULAR TRADITIONAL HUNGARIAN DISH is typically made with whole pieces of chicken slowly simmered in a luscious paprika-laced sauce. My recipe rewards you with the same sweet silky red sauce, but I've swapped in skinless breast meat to slash the time (and the fat). Imported sweet Hungarian or Spanish paprika will give you the nicest, most authentic result.*

MAKES 4 SERVINGS

4 boneless, skinless chicken breasts (about 1 pound)

1/3 cup low-fat sour cream

1 teaspoon cornstarch

2 teaspoons oil

3/4 cup diced onion

1 red bell pepper, diced

2 teaspoons minced garlic

1 tablespoon sweet paprika

1 (15-ounce) can diced tomatoes with juice

1 cup reduced-sodium chicken broth

1/2 teaspoon salt

1/2 teaspoon black pepper

1. Wrap the chicken breasts in plastic wrap, and gently pound to 1/4-inch thickness. In a small bowl, whisk together the sour cream and cornstarch. Set aside.

2. Spray a large nonstick skillet with cooking spray and place over medium heat. Add the chicken and cook for 3 to 4 minutes, or until lightly browned. Turn, and cook for 3 to 4 more minutes or until almost cooked through. Transfer to a plate.

3. Add the oil to the skillet and reduce the heat to medium-low. Add onion, bell pepper, and garlic, and cover. Cook for 3 minutes, stirring occasionally, until the onion has softened. Stir in paprika, tomatoes, and broth, and bring to a boil. Reduce heat to medium-low and simmer for 10 minutes, stirring occasionally. Return chicken and any juices to the skillet. Cover and cook for 5 minutes, or until chicken is cooked through.

4. Transfer chicken to a platter, stir the sour cream mixture into the sauce, and simmer briefly on low to incorporate. Pour the sauce over the chicken and serve.

**NUTRITION INFORMATION PER SERVING:** (1 chicken breast with sauce) Calories 240 | Carbohydrate 13g (Sugars 8g) | Total Fat 7g (Sat Fat 2.5g) | Protein 29g | Fiber 3g | Cholesterol 75mg | Sodium 680mg | Food Exchanges: 3½ Lean Meat, 1½ Vegetable | Carbohydrate Choices: 1 | Weight Watcher Smart Point Comparison: 3

# 5-Ingredient Balsamic Braised Chicken Thighs

*THE NEXT TIME CHICKEN THIGHS ARE ON SALE, GRAB 'EM. A handful of ingredients and 15 short minutes are all it takes to make these juicy chicken thighs bathed in a sauce of balsamic vinegar accented with fresh orange flavor. Serve with fresh steamed broccoli or asparagus and rice or noodles to sop up the citrusy sauce.*

MAKES 4 SERVINGS

1½ pounds boneless, skinless chicken thighs, trimmed

½ teaspoon salt

¼ teaspoon black pepper

2 teaspoons canola oil

¼ cup balsamic vinegar

1 large orange, sliced into 12 wedges

1 tablespoon butter

3 tablespoons chopped fresh parsley

1. Pound chicken slightly to create a uniform thickness if needed, and season with salt and pepper. Heat the oil in a large nonstick skillet over medium-high heat. Add the chicken and cook for 2 to 3 minutes per side, or until well browned.

2. Reduce the heat to medium and add balsamic vinegar. Turn chicken to coat with vinegar, cover, and cook for 4 minutes, or until done. Uncover the skillet, transfer chicken to a serving platter, and cover to keep warm.

3. Add orange wedges to the pan, and with a fork, press on about half of the wedges to release their juice. Add butter, stir, and cook for 2 to 3 minutes, or until orange rinds have softened. Pour the sauce (with the orange wedges) over the chicken and garnish with chopped parsley.

**NUTRITION INFORMATION PER SERVING:** (1 large or 2 small thighs) Calories 230 | Carbohydrate 8g (Sugars 7g) | Total Fat 10g (Sat Fat 4g) | Protein 24g | Fiber 1g | Cholesterol 85mg | Sodium 390mg | Food Exchanges: 3½ Lean Meat, ½ Carbohydrate | Carbohydrate Choices: ½ | Weight Watcher Smart Point Comparison: 6

# Teriyaki Fried Chicken

SEE PAGE 325

*SO MUCH FLAVOR IN SO LITTLE TIME! This dish is fashioned after Chicken Katsu, a dish from Japan consisting of fried chicken served with a thick, sweet sauce called katsu. The dish is popular here in the US in Hawaiian barbecue shacks and Japanese restaurants where you'll find the fried chicken cutlets served with teriyaki sauce for dipping. For my quick and easy take I've gone one step further and built the teriyaki flavor right in! This fast dish has flavor to last for days. . . .*

MAKES 4 SERVINGS

4 boneless, skinless chicken breasts (about 1 pound)

¼ cup reduced-sodium Teriyaki sauce

4 teaspoons brown sugar

½ teaspoon grated or minced ginger

½ cup Panko bread crumbs

3 tablespoons plain bread crumbs

2 teaspoons oil

¼ teaspoon garlic powder

1. Preheat the oven to 425°F. Cover the chicken breasts in plastic wrap and gently pound to ¼-inch thickness.

2. In a medium bowl, combine teriyaki sauce, brown sugar, and ginger. Add the chicken breasts to the sauce mixture and toss to coat. Let chicken marinate for 5 to 10 minutes (but not longer).

3. In a small bowl, mix together the Panko, breadcrumbs, oil, and garlic powder. Roll the chicken breasts in the breadcrumb mixture and place on a baking sheet. Spray tops with cooking spray and bake for 12 to 15 minutes, or until chicken is golden brown. Serve with an extra drizzle of Teriyaki sauce, if desired.

**DARE TO COMPARE:** According to L&L Hawaiian Barbecue, a "mini" Hawaiian Lunch plate of Chicken Katsu, macaroni salad, and rice has 1,190 calories. Instead, pair this recipe with the Creamy Potato Mac Potluck Salad (page 149) and a ½ cup serving of instant brown for less than 400 calories!

**NUTRITION INFORMATION PER SERVING:** (1 chicken breast) Calories 205 | Carbohydrate 16g (Sugars 7g) | Total Fat 4g (Sat Fat 0.5g) | Protein 25g | Fiber 0g | Cholesterol 65mg | Sodium 560mg | Food Exchanges: 3½ Lean Meat, 1 Starch | Carbohydrate Choices: 1 | Weight Watcher Smart Point Comparison: 3

# Chicken Tikka Masala

*MY BOYS LOVE THE CHICKEN TIKKA MASALA FROM OUR LOCAL INDIAN RESTAURANT, but as it is made with heavy cream, I couldn't resist creating a healthier version. After several attempts I learned the ticket to delivering traditional tikka masala taste quickly is to use garam masala, an Indian spice mixture of over a dozen spicy, sweet, and earthy spices, including cardamom, cumin, and cinnamon. Look for it with the rest of the spices. Tender, creamy and spiced just right, I'm happy to say this version is now loved just as much!*

MAKES 4 SERVINGS

1 pound chicken tenders

2 teaspoons oil

1 cup finely chopped onion

1 tablespoon minced ginger

3 garlic cloves, minced

2 teaspoons garam masala

Pinch of cayenne pepper (optional)

1 (8-ounce) can tomato sauce

2 teaspoons lemon juice

1/4 cup nonfat half-and-half

Chopped fresh cilantro, for garnish

1. Spray a large nonstick skillet with cooking spray and heat over medium high heat. Add the chicken and cook for 2 to 3 minutes per side, or until well browned and barely cooked through. Transfer the chicken to a plate.

2. Add the oil to the skillet and reduce heat to medium. Add the onion, ginger, and garlic, and cover. Cook for 3 minutes, or until the onions soften, stirring occasionally. Stir in garam masala and optional cayenne, and cook for 15 seconds. Reduce heat to medium low, and stir in tomato sauce, lemon juice, and 1/3 cup of water. Simmer, partially covered, for 5 minutes or until sauce slightly thickens, stirring occasionally.

3. Stir in the half-and-half, and return the chicken and any juices to the skillet. Cover, and cook for 3 minutes, or until chicken is cooked through and sauce re-thickens. Sprinkle with the cilantro and serve.

**DARE TO COMPARE:** Wholesome or not? A 5 oz. serving of chicken tikki Masala from Whole Foods comes with 18 grams of fat—54% of the total calories.

**NUTRITION INFORMATION PER SERVING:** (4-ounces chicken plus sauce) Calories 190 | Carbohydrate 11g (Sugars 5g) | Total Fat 4g (Sat Fat 0.5g) | Protein 26g | Fiber 2g | Cholesterol 65mg | Sodium 450mg | Food Exchanges: 3 1/2 Lean Meat, 2 Vegetable | Carbohydrate Choices: 1 | Weight Watcher Smart Point Comparison: 1

# 2-Minute Greek Lemon Chicken

*POUNDING THE CHICKEN VERY THIN AND COOKING IT IN A HOT PAN IS THE SECRET* to this moist and zesty 2-minute chicken, and the combination of Mediterranean flavors—lemon zest, oregano, garlic, and olive oil—is as enticing as it is good for you. Serve this dish with Instant Brown Rice Pilaf (page 199) or One-Pot Spaghetti and Spinach (page 195) for a quick 15-minute meal. A squeeze of lemon juice is the perfect finishing touch.

MAKES 2 SERVINGS

2 (5-ounce) boneless, skinless chicken breasts

¾ teaspoon lemon zest

½ teaspoon dried oregano

½ teaspoon dried parsley

¼ teaspoon garlic salt

⅛ teaspoon black pepper

½ teaspoon olive oil

1. Cover chicken in plastic wrap and gently pound to between ⅛- and ¼-inch thickness. (If breast is very thick, you can make a lengthwise cut (stopping before cutting it all the way through), and open it like a book, and then pound it lightly.)

2. In a small bowl, combine the next 5 ingredients (lemon zest through pepper). Rub the oil on one side of each of the breasts, turn, and rub the herb mixture on the other side.

3. Spray a medium nonstick skillet with cooking spray and place over high heat. Place the chicken in the skillet, seasoned-side up, and cook until almost cooked through, about 1 minute. Turn the chicken and cook for 30 seconds or chicken is until cooked through.

**Marlene Says:** *Move this to the grill or mix and match the herbs as you please. Fresh rosemary, dried thyme, or Herbes de Provence are all wonderful choices.*

**NUTRITION INFORMATION PER SERVING: (1 chicken breast)** Calories 160 | Carbohydrate 0g (Sugars 0g) | Total Fat 3g (Sat Fat 0.5g) | Protein 30g | Fiber 0g | Cholesterol 80mg | Sodium 200mg | Food Exchanges: 4½ Lean Meat | Carbohydrate Choices: 0 | Weight Watcher Smart Point Comparison: 0

# Bourbon Chicken and Broccoli Stir-Fry

*WHEN IT COMES TO QUICK AND EASY COOKING, you just can't beat a dazzling stir-fry. This one combines tender chicken and crunchy broccoli with a sweet Chinese "bourbon" sauce (no bourbon required!). I chop my own carrots and onions and use bagged broccoli florets for ease. For extra ease you can purchase all the veggies ready to cook. Either way, have everything ready before firing up the skillet as this just takes minutes to cook.*

MAKES 4 SERVINGS

1/2 cup light or regular apple juice

1/4 cup reduced-sodium soy sauce

1 tablespoon molasses

1 tablespoon cornstarch

1 1/4 teaspoons minced ginger

1/2 teaspoon minced garlic

1 cup carrots, thinly sliced on the diagonal

2 teaspoons oil

1 cup sliced onion

1 pound boneless, skinless chicken breast, thinly sliced

4 cups broccoli florets

1/4 teaspoon black pepper

1. In a small bowl, whisk together first 6 ingredients (apple juice through garlic). Place carrots in a microwave-safe bowl, cover with plastic wrap, and microwave on high for 1 minute.

2. Heat the oil in a large nonstick skillet or wok over medium-high heat. Add onion and stir-fry for 2 to 3 minutes or until it starts to turn translucent. Add chicken and cook for 2 to 3 minutes, or until barely done. Add the carrots and broccoli to the pan, and stir to combine.

3. Pour in the sauce, cover, and cook for 3 minutes. Uncover pan, and stir until sauce coats ingredients and broccoli is tender. Sprinkle with black pepper and serve.

**DARE TO COMPARE:** An order of Beef and Broccoli from P.F. Chang's has 669 calories, including a whopping 35 grams of fat and 3,260 milligrams of sodium!

**NUTRITION INFORMATION PER SERVING:** (1 1/2 cups) Calories 200 | Carbohydrate 19g (Sugars 11g) | Total Fat 2g (Sat Fat 0g) | Protein 27g | Fiber 4g | Cholesterol 65mg | Sodium 610mg | Food Exchanges: 3 1/2 Lean Meat, 2 Vegetable, 1/2 Carbohydrate | Carbohydrate Choices: 1 | Weight Watcher Smart Point Comparison: 1

# Slow-Cooker Creamy Chicken and Biscuit Stew

*THIS EASY, CREAMY, RIB-STICKING STEW (which will remind you of chicken pot pie) is as comforting as a warm hug on a cold day. Colorful frozen vegetables and ready-made biscuits cancel out prep time, and the slow cooker does the rest of the work. Add a fresh green salad and dinner is done!*

**MAKES 6 SERVINGS**

¾ teaspoon poultry seasoning

½ teaspoon garlic powder

1 (11-ounce) bag frozen mixed vegetables

1½ pounds boneless, skinless chicken tenders

2 (10-ounce) cans reduced-fat cream of chicken soup

2 cups slender cut frozen green beans

1 (7.5-ounce) can refrigerated biscuits*

Salt and black pepper, to taste

1. Layer the poultry seasoning, garlic powder, mixed vegetables, and chicken in the bottom of a 4- to 6-quart slow cooker. Top with soup and 1 cup of water, and stir to combine. Cover, and cook on low for 3 to 3½ hours. Open the lid and using 2 forks, shred the chicken into medium-sized pieces (if the chicken does not easily shred, cover and cook longer). Stir in the green beans, and re-cover.

2. Place the biscuits on a flat surface. Press to flatten them slightly, and cut each biscuit into 3 or 4 strips. Place biscuit strips in the slow cooker, pressing some into the stew, and leaving some on top, cover, and cook for 90 minutes on high, or until the biscuits are plump and cooked in the center. Add salt and pepper to taste.

**Marlene Says:** *I use Pillsbury Buttermilk Biscuits. The chicken tenders ensure tender chicken (in less time), but skinless, boneless chicken breasts can be used. Prep the same way and cook on low for 5½ hours, shred chicken, add beans and biscuits, and then cook on high for 90 minutes.*

**NUTRITION INFORMATION PER SERVING:** (1½ cups) Calories 320 | Carbohydrate 41g (Sugars 7g) | Total Fat 4g (Sat Fat 1g) | Protein 31g | Fiber 5g | Cholesterol 70mg | Sodium 750mg | Food Exchanges: 4 Lean Meat, 2 Starch, 2 Vegetable | Carbohydrate Choices: 2½ | Weight Watcher Smart Point Comparison: 5

# Jalapeño Popper Chicken

*CREAMY, CHEESY GOODNESS AND THE MILD HEAT OF JALAPEÑO PEPPERS made this a crave-worthy winner with my crew. Instead of being stuffed, these quickly sautéed chicken breasts are covered with the ooey, gooey popper filling and topped with crunchy, buttery panko breadcrumbs for the requisite fried crunch. Oh my goodness is right! I like to serve this with my Last-Minute Roasted Red Potatoes (page 192).*

MAKES 4 SERVINGS

⅔ cup shredded reduced-fat cheddar cheese

¼ cup light tub-style cream cheese

¼ cup light sour cream

1 tablespoon finely chopped jarred jalapeño pepper

¼ cup plus 1 tablespoon Panko breadcrumbs, divided

1 teaspoon butter, melted

½ teaspoon garlic salt, divided

4 boneless, skinless chicken breasts (about 1¼ pounds)

1. In a medium bowl, mix together the cheeses, sour cream, and jalapeño. Place a small skillet over medium heat and add the Panko, melted butter, and ¼ teaspoon garlic salt. Stir to combine, and heat for about 5 minutes, or until crumbs are lightly browned. Remove from heat and set aside.

2. Wrap the chicken breasts in plastic wrap and gently pound to ¼-inch thickness. Sprinkle remaining ¼ teaspoon garlic salt over chicken breasts. Spray a large nonstick skillet with cooking spray and place over medium-high heat. Add the chicken and cook for 2 to 3 minutes on each side, until well browned and barely cooked through.

3. Spoon 3 tablespoons of the cheese mixture onto each chicken breast. Add a few tablespoons of water to the skillet, cover, and cook for 1 minute, or until chicken is cooked through and topping is melted. Sprinkle each breast with 1 tablespoon of the Panko crumbs and serve.

**NUTRITION INFORMATION PER SERVING:** (1 chicken breast) Calories 235 | Carbohydrate 5g (Sugars 2g) | Total Fat 9g (Sat Fat 4g) | Protein 31g | Fiber 0g | Cholesterol 105mg | Sodium 490mg | Food Exchanges: 4 Lean Meat, ½ Carbohydrate | Carbohydrate Choices: 0 | Weight Watcher Smart Point Comparison: 3

# Anytime Turkey Meatballs

SEE PAGE **325**

*WHY BUY SPONGY OR SALTY FROZEN MEATBALLS when it is so easy to make tastier, healthier ones yourself? This is my everyday go-to basic turkey meatball recipe. After preparing, store them uncooked in the fridge for several days, or bag and freeze them for several months. It's always good to have meatballs at the ready! Be sure to try them with Grape Jelly BBQ Sauce (page 95).*

**MAKES 24 SERVINGS**

20 ounces lean ground turkey

1/2 cup dry breadcrumbs

1/4 cup fresh chopped parsley

1 large egg

3 tablespoons dried minced onion

2 tablespoons low-fat milk

2 tablespoons Worcestershire sauce

2 tablespoons grated Parmesan cheese

1 teaspoon garlic salt

1/2 teaspoon black pepper

1. Preheat the oven to 400°F. Line a sheet pan with foil, spray lightly with cooking spray, and set aside.

2. In a large bowl, with a spoon or with your hands, gently mix all of the ingredients together until combined.

3. Roll meat mixture into twenty-four 1½-inch meatballs and place on a baking sheet. Bake for 15 minutes or until tops and bottoms are browned, and meat is cooked through.

**Marlene Says:** *You can cook them directly from frozen, or move them to the fridge the night before for faster last-minute cooking. See page 100 for more freezer tips.*

**NUTRITION INFORMATION PER SERVING: (1 meatball)** Calories 50 | Carbohydrate 2g (Sugars 0g) | Total Fat 2.5g (Sat Fat 1g) | Protein 5g | Fiber 0g | Cholesterol 25mg | Sodium 115mg | Food Exchanges: 1 Lean Meat | Carbohydrate Choices: 0 | Weight Watcher Smart Point Comparison: 1

# Stuffin' Crusted Turkey Sheet Pan Supper

*GET READY TO ENJOY THE GREAT TASTE OF THANKSGIVING DINNER* at any time of the year with this quick 350-calorie sheet pan meal. Speedy stuffing-topped turkey cutlets cook on one sheet pan and fabulous fresh green beans cook simultaneously on another—and 20 minutes later; you've got an entire dinner on the table! If your market doesn't sell turkey cutlets, just slice two turkey tenderloins (about 8 ounces each) in half horizontally to form the cutlets. To crush fennel seeds, chop them with a chef's knife.

MAKES 4 SERVINGS

1 pound fresh green beans

1 teaspoon olive oil

1/4 teaspoon garlic salt with parsley

1 box reduced-sodium chicken stuffing mix

1 tablespoon margarine or butter

1 teaspoon fennel seeds, crushed

1/4 teaspoon black pepper

3 tablespoons low-sugar raspberry jam

2 tablespoons Dijon mustard

4 turkey cutlets, about 1/4 inch thick (about 1 pound)

1. Preheat the oven to 425°F, and place 2 racks in the oven, evenly spaced. Line 2 sheet pans with foil and set aside. In a large bowl, combine the green beans with olive oil and salt, and toss to coat. Transfer beans to one of the sheet pans.

2. In a large bowl, combine the stuffing mix, margarine, fennel seeds, and black pepper. Boil 1$\frac{2}{3}$ cups water, pour it over the stuffing mix, and stir lightly to combine. Let stuffing sit for 5 minutes.

3. In a small bowl, combine the jam and mustard. Place the turkey on one of the sheet pans, spread each piece with the jam mixture, and top each tenderloin with 3/4 cup stuffing mix. Spray tenderloins with cooking spray and transfer pan to the top oven rack. Place the green beans on the lower rack. Bake for 17 minutes, or until stuffing is browned and turkey and green beans are cooked.

**NUTRITION INFORMATION PER SERVING:** (1 cutlet plus 1/4 green beans) Calories 350 | Carbohydrate 44g (Sugars 10g) | Total Fat 5g (Sat Fat 0.5g) | Protein 31g | Fiber 5g | Cholesterol 60mg | Sodium 720mg | Food Exchanges: 3 1/2 Lean Meat, 2 Starch, 1 Vegetable, 1/2 Carbohydrate | Carbohydrate Choices: 3 | Weight Watcher Smart Point Comparison: 6

# Turkey Taco Casserole

*WHO DOESN'T LOVE A GOOD TACO CASSEROLE? A handful of smart swaps was all it took to take the original recipe from flabby to fit with this meaty, cheesy, layered Mexican casserole recipe. From start to finish, it takes about 30 minutes, but you can also make it ahead of time. Simply layer it up, cover, place in the fridge, and bake when you're ready. Just add about 10 extra minutes to the baking time.*

**MAKES 6 SERVINGS**

½ cup light sour cream

¾ cup low-fat cottage cheese

½ cup chopped onions

1 small red bell pepper, chopped

12 ounces lean ground turkey

1 recipe DIY Taco Seasoning (page 312) or 1 reduced-sodium packet

1 (8-ounce) can tomato sauce

1 (15-ounce) can black beans, rinsed and drained

1 cup low-fat tortilla chips

¾ cup shredded reduced-fat cheddar cheese

1. Preheat the oven to 375°F. Lightly spray a 2-quart casserole dish with cooking spray and set aside. In a medium bowl, combine the sour cream and cottage cheese; set aside.

2. Place a medium nonstick skillet over medium high heat. Add onions and bell pepper and cook, stirring, for 2 minutes. Add turkey and cook 2 minutes more, or until turkey is lightly browned. Stir in seasoning, sauce, and beans. Cook for 2 minutes to incorporate spices.

3. Place chips in the bottom of casserole dish, breaking chips to flatten. Top chips with meat mixture, and spread sour cream mixture over meat. Sprinkle with cheese. Bake, uncovered, for 20 minutes, or until cheese has melted and filling is bubbly.

**DARE TO COMPARE:** The original recipe for this casserole clocked in at 540 calories per serving, with twice the sodium and four times the fat.

**NUTRITION INFORMATION PER SERVING:** (⅙ casserole) Calories 260 | Carbohydrate 21g (Sugars 6g) | Total Fat 9g (Sat Fat 4g) | Protein 23g | Fiber 5g | Cholesterol 55mg | Sodium 540mg | Food Exchanges: 3 Lean Meat, 1 Starch, ½ Vegetable | Carbohydrate Choices: 1 | Weight Watcher Smart Point Comparison: 4

# BEEF & PORK

# beef & pork

# *For the Love of*
## { PERFECTLY COOKED MEAT }

If you love meat, there is nothing more mouthwatering than a juicy burger, a tender steak, or a plump pork chop. Luckily, marvelous meat entrees like these are not only quick and easy to cook, when prepared with lean cuts of meat; they can be good for you too!

When cooking meat, determining "doneness" can be difficult, as the look on the outside is not always an accurate indicator of how well cooked it is on the inside. With the exception of stir-fries or long simmered dishes, the best way to determine the doneness of meat is to use a thermometer. Here are some tips to help you ensure the meat dishes in this book (and your own!) are always cooked to perfection.

### MARLENE'S COOKED TO PERFECTION TIPS

✦ Invest in an inexpensive instant-read food thermometer. They're easy to use, work well on all cuts of meats, and deliver accurate readings faster than traditional meat thermometers. (Note: Unlike a traditional meat thermometer, do not leave it in the meat while it cooks.)

✦ To get an accurate temperature, insert the thermometer into the thickest part of the meat (making sure not to touch any bones). On thin cuts or burgers, insert the thermometer into the meat lengthwise through the side to ensure enough of the thermometer is inserted into the meat. If needed, use tongs to hold the meat steady.

✦ To determine when the meat is done, use the chart below.* On average, the temperature of steaks, burgers, and roasts rises anywhere from 5 to 10 degrees as they rest. "Medium" meat will still be slightly pink when rested.

✦ Be sure to let the meat rest after cooking. A short 5 to 10 minute rest can decrease the juices lost in carving (or eating) by as much as 40%.

| DESIRED DONENESS | COOK UNTIL IT REGISTERS | FINAL REST TEMPERATURE |
|---|---|---|
| **BEEF** | | |
| Medium-Rare | 125 to 130 degrees | 130 to 135 degrees |
| Medium | 135 to 140 degrees | 140 to 145 degrees |
| Medium-Well | 145 to 155 degrees | 150 to 160 degrees |
| **PORK** | | |
| Medium | 140 to 145 degrees | 145 to 150 degrees |
| Well Done | 150 to 155 degrees | 155 to 160 degrees |

*For food safety, the government recommends that steak and pork be cooked to a minimum temperature of 145°F (and then rested), and ground meats to 160°F.

# Everyday Marinated Steak

*THE BIGGEST MISCONCEPTION ABOUT MARINATING MEAT is that it will tenderize and/or add juiciness to the meat. The truth is that a marinade only adds flavor at/or near the surface because it cannot penetrate the meat, even if the meat marinates for hours. Fortunately, as little as 20 minutes are required for this truly mouthwatering marinade to do its job and add fabulous flavor to any steak (or chicken). A thin cut steak like flank steak cooks up in less than 10 minutes!*

### MAKING 6 SERVINGS

¼ cup reduced-sodium soy sauce

2 tablespoons dry sherry

1 tablespoon brown sugar

1 tablespoon sesame oil

1 teaspoon ground ginger

¼ teaspoon garlic powder

¼ teaspoon onion powder

1½ pounds lean flank steak

1. For the marinade, in a small bowl, combine the first 7 ingredients (soy sauce through onion powder). Transfer to a large zip-top bag, add steak, seal, and turn to coat the meat. Let stand at room temperature, turning occasionally, for 20 to 30 minutes. (Or refrigerate for up to 4 hours, and remove from the refrigerator 30 minutes before cooking.)

2. Preheat the grill to medium-high. Lightly oil the grill grate. Remove steak from the marinade, and shake off excess. Grill steak, with the lid closed, for 3 to 4 minutes, or until the underside is browned. Turn steak and grill for 4 to 5 minutes for medium-rare. (See chart on page 228.)

3. Remove the steak from the grill and let rest for 5 minutes. To serve, cut steak across the grain into thin slices. Serve the steak drizzled with the carving juices.

**Marlene Says:** *To AIR FRY the steak, preheat the air fryer to 400°F. Air-fry the marinated steak for 5 minutes, turn and cook 5 to 7 minutes, or until the steak is done to your liking (see chart on page 228).*

**NUTRITION INFORMATION PER SERVING:** (3 ounces cooked) Calories 190 | Carbohydrate 1g (Sugars 1g) | Total Fat 7g (Sat Fat 3g) | Protein 24g | Fiber 0g | Cholesterol 60mg | Sodium 210mg | Food Exchanges: 3½ Lean Meat | Carbohydrate Choices: 0 | Weight Watcher Smart Point Comparison: 4

# Swedish Meatballs with Sour Cream Gravy

*THE ORIGIN OF MEATBALLS CAN BE TRACED BACK TO CHINA during the Qin Dynasty in 207 BCE! Today almost every country can boast a meatball recipe. Swedish-style meatballs, though, are one of my favorites. Delicately flavored with warm spices, and lavishly smothered in a luscious sour cream sauce, these easy-to-make quick-cooking meatballs are a comforting dinner. Serve them with boiled potatoes or noodles to take advantage of the "only-tastes-sinful" sauce.*

**MAKES 4 SERVINGS**

½ pound lean ground beef

½ pound lean ground pork

⅓ cup dry breadcrumbs

1 large egg, beaten

2 tablespoons grated onion

½ teaspoon salt

¼ teaspoon ground nutmeg

¼ teaspoon ground allspice

¼ teaspoon black pepper

1¼ cups reduced-sodium beef broth, divided

1½ tablespoons instant flour (like Wondra)

½ cup light sour cream

2 tablespoons chopped fresh parsley

1. To make the meatballs, in a large bowl, combine the first 9 ingredients (beef through black pepper) plus 2 tablespoons of water. Mix lightly with a fork until the ingredients are fully mixed together. Using your hands, divide and roll the mixture into 16 meatballs, about 1¼ inches in diameter.

2. In a large nonstick skillet over medium-high heat, add 1 cup broth and bring to a simmer. Reduce heat to medium-low, gently add meatballs, and cover. Simmer for 15 to 20 minutes, or until meatballs are cooked through, turning occasionally. (If you want to serve noodles with your meatballs, now is a good time to cook them.) With a slotted spoon, transfer the meatballs to a large serving bowl and cover to keep warm.

3. Sprinkle the flour into the pan, whisk well, and simmer for 1 minute over medium heat. Add remaining ¼ cup broth, reduce heat to low, add the sour cream, and whisk until smooth; do not boil. Season the sauce with additional salt and pepper, if desired. Pour sauce over meatballs, sprinkle with parsley, and serve.

**NUTRITION INFORMATION PER SERVING: (4 meatballs + ⅓ cup sauce)** Calories 280 | Carbohydrate 12g (Sugars 3g) | Total Fat 11g (Sat Fat 5g) | Protein 29g | Fiber 1g | Cholesterol 80mg | Sodium 490mg | Food Exchanges: 4 Lean Meat, ½ Starch, ½ Fat | Carbohydrate Choices: 1 | Weight Watcher Smart Point Comparison: 7

# 15-Minute Upside-Down Shepherd's Pie

*WHAT ONCE TOOK HOURS NOW TAKES MINUTES with this creative spin on the classic shepherd's pie. What's more, you don't have to serve it all at once. To serve two (or even just you), microwave only one potato and refrigerate or freeze the remaining meat and veggie mixture for another meal. You can also make the "shepherd" topping earlier in the day and refrigerate it until dinner. A simple green salad is a nice accompaniment to this all-in-one dinner.*

**MAKES 4 SERVINGS**

2 large potatoes (about 1½ pounds)

1 small onion, chopped

12 ounces lean ground beef

1¼ cups reduced-sodium beef broth

2 teaspoons cornstarch

2 cups frozen peas and carrots

2 tablespoons tomato paste

1 tablespoon Worcestershire sauce

1 teaspoon garlic salt with parsley

½ teaspoon thyme

¼ cup light sour cream

4 teaspoons margarine or butter

1. Pierce the potatoes with a fork, and place in the microwave. Cook on high for 8 to 9 minutes, or until tender when pierced with a fork.

2. While potatoes are cooking, spray a large nonstick skillet with cooking spray and place over medium-high heat. Add onion, crumble in beef, and cook for 5 minutes, or until the meat is browned. Whisk together broth and cornstarch and add it to the skillet with next 4 ingredients (peas and carrots through garlic salt). Crush thyme in with your fingers, reduce heat to medium, and simmer for 5 minutes, stirring occasionally, until the sauce thickens slightly.

3. Slice the potatoes in half lengthwise, and place each half on a plate. With a fork, fluff potato pulp and mix 1 tablespoon sour cream and 1 teaspoon margarine into each potato half. Spoon ¾ cup of meat mixture over each "mashed potato" and serve.

**NUTRITION INFORMATION PER SERVING:** (½ potato + toppings) Calories 345 | Carbohydrate 39g (Sugars 8g) | Total Fat 9g (Sat Fat 4) | Protein 26g | Fiber 5g | Cholesterol 45mg | Sodium 460mg | Food Exchanges: 2½ Lean Beef, 2 Starch, 1 Vegetable | Carbohydrate Choices: 2 | Weight Watcher Smart Point Comparison: 9

# Chinese Pepper Steak

*THIS MAKEOVER OF THE CLASSIC CHINESE STIR-FRY DISH scored big kudos from my kitchen staff on the day we made it—and even more from my husband when he ate the leftovers for lunch the next day! It gets its name from the combination of spicy black pepper and sweet, fresh bell peppers, and while packed with tons of flavor, this quicker-than-takeout favorite packs 85% less sodium than the typical restaurant version. (I use the higher amount of black pepper, but it does add a kick.)*

MAKES 4 SERVINGS

3 tablespoons reduced-sodium soy sauce, divided

2 teaspoons cornstarch

1 pound lean boneless sirloin, partially frozen

2/3 cup reduced-sodium beef stock

2 teaspoons granulated sugar

1/2 to 3/4 teaspoon black pepper

1 medium onion, cut into thin slices

4 stalks celery, sliced diagonally, leaves reserved

2 medium bell peppers (one red and one green), chopped

2 teaspoons minced garlic

1 1/2 teaspoons minced ginger

1. In a medium bowl, whisk together 2 tablespoons soy sauce and the cornstarch. Thinly slice steak across the grain, add to sauce mixture, and stir to coat. Let sit for 10 minutes. In a small bowl, whisk together stock, remaining soy sauce, sugar, and black pepper, and set aside.

2. While the steak marinates, prep the vegetables. Spray a large nonstick skillet with cooking spray and place over medium-high heat. Add half of the beef, and stir-fry for 3 to 4 minutes, or just until no longer pink. Remove beef from skillet, cook remaining beef, and remove from skillet.

3. Add the onion and celery to the skillet and cook for 3 minutes, or until slightly softened. Add bell pepper, garlic, and ginger, and cook for 3 more minutes. Pour in the broth mixture and let simmer for 2 minutes. Add the beef to the skillet, stirring well to coat. Garnish with chopped celery leaves and serve.

**DARE TO COMPARE:** A single order of the Wok Classic Pepper Steak at P.F. Chang's has 660 calories, 37 grams of fat, and is saturated with 3,210 milligrams of sodium.

**NUTRITION INFORMATION PER SERVING (1 1/2 cups):** Calories 230 | Carbohydrate 14g (Sugars 7g) | Total Fat 7g (Sat Fat 3g) | Protein 33g | Fiber 3g | Cholesterol 100mg | Sodium 495mg | Food Exchanges: 3 1/2 Lean Meat, 2 Vegetables | Carbohydrate Choices: 1 | Weight Watcher Smart Point Comparison: 4

# Pan-Seared Filet Mignon with Rosemary Red Wine Sauce

*THERE'S NOTHING AS EASY AND ELEGANT AS A MOUTHWATERING FILET MIGNON when you want to create a memorable meal. Filet mignon is the most tender lean cut of beef, and as such a favorite of mine to cook. It's great on the grill, but for this easy weeknight recipe, romantically made for two, I keep it on the kitchen stove. While the steak rests, the seasoned pan is perfect for creating a delectable sauce. Don't fret if you don't have fresh rosemary: Simply substitute a pinch of crushed dried thyme leaves. Who said special couldn't be speedy?*

SERVES 2

2 (5-ounce) filet mignons, at room temperature

Salt and black pepper, to taste

2 teaspoons butter

¼ cup minced shallot

¼ teaspoon finely minced rosemary

½ teaspoon cornstarch

½ cup reduced-sodium beef broth

¼ cup red wine

1. Pat steaks dry with clean paper towels and season each side with salt and black pepper.

2. Place a medium nonstick pan over medium-high heat. Add the steaks and cook 3 to 4 minutes, or until steak is well browned, flip, and cook for an additional 3 minutes (or until 130°F for medium-rare). Remove steaks from pan, place on a plate, and cover with foil.

3. Add the butter to the pan, and then shallot, and cook over medium heat for 3 minutes or until softened. Stir in the rosemary. Stir the cornstarch into the beef broth and add to the pan. Cook for 1 minute or until broth reduces slightly and clears. Add the wine and any accumulated juices on the plate and continue to cook for 1 more minute. Season with additional pepper to taste and pour over steaks before serving.

**NUTRITION INFORMATION PER SERVING: (1 steak)** Calories 230 | Carbohydrate 8g (Sugars 8g) | Total Fat 7g (Sat Fat 2.5g) | Protein 34g | Fiber 0g | Cholesterol 115mg | Sodium 180mg | Food Exchanges: 4½ Lean Meat | Carbohydrate Choices: ½ | Weight Watcher Smart Point Comparison: 5

# Slow Cooker Balsamic BBQ Beef

*MOVE OVER PULLED PORK, this saucy, versatile barbecued shredded beef is just as tasty—and healthier to boot! Serve it plated with sides, atop a baked potato or a crunchy green salad, stuffed into a sandwich or taco, or rolled into a burrito. You can simply dump everything all at once into the slow cooker, but I find taking a few minutes to brown the beef pays off in flavor.*

MAKES 8 SERVINGS

3 pound bottom round roast

1 teaspoon salt

1 teaspoon black pepper

1 teaspoon canola oil (optional)

1/2 cup chopped onion

4 garlic cloves, chopped

1/4 cup balsamic vinegar

1/4 cup tomato paste

2 tablespoons light brown sugar

1 teaspoon liquid smoke

1. If desired, spray a medium nonstick skillet with oil and heat over medium-high heat. Sprinkle salt and pepper over beef, add it to skillet, and cook, turning occasionally, for 5 to 6 minutes, or until browned on all sides (or brown using slow cooker instructions). Transfer beef to a 4- to 6-quart slow cooker. Add onion and garlic to the cooker.

2. In a small bowl or measuring cup, whisk together the remaining ingredients with 1 cup of water. Pour sauce over beef, cover, and cook on low for 7 to 8 hours, or 3½ to 4 hours on high, or until beef is fork-tender.

3. Transfer beef to a carving board and tent it with foil. Pour cooking liquid into a large saucepan. Bring to a boil over high heat and cook for 8 to 10 minutes, stirring occasionally, until sauce has reduced by half. Shred the beef with two forks and stir it into the sauce.

   **Marlene Says:** *This recipe yields about 5 cups of shredded beef. Store leftovers in the fridge for up to 4 days or up to a month in the freezer (portioned if you like).*

**NUTRITION INFORMATION PER SERVING:** (²/₃ cup) Calories 210 | Carbohydrate 5g (Sugars 4g) | Total Fat 7 g (Sat Fat 3g) | Protein 31g | Fiber 0g | Cholesterol 85mg | Sodium 360mg | Food Exchanges: 4 Lean Meat | Carbohydrate Choices: 0 | Weight Watcher Smart Point Comparison: 5

# 4-Ingredient Sweet and Spicy Pork Chops

*SRIRACHA, PRONOUNCED "SEE-RAH-CHA," is a hot sauce that has taken the food world by storm. Originally from Thailand, and relatively unknown in the West until a few years ago, the fiery red sauce can now be found everywhere, and on everything—from burgers and pizza to tacos, chips, and even candy. The main ingredient is red jalapeño chili purée, which is rounded out with sugar, salt, vinegar, and a touch of garlic. In this oh-so-simple 15-minute recipe, the richly flavored spicy kick of Sriracha is the perfect counterpoint to the soothing sweetness of honey.*

### MAKES 2 SERVINGS

2 (5-ounce) lean pork chops

Pinch of salt

Pinch of black pepper

1 tablespoon honey

2 teaspoons Sriracha sauce

1 teaspoon canola oil

1. Season pork chops with salt and pepper. In a very small bowl or cup, mix together honey, Sriracha, and 1 tablespoon of water.

2. Heat the oil in a nonstick skillet over medium-high heat. Add the pork chops and cook for 2 minutes, or until nicely browned on the bottom. Turn the chops, cook for 1 minute, and pour the honey mixture into the pan. Cook the chops for 3 to 4 more minutes until the sauce thickens and coats the chops, basting as necessary.

**Marlene Says:** *Sriracha can be used as you would any hot sauce. It's low in sodium and calorie-free. Just a few drops are all it takes to kick up the flavor in ketchup, mayonnaise, cocktail sauce, egg dishes, and casseroles. Look for Sriracha in the Asian food section of your local market.*

**NUTRITION INFORMATION PER SERVING: (1 chop)** Calories 230 | Carbohydrate 8g (Sugars 8g) | Total Fat 7g (Sat Fat 2.5g) | Protein 34g | Fiber 0g | Cholesterol 115mg | Sodium 180mg | Food Exchanges: 4½ Lean Meat | Carbohydrate Choices: ½ | Weight Watcher Smart Point Comparison: 5

# Fuss-Free Sheet Pan Fajitas

*WITH THIS FUSS-FREE COOKING TECHNIQUE, ALL YOU NEED IS A SINGLE SHEET PAN to create great-tasting fajitas. I have always grilled the meat and cooked the veggies separately, so I was a bit skeptical when I came across a similar recipe—but it works. Everything comes out perfectly cooked, and best of all, the oven does most the work! You just need to tuck the meat and veggies into warmed tortillas, serve with your favorite fajita fix-ins, and wait for the compliments.*

MAKES 4 SERVINGS

1/4 cup lime juice

1 tablespoon olive oil

1 tablespoon minced garlic

2 teaspoons reduced-sodium soy sauce

1 teaspoon ground cumin

1/2 teaspoon liquid smoke

1/4 teaspoon chili powder

1/4 teaspoon cayenne pepper

1 pound flank steak

2 large bell peppers, sliced into strips

1 large onion, sliced into strips

Warmed corn or flour tortillas

1. Position an oven rack about 4 inches below the broiler, place another rack in the center position, and preheat the oven to 450°F.

2. In a large bowl, whisk together the first 8 ingredients (lime juice through cayenne). Place steak in a large zip-top bag, pour all but 2 tablespoons of the mixture into the bag, seal, and set aside. Add peppers and onions to the bowl with remaining marinade, stir to coat, and transfer vegetables to a 13 by 18-inch sheet pan. Roast for 10 minutes, or until slightly softened.

3. Remove the pan from oven and turn on the broiler. Push the vegetables to the sides of the pan, remove steak from the marinade, allowing excess to drain, and place steak in the center of the pan. Place pan to the top rack and broil steak for 3 to 5 minutes per side, or until a meat thermometer registers 135°F (for medium-rare). Let the steak rest for 10 minutes, and slice thinly against the grain. Assemble the fajitas and serve.

**Marlene Says:** *Warm the tortillas in the microwave or wrapped in foil on the bottom oven rack while cooking the veggies and meat.*

**NUTRITION INFORMATION PER SERVING:** (without tortillas) Calories 225 | Carbohydrate 10g (Sugars 5g) | Total Fat 9g (Sat Fat 3g) | Protein 27g | Fiber 2g | Cholesterol 90mg | Sodium 220mg | Food Exchanges: 3 1/2 Lean Meat, 1 1/2 Vegetable | Carbohydrate Choices: 1/2 | Weight Watcher Smart Point Comparison: 3

# Sheet Pan Pork and Vegetable "Stir Fry"

*STIR-FRY ON A SHEET PAN? ABSOLUTELY! Seriously, walk away from your wok and let your broiler do the work. The broiler cooks the veggies and the meat quickly, while keeping the taste and texture you'd expect from a traditional stove-top stir fry. Lean strips of pork and colorful veggies cooked in an enticing soy and ginger sauce make this a family favorite.*

MAKES 4 SERVINGS

1 to 1¼ pound pork tenderloin, halved lengthwise

4 tablespoons reduced-sodium soy sauce, divided

1 tablespoon honey

1 teaspoon minced ginger, divided

8 ounces snow peas, trimmed

2 medium carrots, peeled and julienned

2 medium red bell peppers, thinly sliced

1 medium red onion, thinly sliced

Black pepper, to taste

1. Place the pork on a cutting board and slice horizontally most of the way through (allowing it to open flat like a book). In a large zip-top bag, combine 2 tablespoons soy sauce, honey, ½ teaspoon ginger, and the pork. Close the bag, massage marinade onto the meat, and set aside.

2. Position the oven rack in the middle of the oven, about 6 inches below the broiler, and turn on broiler. Place the vegetables onto a large rimmed baking sheet and toss with the remaining 2 tablespoons soy sauce and ½ teaspoon ginger. Place pan in oven and broil vegetables for 5 minutes.

3. Remove pan from oven, stir vegetables, and make room for pork in center of the pan by pushing aside some of the veggies (it's okay if the meat lays on some). Remove pork from marinade, reserving marinade, and place pork on the pan. Broil for 6 to 7 minutes, or until well browned. Pull pan from the oven, stir vegetables, turn pork, and place the pan back under the broiler for 2 more minutes, or until meat thermometer reads 145°F.

3. While the pork cooks, transfer the marinade from the bag into a bowl and microwave on high for 1 minute. Place cooked vegetables onto a large platter. Slice pork into thin slices, add to the vegetables, and top with cooked marinade. Toss together if desired, and add black pepper to taste.

**NUTRITION INFORMATION PER SERVING:** (1½ cups) Calories 270 | Carbohydrate 20g (Sugars 12g) | Total Fat 6g (Sat Fat 2g) | Protein 36g | Fiber 4g | Cholesterol 90mg | Sodium 610mg | Food Exchanges: 3½ Lean Meat, 2 Vegetable | Carbohydrate Choices: 1 | Weight Watcher Smart Point Comparison: 4

# Pork Tenderloin with Orange Marmalade Sauce

*I LOVE LEAN, TASTY PORK TENDERLOIN and have cooked it in just about every way you can imagine, but it wasn't until I created this recipe that I cooked one whole on the stovetop. Wow, I should have done it sooner. Simply sear the tenderloin in a pan, add stock, and simmer for 15 minutes, and it's done. Add a delectable orange sauce and you have a company-worthy entrée in under 30 minutes!*

MAKES 4 SERVINGS

2 teaspoons canola oil

1¼ pounds pork tenderloin

Salt and black pepper, to taste

¾ cup reduced-sodium chicken stock, divided

1 teaspoon Dijon mustard

3 tablespoons orange marmalade

Scant ½ teaspoon dried thyme

1. In a large nonstick skillet, heat oil over medium high heat. Season the pork with salt and pepper to taste. Add pork to the skillet and brown well on all sides.

2. Reduce heat to medium, add ½ cup chicken stock, cover skillet, and simmer for 15 minutes, or until meat thermometer reads 145°F. Remove pork from pan and loosely cover with foil to keep warm.

3. Add mustard to the pan juices and whisk until smooth. Whisk in marmalade, crush the thyme in with your fingers, and add remaining ¼ cup chicken stock. Simmer, whisking occasionally, until the sauce thickens and coats the back of a spoon. Adjust pepper to taste. To serve, slice the pork on a diagonal and arrange on a platter, topping with orange sauce.

**Marlene Says:** *Pork tenderloins range in size from 1 to 2 pounds. To cook one larger than 1¼ pounds, allow extra time and use a meat thermometer to ensure it's done.*

**NUTRITION INFORMATION PER SERVING:** (4 ounces cooked pork + sauce) Calories 210 | Carbohydrate 5g (Sugars 4g) | Total Fat 7g (Sat Fat 2g) | Protein 29g | Fiber 0g | Cholesterol 80mg | Sodium 190mg | Food Exchanges: 4 Lean Meat | Carbohydrate Choices: ½ | Weight Watcher Smart Point Comparison: 5

# Autumn Apple Pork Chop Skillet

*WHILE THE AROMAS OF THIS HEARTY DISH SAY "AUTUMN," it would be a shame to not enjoy it all year round. Thin-cut boneless pork chops hasten the cooking time, while sweet apple juice keeps them moist. I like to serve these with noodles and thinly shredded green cabbage that is simply sautéed with a little oil, butter, salt, dill, and celery seeds (you'll find the recipe for Warm Cabbage Slaw on page 190).*

**MAKES 4 SERVINGS**

4 (5-ounce) thin cut boneless pork chops

1 teaspoon dried sage leaves

½ teaspoon salt

¼ teaspoon black pepper

2 medium apples, peeled, cored, and each cut into 8 wedges

2 teaspoons butter

2 tablespoons minced shallot

1 cup regular or light apple juice

1 tablespoon all-purpose flour

1 teaspoon Dijon mustard

1. Pat the pork chops dry with paper towels and evenly sprinkle with sage, salt, and pepper. Spray a large nonstick skillet with cooking spray and place over medium-high heat. Add chops and cook for 2 minutes per side, or until lightly browned. Remove chops from skillet, place on plate, and set aside.

2. Add the apples and butter to the skillet. Cook over medium heat, stirring occasionally, for 3 to 4 minutes or until apples are lightly browned. Add shallot and cook for 2 minutes, or until softened. In a medium bowl, whisk together apple juice, flour, and mustard. Pour into skillet and bring to a simmer.

3. Return chops to the skillet, reduce heat to medium-low, and cook for 3 minutes. Turn chops and cook until sauce is slightly thickened. Transfer the chops to a platter, top with apples and sauce, and serve.

**Marlene Says:** *With 24 grams of sugar per cup, regular apple juice is high in sugar as a beverage but adds a richer flavor to this sauce. It's easy to buy by the can for recipes like this. Subtract 3 grams of sugar if you use light apple juice.*

**NUTRITION INFORMATION PER SERVING: (1 chop + ¼ sauce)** Calories 270 | Carbohydrate 16g (Sugars 12g) | Total Fat 8g (Sat Fat 4g) | Protein 31g | Fiber 1g | Cholesterol 85mg | Sodium 380mg | Food Exchanges: 4 Lean Meat, 1 Fruit | Carbohydrate Choices: 1 | Weight Watcher Smart Point Comparison: 6

# Slow and Easy Pork Chili Verde

*SAUCY, SCINTILLATING SLOW-COOKED PORK CHILI VERDE is a lean and tasty alternative to fat-laden pork carnitas. Just like carnitas, it can be served by itself (accompanied by rice or warm tortillas) or as a filling for tacos, burritos, or quesadillas. And it takes only minutes to prep. I usually cook it on the stovetop, but you can also cook in a slow cooker. Just add all the ingredients to your slow cooker, and cook for 2 to 4 hours on high or 7 to 8 hours on low. The meat is done when it pulls apart easily.*

MAKES 4 SERVINGS

1 teaspoon canola oil

1 cup chopped onion

1½ teaspoons minced garlic

1 pound pork tenderloin, cut into ¾-inch cubes

¾ cup jarred salsa verde sauce

1 (4-ounce) can fire-roasted green chiles

¾ teaspoon ground cumin

½ teaspoon dried oregano

¼ teaspoon salt

2 teaspoons cornmeal

1. Heat the oil in a large soup pot over medium heat. Add onions and sauté for 5 minutes or until soft. Add the garlic and cook for 1 minute. Add the next 6 ingredients (pork through salt) plus ½ cup water, and simmer for one hour.

2. Whisk in the cornmeal and cook for another 5 minutes, or until thickened.

**DARE TO COMPARE:** Made with pork shoulder instead of pork tenderloin, a serving of this dish would have 280 calories, 18 grams of fat (including 6 grams saturated fat), and 6 *less* grams protein.

**NUTRITION INFORMATION PER SERVING:** (1 cup) Calories 190 | Carbohydrate 9g (Sugars 3g) | Total Fat 5g (Sat Fat 1g) | Protein 25g | Fiber 2g | Cholesterol 65mg | Sodium 420mg | Food Exchanges: 3 Lean Meat, 1 Vegetable | Carbohydrate Choices: ½ | Weight Watcher Smart Point Comparison: 4

# SEAFOOD & MEATLESS ENTRÉES

## seafood & meatless entrées

# Tilapia Piccata

*OF ALL THE RECIPES IN MY EAT WHAT YOU LOVE COOKBOOKS, MY FATHER LOVED my fish and seafood recipes best. On visits home, this is a last-minute dish I fondly remember whipping up for him and my "I don't really like fish" mother—and it was always a hit. An easy, yet fancy way to serve it is to prepare the One-Pot Spaghetti with Spinach (page 195), place it on a large platter, top with the fish, and garnish with lemon slices.*

MAKES 4 SERVINGS

4 (5-ounce) tilapia fillets (about 1¼ pounds)

¼ cup all-purpose flour

1 tablespoon olive oil

½ cup reduced-sodium chicken broth

¼ cup white wine

Juice of 1 large lemon

1 tablespoon capers

1 tablespoon butter or margarine

2 tablespoons fresh chopped Italian parsley

1. Lightly coat the fish with flour. Heat the oil in a large nonstick skillet over medium-high heat. Add the fish and cook for 3 to 4 minutes, or until underside is lightly browned, spray the tops lightly with cooking spray, flip, and cook until cooked through. Transfer to a plate and cover.

2. Pour the broth, wine, and lemon juice into the skillet, whisking in the bits from the bottom of the pan. Whisk the sauce until slightly thickened and swirl the butter into the sauce. Pour the sauce over the fish fillets and top with fresh parsley.

**DARE TO COMPARE:** Who knew a light Italian dish could be so heavy? A plate of Chicken Piccata at California Pizza Kitchen has 1,630 calories, over 70 grams of fat, and 2,140 milligrams of sodium.

**NUTRITION INFORMATION PER SERVING:** (1 fillet) Calories 210 | Carbohydrate 6g (Sugars 1g) | Total Fat 8g (Sat Fat 3.5g) | Protein 29g | Fiber 0g | Cholesterol 40mg | Sodium 210mg | Food Exchanges: 4 Lean Meat, ½ Carbohydrate | Carbohydrate Choices: ½ | Weight Watcher Smart Point Comparison: 3

# Chicken Fried Fish with Buttermilk Dressing

**AIR FRY!**
SEE PAGE **325**

*IF VERSATILE, MILD-TASTING TILAPIA has not stolen the "chicken of the sea" moniker from tuna fish yet, this recipe should seal the deal. Here, tilapia gets the royal "chicken fried" treatment—and the result is fish-tastic! Wonderfully crispy and flavorful on the outside, and moist and mild on the inside, even die-hard fish haters love it. Thinned Buttermilk Scallion Dressing (309) tastefully replaces the customary cooked gravy with ease.*

**MAKES 4 SERVINGS**

4 (5-ounce) tilapia fillets (about 1¼ pounds)

5 tablespoons all-purpose flour, divided

½ cup low-fat buttermilk

1 large egg white

½ teaspoon baking soda

1¼ cups finely crushed cornflake crumbs

1 teaspoon reduced-sodium seasoned salt

½ teaspoon dried thyme

½ teaspoon black pepper

½ teaspoon garlic powder

4 teaspoons canola oil, divided

1 recipe Buttermilk Scallion Dressing (page 309)

1. Preheat the oven to 400°F. Line a baking sheet with foil and set aside. Place 3 tablespoons of flour on a plate. In shallow bowl, whisk together buttermilk, egg white, and baking soda. In another shallow bowl, mix the cornflake crumbs with remaining 2 tablespoons flour, seasoned salt, thyme, pepper, and garlic powder.

2. Heat 2 teaspoons oil in a large nonstick skillet over medium-high heat. Coat 2 fillets with flour, dip into buttermilk mixture, allowing excess to drip off, and roll in crumbs. Sauté for 1½ to 2 minutes, or until underside is golden brown. Spray top with cooking spray and turn. Cook 2 minutes or until the bottom is lightly browned.

3. Transfer fish to prepared baking sheet. Repeat with remaining 2 teaspoons oil and 2 fish fillets. Bake fillets for 5 minutes, or until cooked through. Thin buttermilk dressing with one tablespoon water and drizzle each fillet with 3 tablespoons dressing.

**Marlene Says:** *I keep a bag of frozen tilapia loins from the club store in my freezer at all times. They average 4 to 5 ounces each, are individually wrapped, and thaw in just minutes.*

**NUTRITION INFORMATION PER SERVING: (1 fillet)** Calories 270 | Carbohydrate 22g (Sugars 3g) | Total Fat 9g (Sat Fat 2g) | Protein 26g | Fiber 1g | Cholesterol 25mg | Sodium 695mg | Food Exchanges: 4 Lean Meat, 1 Starch, ½ Fat | Carbohydrate Choices: 1½ | Weight Watcher Smart Point Comparison: 5

# 5-Ingredient Spinach-Stuffed Salmon

*THIS DISH IS A SLIGHTLY ADAPTED VERSION OF A RECIPE BY A VERY TALENTED COLLEAGUE of mine, Michelle Dudash, created for her fabulous cookbook, Clean Eating for Busy Families. The first time I made it I did so for two very last-minute dinner guests. Remarkably, less than 30 minutes after I extended the invitation I had an elegant meal on every plate. My guests couldn't have been more delighted— or impressed! Instant Brown Rice Pilaf (page 199) and microwaved carrots are easy plate partners.*

MAKES 4 SERVINGS

2 cups finely chopped fresh spinach

3 tablespoons light mayonnaise

2 tablespoons Panko breadcrumbs

2 tablespoons grated Parmesan cheese

1/4 teaspoon black pepper

1/8 teaspoon salt

4 (5-ounce) thick, center-cut, skin-on salmon fillets

1. Preheat the oven to 375°F. Line a baking sheet with foil and set aside. In a small bowl, combine first 6 ingredients (spinach through salt).

2. Cut a slit lengthwise along the top of each piece of salmon, taking care to not cut completely through. Pull sides apart and spoon 3 tablespoons of the spinach mixture into the middle of the slit, and smooth the filling into a mound.

3. Transfer fillets to the baking sheet, and bake for 17 minutes, or until the center of the fillet is cooked through. Use a spatula to remove skin before serving.

**Marlene Says:** *Salmon is high not only in heart-healthy Omega-3 fatty acids, but in unique, high-quality proteins. The powerful combo makes salmon good for your brain, bones, eyes, and mood! Wild Atlantic Salmon has 8 grams of fat in a 4-ounce cooked portion, while farm-raised has 13 grams of fat. This recipe was analyzed using the average of the two.*

**NUTRITION INFORMATION PER SERVING: (1 fillet)** Calories 225 | Carbohydrate 3g (Sugars 0g) | Total Fat 13g (Sat Fat 1.5g) | Protein 26g | Fiber 0g | Cholesterol 75mg | Sodium 300mg | Food Exchanges: 4 Medium Fat Meat, 1/2 Fat | Carbohydrate Choices: 0 | Weight Watcher Smart Point Comparison: 2

# Almost Bang Bang Shrimp

*BONEFISH GRILL SPECIALIZES IN TWO THINGS: seafood, and according to their website, "incredible food served daily." There is no denying the two came together when they created their wildly popular Bang Bang Shrimp appetizer. Crispy, creamy, sweet, and spicy, it's a shrimp lover's feast all rolled into one delectable dish. If I dare say, with a fraction of the calories, fat and sodium, this is one bangin' good slimmed-down makeover.*

**MAKES 4 SERVINGS**

1 pound peeled, tail-on large shrimp (about 21 to 25)

1 tablespoon cornstarch

1/4 cup light mayonnaise

1 tablespoon honey

1 1/2 teaspoons Sriracha chili sauce

1/8 teaspoon red chili flakes

2 teaspoons canola oil, divided

2 tablespoons thinly sliced green onion (green part only)

Shredded lettuce or Napa cabbage for serving

1. In a medium bowl, place the shrimp, sprinkle with cornstarch, and stir to coat. In a large bowl, whisk together the next 4 ingredients (mayonnaise through chili flakes).

2. Heat 1 teaspoon oil in a large non-stick skillet over medium-high heat. Add half the shrimp and sauté for 1 1/2 minutes, flip, and cook for 1 to 2 minutes. Transfer shrimp to bowl of Sriracha mixture. Heat the remaining oil, cook the remaining shrimp, and add to the bowl.

3. Top shrimp with green onion, and stir gently to coat. Spoon shrimp onto bed of lettuce or cabbage and serve. (Top with an additional pinch of red chili flakes for a spicier dish).

**DARE TO COMPARE:** An appetizer order of Bang Bang Shrimp has 840 calories, 65 grams of fat, and a hefty 2,180 milligrams of sodium. Love this? Split the recipe into two servings (like we often do) and you still slash 62% of the calories, 70% of the sodium, and 80% of the usual fat.

**NUTRITION INFORMATION PER SERVING:** (1/4 recipe) Calories 160 | Carbohydrate 7g (Sugars 5g) | Total Fat 7g (Sat Fat 1g) | Protein 17g | Fiber 1g | Cholesterol 160mg | Sodium 340mg | Food Exchanges: 3 Lean Meat, 1/2 Carbohydrate | Carbohydrate Choices: 1/2 | Weight Watcher Smart Point Comparison: 3

# Sheet Pan Salmon

*THIS SHEET PAN RECIPE IS TRULY STELLAR. Seasoned green beans and tomatoes get a quick-cook jump-start on a sheet pan before salmon is added to the same pan. The end result is a gorgeous one-pan display of perfectly cooked beans, succulent salmon, and juicy pan-roasted tomatoes (that are even more delectable when eaten together with the salmon). To add fuss-free roasted potatoes to the meal, see the Marlene Says below. Make this for guests; I guarantee they will be impressed.*

**MAKES 4 SERVINGS**

12 ounces fresh green beans, trimmed

1 cup cherry or grape tomatoes

1/2 medium red onion, sliced into 1/4-inch half moons

1 teaspoon lemon zest

1 teaspoon olive oil

3/4 teaspoon garlic salt, divided

4 (5-ounce) salmon fillets (about 3/4 inch thick)

1/8 teaspoon black pepper, or to taste

1 lemon, sliced into 1/4-inch slices

1. Preheat the oven to 375°F; place rack in the center of the oven. In a large bowl, toss together the first 5 ingredients (green beans through oil), plus 1/2 teaspoon garlic salt. Spread in an even layer on a 13-inch by 18-inch sheet pan and bake for 15 minutes.

2. While the vegetables are roasting, season the salmon with pepper and remaining 1/4 teaspoon garlic salt. Remove pan from oven, push the vegetables to the sides of the pan, and place the salmon in the center of the pan. Top the salmon and vegetables with lemon slices, and bake for 10 minutes, or until fish flakes apart easily.

**Marlene Says:** *To roast potatoes simultaneously, toss 4 to 6 small red potatoes into the microwave and cook on high for 5 minutes, or until almost cooked, but still firm. Quarter the potatoes, toss with 1 teaspoon olive oil and salt to taste, and transfer to another sheet pan. Place the sheet pan on a rack beneath the sheet pan salmon and bake for 15 to 20 minutes or until cooked through.*

**NUTRITION INFORMATION PER SERVING:** (1 fillet + 1/4 vegetables) Calories 260 | Carbohydrate 10g (Sugars 4g) | Total Fat 12g (Sat Fat 2g) | Protein 28g | Fiber 4g | Cholesterol 70mg | Sodium 240mg | Food Exchanges: 4 Medium Fat Meat, 2 Vegetables | Carbohydrate Choices: 1/2 | Weight Watcher Smart Point Comparison: 0

# Bacon-Wrapped Rosemary Cod

*YOU CAN USE ALMOST ANY FISH THAT SWIMS IN THE OCEAN when making this impressive no-fuss, 20-minute, company-worthy recipe (yes, I said 20 minutes, and company worthy!). Salmon, halibut, and tilapia all work equally well. It has become a go-to staple for my husband and me, but rest assured, it can be doubled (or even tripled). My trick to keep the fish moist and flakey is to add a small amount of liquid at the end of the cooking time. The steam works wonders.*

MAKES 2 SERVINGS

1 tablespoon Dijon mustard

1 tablespoon light mayonnaise

2 teaspoons cider vinegar

2 teaspoons honey

1/2 teaspoon minced fresh rosemary

2 slices center-cut bacon

2 (5-ounce) cod fillets

2 fresh rosemary sprigs

1. In a small microwave-safe bowl, whisk together the first 5 ingredients (Dijon through rosemary) plus 1 tablespoon water. Heat for 30 seconds in the microwave and set aside.

2. Lay out the bacon on a cutting board stretching the ends to slightly lengthen them. Lay the cod pieces on the board, top each with a rosemary sprig, and wrap each with one slice of bacon. (I like to start across the top of the fish, wrap it underneath the bottom, and then back slightly askew across the top to get a double width of bacon on top.)

3. Spray a medium nonstick skillet with cooking spray and heat over medium heat. Transfer fish to the skillet, rosemary-side down, and cook for 4 minutes, or until the underside of the bacon is crisp. Flip and cook for 3 to 4 minutes, or until the bacon on the bottom is crisp. Add 1 tablespoon of water to the pan, cover, and cooke for 1 additional minute, or until the fish is cooked through. Top each fillet with half of the mustard sauce, and serve.

**Marlene Says:** *The Amazing Zucchini "Butter" (page 202) is truly excellent with this dish, and can be made concurrently or ahead of time—as can the preparation of the fish through step 2. Cover and place it in the fridge if it will not be cooked for more than one hour.*

**NUTRITION INFORMATION PER SERVING: (1 fillet)** Calories 205 | Carbohydrate 8g (Sugars 6g) | Total Fat 6g (Sat Fat 1.5g) | Protein 30g | Fiber 0g | Cholesterol 75mg | Sodium 450mg | Food Exchanges: 4 Lean Meat, 1 Fat, 1/2 Carbohydrate | Carbohydrate Choices: 1/2 | Weight Watcher Smart Point Comparison: 2

# Flash Broiled Fish with 1-Minute Seafood Hollandaise

*THERE ARE PLENTY OF QUICK AND EASY BASIC WEEKNIGHT DISHES, but few are as fast, easy, and impressive as this entrée. As the saying goes, "The secret's in the sauce." In this case, the sauce is a luxurious hollandaise-like sauce seasoned to perfection to compliment the quickly broiled fish—and no one will be the wiser that you cooked it in just one minute! Instant Brown Rice Pilaf (page 199) or 10-Minute Broccoli and Parmesan Couscous (page 198) pair well with this guest-worthy dish.*

MAKES 4 SERVINGS

¼ cup light mayonnaise

¼ cup light sour cream

¼ cup liquid egg substitute

¼ teaspoon dried dill

1 tablespoon fresh lemon juice

¼ teaspoon Old Bay seasoning

4 (5-ounce) firm white fish fillets, like tilapia, halibut, or cod

1. Position the oven rack about 6 inches below the broiler, and turn on the broiler.

2. Place first 6 ingredients (mayonnaise through Old Bay) in a small saucepan and set aside. Line a baking sheet with foil and coat with cooking spray. Arrange fish fillets on foil, spray lightly with cooking spray, and broil for 2 to 3 minutes on each side, depending on thickness. (Fish is fully cooked when the center flakes easily with a fork.)

3. As soon as you pull the fish out of the oven, place the saucepan over low heat and heat the sauce, whisking for 1 minute, or until mixture is hot and coats a spoon. Pour 3 tablespoons sauce over each fish fillet and serve.

**Marlene Says:** *Like any hollandaise, this sauce is best served immediately and should not be re-heated.*

**NUTRITION INFORMATION PER SERVING:** (1 fillet + sauce) Calories 200 | Carbohydrate 2g (Sugars 0g) | Total Fat 7g (Sat Fat 3g) | Protein 31 g | Fiber 0g | Cholesterol 35mg | Sodium 220mg | Food Exchanges: 4½ Lean Meat | Carbohydrate Choices: 0 | Weight Watcher Smart Point Comparison: 2

# Any Day Salmon Cakes with Homemade Tartar Sauce

*A QUICK "SHOPPING TRIP" INTO THE CUPBOARD and a couple of items delivered from the fridge is all it takes to create this delicious entrée in a flash. After testing these slim protein-packed salmon cakes with various seasonings, the hands-down winner was classic seafood seasoning (including a pop of freshness from lemon zest). Once made, the patties can be wrapped and refrigerated for up to three days.*

MAKES 4 SERVINGS

1/4 cup light mayonnaise, divided

3 tablespoons low-fat plain Greek yogurt

1 teaspoon capers, drained and chopped

1/4 teaspoon dried dill

2 (6-ounce) cans pink salmon*, rinsed and drained

3 tablespoons chopped green onion

1 large egg white, lightly beaten

1 teaspoon lemon zest

1/2 teaspoon garlic powder

1/2 teaspoon Old Bay seasoning

1/2 teaspoon paprika

1/3 cup plain dry breadcrumbs, divided

1. For tartar sauce, in a small bowl combine 2 tablespoons mayonnaise, yogurt, capers, and dill. Set aside.

2. In a medium bowl combine the salmon, green onion, egg white, zest, garlic powder, Old Bay, paprika, 2 tablespoons breadcrumbs, and 2 tablespoons mayonnaise. Stir well to combine. Shape mixture into 4 patties about 1/4 inch thick. Lightly dust both sides with remaining breadcrumbs.

3. Coat a large nonstick skillet with cooking spray and place over medium heat. Add the salmon cakes and cook for 5 minutes per side, or until lightly browned and warmed through. Serve with tartar sauce.

**Marlene Says:** *Canned salmon varies greatly in quality and taste. Pink salmon is the mildest in color and taste, while sockeye offers a richer taste—and more fat. When using sockeye salmon, decrease the mayonnaise by one tablespoon and increase the breadcrumbs by the same amount.*

**NUTRITION INFORMATION PER SERVING:** (1 salmon cake with sauce) Calories 150 | Carbohydrate 7g (Sugars 1g) | Total Fat 4.5g (Sat Fat 0g) | Protein 22g | Fiber 0g | Cholesterol 30mg | Sodium 420mg | Food Exchanges: 3 Lean Meat, 1/2 Carbohydrate | Carbohydrate Choices 1/2 | Weight Watcher Smart Point Comparison: 1

# 15-Minute Shrimp and Couscous Skillet

*SHRIMP IN TOMATO SAUCE, TOPPED WITH TANGY FETA, is one of the national dishes of Greece. It is also one of the fastest and most delicious meals you can prepare. It's often baked, but I love this quick skillet rendition served over quick-cooking couscous. To serve it the Mediterranean way, garnish with fresh lemon wedges.*

MAKES 4 SERVINGS

2 teaspoons olive oil

1 large zucchini, diced

2 teaspoons minced garlic

1 (15-ounce) can chopped tomatoes, with juices

1/3 cup dry white wine or dry vermouth

1 teaspoon dried oregano

Scant 1/8 teaspoon hot red pepper flakes

Scant 1/4 teaspoon salt

1 pound medium shrimp, peeled and deveined

1/4 cup crumbled feta cheese

2/3 cup dry couscous

1. Spray a large nonstick skillet with cooking spray and place over medium-high heat. Add oil to the skillet, add zucchini, and cook for 3 minutes, stirring, until the zucchini starts to soften. Stir in garlic and cook for 30 seconds. Add tomatoes, wine, oregano, and pepper flakes, and bring to a simmer. Reduce heat to medium-low, cover, and simmer for 5 minutes. Add shrimp to the pan, and cook for 5 more minutes, stirring occasionally. Turn off heat and top with feta.

2. While the shrimp cooks, in a medium bowl (or small saucepan) bring 1 cup water to a boil. (I do it in the microwave.) Stir in the couscous, cover, and let sit 5 minutes.

3. Fluff the couscous with a fork. Divide among bowls and add tomatoes and shrimp.

**NUTRITION INFORMATION PER SERVING:** (1 1/3 cups) Calories 260 | Carbohydrate 24g (Sugars 5g) | Total Fat 5g (Sat Fat 2g) | Protein 22g | Fiber 3g | Cholesterol 170mg | Sodium 560mg | Food Exchanges: 3 1/2 Lean Meat, 1 Starch, 1 Vegetable | Carbohydrate Choices: 1 1/2 | Weight Watcher Smart Point Comparison: 6

# Teriyaki Fish Foil Packets

*FOR MOIST AND TENDER FISH (SANS DISHES!), it's hard to beat a foil packet. The packet steams the enclosed fish, sealing in the juices and infusing the flavor of any seasonings or sauce you choose to add. This particular quick-fix packet is one of my favorites. It combines mild tilapia with a teriyaki-style sauce and colorful veggies, and cooks in just 10 minutes. A side serving of rice is a nice addition.*

MAKES 2 SERVINGS

2 (5-ounce) tilapia filets

1/2 cup julienned zucchini

1/2 cup julienned carrots

1/2 cup julienned red
bell pepper

1 teaspoon minced garlic

2 teaspoons minced ginger

1 tablespoon reduced-sodium
soy sauce

1 1/2 teaspoons rice vinegar

1 1/2 teaspoons hoisin sauce

1. Preheat the oven to 450°F. Place each piece of fish in the center of 12 x 18-inch sheet of foil and top each with half of the zucchini, carrots, and bell pepper.

2. In a small bowl whisk together the soy sauce, vinegar, and hoisin. Pour half the sauce over each packet. Fold up the sides of foil around the fish and crimp into two airtight packets.

3. Transfer packets to a sheet pan and bake for 10 minutes. Remove from oven and immediately open the packets, taking care to avoid the steam, and serve.

**Marlene Says:** *The packets can be prepared up to a day ahead of time. Bring to room temperature before cooking, or simply add an additional 5 minutes to the baking time.*

**NUTRITION INFORMATION PER SERVING: (1 packet)** Calories 180 | Carbohydrate 8g (Sugars 3g) | Total Fat 5g (Sat Fat 1.5g) | Protein 27g | Fiber 2g | Cholesterol 30mg | Sodium 370mg | Food Exchanges: 4 Lean Meat, 1/2 Carbohydrate | Carbohydrate Choices: 1/2 | Weight Watcher Smart Point Comparison: 0

# Creamy Vegetable Enchiladas

*MEAT-FILLED ENCHILADAS DON'T HAVE A THING OVER THESE tasty black bean, corn-and-spinach stuffed enchiladas (with an impressive 11 grams of fiber each!). The filled tortillas can be frozen before baking, but it is best to do so without the green chili cream sauce. Make it separately, or make it and store it in the refrigerator, and then pour it over the enchiladas just prior to baking (see page 100 for more freezer tips).*

**MAKES 8 SERVINGS**

¾ cup light sour cream

2 teaspoons all-purpose four

¾ cup reduced-sodium chicken broth

1 (4-ounce) can fire-roasted diced green chilies

½ teaspoon garlic salt

1 (10-ounce) package frozen spinach

1⅓ cups frozen corn

1 (14.5-ounce) can black beans, drained and rinsed

1½ cups reduced-fat Mexican blend cheese, divided

3 green onions, chopped (green and white parts separated)

1 teaspoon ground cumin

8 (8-inch) reduced-carb high-fiber flour tortillas

1. Preheat the oven to 375°F. In a small bowl, whisk together the sour cream and flour. In a small saucepan, add broth, green chilies, and garlic salt, and bring to a simmer over medium heat. Whisk in sour cream mixture and simmer for 2 minutes, or until thickened, continuing to whisk while cooking. Set sauce aside.

2. Place spinach in a medium microwave-safe bowl, and cook according to package directions. Drain and squeeze dry. Stir in the corn, black beans, 1 cup cheese, the white parts of green onion, and cumin. Stir in ½ cup of sauce.

3. Top each tortilla with ½ cup of filling, roll the tortilla to cover filling, and place in a 13 x 9 x 2-inch baking pan seam-side down. Pour remaining sauce over enchiladas, top with remaining ½ cup cheese, and garnish with green part of green onions. Cover with foil and bake for 20 minutes, or until cheese is melted and enchiladas are heated through.

**NUTRITION INFORMATION PER SERVING:** (1 enchilada) Calories 250 | Carbohydrate 35g (Sugars 3g) | Total Fat 9g (Sat Fat 5g) | Protein 15g | Fiber 11g | Cholesterol 20mg | Sodium 590mg | Food Exchanges: 1½ Lean Meat, 1½ Carbohydrate, 1 Vegetable, 1 Fat | Carbohydrate Choices: 2 | Weight Watcher Smart Point Comparison: 6

# Megan's Marvelous Zucchini Pie

*THIS DELECTABLE VEGETABLE PIE IS AS WONDERFUL AS ITS NAMESAKE, my kitchen assistant Megan, who made it on the day we tested it. The rest of my helpers and I began oohing and ahhing over the golden cheese-laced chili-flecked beauty as soon as it came out of the oven. After one bite, we swooned. This pie can be served warm or at room temperature for breakfast, lunch, or dinner. The truth is, it's marvelous no matter when or how you eat it.*

MAKES 8 SERVINGS

½ package refrigerated piecrust

1 teaspoon canola oil

2 large zucchini (about 1¼ pounds)

½ medium onion, chopped

½ teaspoon salt

¼ teaspoon black pepper

2 teaspoons minced garlic

⅔ cup frozen corn

1 (4-ounce) can fire-roasted green chilies

2 large eggs

1½ cups shredded reduced-fat mozzarella cheese

1. Preheat the oven to 375°F. Place the pie dough on a lightly floured surface, and lightly roll out to an 11-inch-diameter round. Place the piecrust into a 9-inch pie pan and crimp the edges. Refrigerate while preparing filling.

2. Slice the zucchini in half lengthwise and crosswise in thin slices (you should have about 5 cups). Heat the oil in a large, nonstick skillet over medium heat. Add the zucchini, onion, salt, and pepper, and cook for 10 minutes, stirring occasionally, until vegetables are soft, but not limp. Add garlic, corn, and chilies and cook for 2 minutes. Let cool slightly.

3. While zucchini cools, in large bowl whisk the eggs and stir in mozzarella. Stir in the slightly cooled zucchini mixture and spoon into prepared crust. Bake for 27 to 30 minutes, or until crust is golden brown and filling is set. Let cool for 10 minutes before serving.

**Marlene Says:** *This pie is still delicious the next day although the bottom crust will be softer, the flavor and texture are as good as the day it was made. A slight re-heat in the microwave is perfect, as are a couple of hits of green hot sauce if you like a little heat.*

**NUTRITION INFORMATION PER SERVING:** Calories 200 | Carbohydrate 18g (Sugars 3g) | Total Fat 9g (Sat Fat 4g) | Protein 12g | Fiber 2g | Cholesterol 55mg | Sodium 450mg | Food Exchanges: 1½ Lean Meat, 1 Vegetable, ½ Carbohydrate, 1 Fat | Carbohydrate Choices: 1 | Weight Watcher Smart Point Comparison: 5

# Hoppin' Jane in a Hurry

*THIS HEARTY STEW IS A FAST AND HEALTHY VERSION of the slow-simmered Southern dish known as Hoppin' John. To makeover the classic comfort food I used canned black-eyed peas to cut the cooking time to 20 minutes, quick-cooking barley to boost the fiber and nutrients, and a touch of liquid smoke to deliver the smoky taste of a ham–sans the sodium and fat. With just 1 gram of fat and 11 grams of fat-blasting fiber, I'll be hopping onto team Jane from now on.*

**MAKES 4 SERVINGS**

½ medium onion, chopped

½ medium green bell pepper, chopped

2 teaspoons minced garlic

½ teaspoon dried thyme

¼ teaspoon black pepper

⅛ teaspoon red pepper flakes

1 (14.5-ounce) reduced-sodium chicken broth, divided

1 (15.5-ounce) can black-eyed peas, drained

¾ cup uncooked quick-cooking barley

½ teaspoon liquid smoke

3 cups chopped collard greens

1. Spray a large soup pot with non-stick cooking spray and place over medium heat. Add first 6 ingredients (onion through red pepper flakes) plus 2 tablespoons chicken broth. Cook, stirring occasionally, for 5 to 7 minutes, or until onions are translucent.

2. Stir in remaining chicken broth, peas, barley, and liquid smoke, and bring to a boil. Add the collards to the top of the pot, reduce heat to low, cover, and simmer for 10 minutes. Turn off heat and let sit for 5 minutes before serving.

**NUTRITION INFORMATION PER SERVING: (1 generous cup)** Calories 245 | Carbohydrate 48g (Sugars 6g) | Total Fat 1 g (Sat Fat 0g) | Protein 13g | Fiber 11g | Cholesterol 0mg | Sodium 260mg | Food Exchanges: 2½ Starch, 1½ Vegetable, 1 Lean Meat | Carbohydrate Choices: 3 | Weight Watcher Smart Point Comparison: 4

# Steak-Style Portobellos

SEE PAGE **325**

*IF YOU'RE LOOKING TO ADD MORE MEATLESS MAINS TO YOUR DIET, or, simply looking for a great mushroom recipe, this one is for you. After thoroughly enjoying a salad at a restaurant with mushroom slices that had the most wonderful steak quality, I was determined to find a way to get the same effect at home. It took a lot of trials, but I am pleased to say I did it—on the grill and in the oven! Whether served in lieu of a steak, sliced and served on a steak, or as my husband prefers, on a burger bun topped with grilled onions and blue cheese, these are some mighty meaty mushrooms!*

**MAKES 2 SERVINGS**

2 tablespoons balsamic vinegar

1 tablespoon olive oil

2 teaspoons Dijon mustard

2 teaspoons low-sodium soy sauce

2 teaspoons minced garlic (2 cloves)

1 teaspoon Worcestershire sauce

¼ teaspoon salt

¼ teaspoon black pepper

2 large portobello mushrooms, stems removed

1. Heat the grill or preheat the oven to 400°F, and line a baking sheet with foil and top with a baking rack.

2. In a medium bowl, combine first 8 ingredients (balsamic through pepper). Brush about 2 teaspoons marinade on each side of the portobellos. Let sit for 10 minutes, with gills up.

3. To grill the mushrooms, place on grill "gill"-side up and cook 6 to 7 minutes until underside is lightly charred. Flip, baste with marinade, and cook for 5 more minutes or until tender when pierced with a knife.

4. To bake, place mushrooms "gill"-side up on rack and bake for 10 minutes. Carefully flip the mushrooms, brush with remaining marinade, and bake for 15 minutes, or until mushrooms are tender.

> **DARE TO COMPARE:** Four ounces of 93% lean ground beef has 170 calories and 7 grams of fat. A 4-ounce (quarter-pound) raw Portobello mushroom has 30 calories and 0 grams of fat.

**NUTRITION INFORMATION PER SERVING:** (1 mushroom) Calories 100 | Carbohydrate 10g (Sugars 4g) | Total Fat 5g (Sat Fat 1g) | Protein 5g | Fiber 4g | Cholesterol 0mg | Sodium 510mg | Food Exchanges: 1 Vegetable, 1 Fat | Carbohydrate Choices: ½ | Weight Watcher Smart Point Comparison: 3

# EASY NO-BAKE DESSERTS

## easy no-bake desserts

# Berry Good Icebox Cake

*FOR ME, THE ICEBOX CAKE IS THE QUEEN OF ICEBOX DESSERTS. There's something magical about the way graham crackers (or cookies) soften and turn into thin layers of "cake" when layered with whipped cream. With no mixing, stirring, or oven required, this cool and creamy classic dessert with its luscious layers of fresh berries, whipped "cream," jam, and graham crackers is a lazy-day cake-making dream come true. Feel free to substitute raspberry jam and raspberries for the strawberries.*

MAKES 9 SERVINGS

6 tablespoons low- or no-sugar added strawberry jam

9 full graham crackers (18 squares)

3 cups light whipped topping, thawed, divided

1 pound thickly sliced fresh strawberries (about 3 cups)

1 cup fresh blueberries

1. Place the jam in a small microwave-safe bowl and microwave on high for 15 seconds, or until mostly melted.

2. Break the sheets of graham crackers in half. Arrange 9 squares on the bottom of an 8-inch square pan. (Note: There will be a small space between the crackers.) Brush 2 tablespoons of jam on the crackers and top with 1½ cups of the whipped topping. Smooth the topping and evenly layer 2 cups of the strawberry slices on top. Repeat with remaining crackers, jam, and whipped topping.

3. Cover, and refrigerate for 8 hours or overnight. Within an hour or two of serving, top with remaining sliced strawberries and blueberries.

**Marlene Says:** *This cake is best eaten within two days of being made as the crackers continue to soften and get mushy.*

**NUTRITION INFORMATION PER SERVING: (1 piece)** Calories 150 | Carbohydrate 25g (Sugars 14g) | Total Fat 4g (Sat Fat 2.5g) | Protein 1g | Fiber 2g | Cholesterol 0mg | Sodium 110mg | Food Exchanges: 1 Carbohydrate, ½ Fruit | Carbohydrate Choices: 1½ | Weight Watcher Smart Point Comparison: 5

# Frosty Peaches and Cream Yogurt Pie

*WITH ONLY FIVE INGREDIENTS, THIS FAST-FIX FROZEN PIE IS JUST PEACHY. Made with the goodness of creamy yogurt and juicy diced peaches, it takes mere minutes to make and stays fresh in the freezer for up to a week (or longer). Allow the pie, or a piece of it, to thaw slightly before eating and you will be blessed with creamy, frosty, melt-in-your mouth peach perfection.*

MAKES 8 SERVINGS

3 (6-ounce) containers light peach yogurt (like Yoplait)

1 tablespoon powdered sugar

½ cup canned peaches, drained and diced

½ (8-ounce) tub light whipped topping, thawed

1 prepared 9-inch graham cracker piecrust

1. In a medium bowl, gently combine the yogurt and powdered sugar. Stir in the peaches and gently fold in the whipped topping.

2. Transfer the filling to the piecrust and smooth the top. Place the pie in the freezer for 30 minutes, or until the top is firm. Cover tightly with foil or plastic wrap and freeze until completely firm. To serve, allow the pie to soften in the refrigerator for 1½ to 2 hours or on the counter for 1 hour before serving for the best texture.

**Marlene Says:** *Feel free to mix and match your favorite yogurt flavors, fruit, and crust. When shopping for yogurt, I have found creamy blended varieties work best (versus fruit on the bottom). Canned peaches are excellent in this pie, but in-season peeled and diced fresh peaches are wonderful as well. The Vanilla Crumb Crust (page 321) is also quite delicious with this pie.*

**NUTRITION INFORMATION PER SERVING:** (1 piece) Calories 170 | Carbohydrate 24g (Sugars 16g) | Total Fat 7g (Sat Fat 2g) | Protein 4g | Fiber 0g | Cholesterol 5mg | Sodium 170mg | Food Exchanges: 1½ Carbohydrate | Carbohydrate Choices: 1½ | Weight Watcher Smart Point Comparison: 6

# Luscious Lemon Pie with Shortbread Crust

*I CREATED THIS PIE FOR THE LEMON LOVERS IN MY FAMILY—AND YOURS! Indulge in a layer of creamy lemon cheesecake sitting on top of a crunchy buttery shortbread crust topped with a layer of smooth and tangy lemon pudding, finished off with whipped topping and fresh blackberries. I guarantee, every sweet, puckery, luscious bite is enough to make you swoon. The no-bake prep is, as they say, as easy as pie.*

---

**MAKES 8 SERVINGS**

¼ cup light cream cheese, softened

¼ cup nonfat cream cheese, softened

2 tablespoons granulated sweetener*

1 medium lemon, zested and juiced

2 cups light whipped topping, thawed

1 prepared shortbread crust** (like Keebler)

1 (4-serving size) package sugar-free instant lemon pudding mix

1½ cups low-fat milk

1 cup fresh blackberries

1. In a medium bowl, with an electric mixer, beat the cream cheeses, sweetener, 2 teaspoons lemon juice, and ½ teaspoon lemon zest until smooth. Fold in ½ cup whipped topping and spread onto bottom of piecrust.

2. Add pudding mix and milk to the bowl and beat until smooth. Stir in 2 tablespoons lemon juice and 1 teaspoon lemon zest. Fold in ⅓ cup whipped topping. Spread the lemon filling over the cream cheese layer.

3. Decorate the top of pie with the remaining whipped topping and blackberries. Refrigerate for at least one hour before serving.

**Marlene Says:** **The Vanilla Crumb Crust on page 321 (or a prepared graham cracker crust) can be substituted for the shortbread crust.*

* See page 36 for sweetener options.

**NUTRITION INFORMATION PER SERVING: (1 piece)** Calories 200 | Carbohydrate 24g (Sugars 11g) | Total Fat 9g (Sat Fat 3.5g) | Protein 5g | Fiber 1g | Cholesterol 5mg | Sodium 250mg | Food Exchanges: 1½ Carbohydrate | Carbohydrate Choices: 1½ | Weight Watcher Smart Point Comparison: 8

# Fresh Strawberry Single-Serving Pies

*HIGH IN SUGAR (AND/OR HIGH FRUCTOSE CORN SYRUP) and low in fresh strawberry taste, store-bought strawberry pie glaze simply can't compete with homemade. Fortunately, a homemade strawberry glaze is quick and easy to make, and you control the amount of sugar. Once made, simply toss with fresh juicy berries to create perfectly portioned individual pies. (If you love strawberry-topped cheesecake, see below for how to add a layer of cheesecake to these little beauties.)*

MAKES 6 SERVINGS

1/3 cup low-sugar strawberry jam

1/3 cup granulated sweetener*

2 teaspoons cornstarch

3 cups fresh strawberries, stemmed and halved

6 mini graham cracker pie shells

Light whipped cream (optional)

1. In a small saucepan, whisk together the jam, sweetener, cornstarch, and 2/3 cup water. Mash enough strawberries to make 1/2 cup and add to the jam mixture. Heat over low heat about 3 minutes or until mixture bubbles and thickens. Let cool to room temperature.

2. In a large bowl, toss the remaining strawberries with the glaze. Evenly divide the strawberries among the 6 pie shells and any glaze left behind. Refrigerate for at least one hour before serving.

**DARE TO COMPARE:** A piece of traditional fresh strawberry pie has 480 calories. Up the ante by adding a layer of cream cheese, and you're looking at 655 calories and a hefty 48 grams of fat. To add the cream cheese layer, mix together 1/4 cup light tub-style cream cheese and 2 tablespoons of light sour cream with 1 tablespoon sweetener and 1 teaspoon powdered sugar. Place 1 tablespoon in the bottom of each crust. (The cream cheese layer adds 30 calories and 3 grams of fat per pie.)

*See page 36 for sweetener options.

**NUTRITION INFORMATION PER SERVING: (1 pie)** Calories 150 | Carbohydrate 25g (Sugars 13g) | Total Fat 5g (Sat Fat 3g) | Protein 1g | Fiber 2g | Cholesterol 0mg | Sodium 110mg | Food Exchanges: 1 Carbohydrate, 1/2 Fruit | Carbohydrate Choices: 1 1/2 | Weight Watcher Smart Point Comparison: 6

# 2-Minute Microwave Pumpkin Pie

*WHEN IT COMES TO BEING AN APPLE OR PUMPKIN PIE FAN, most Americans go for apple. Personally, I'm a bigger pumpkin fan, and specifically, I could eat pumpkin pie filling every day. With this remarkable recipe, I can do just that. It takes only two minutes and a microwave to make a generous single serving of not only delicious, but protein- and nutrient-packed, creamy pumpkin custard! Eat it warm or chill it in the fridge. Either way, don't forget to add a dollop of whipped cream.*

MAKES 1 SERVING

⅓ cup canned pumpkin

3 tablespoons liquid egg substitute (or one large egg, beaten)

2 tablespoons nonfat half-and-half

2 tablespoons granulated sweetener*

1 teaspoon brown sugar

½ teaspoon Favorite Pumpkin Pie Seasoning (page 313) or store bought

½ teaspoon vanilla extract

Light whipped topping or aerosol whipped cream (optional)

1. In a 1-cup or larger microwave-safe bowl, whisk together all of the ingredients. Place in the microwave and cook on high for 2 minutes. (The center may appear a little wet, but the rest of the custard should be almost fully set. It will continue to cook slightly more upon cooling.)

2. Serve warm or cold with a whipped topping, if desired.

**Marlene Says:** *Missing the crust? Enjoy or serve this with a graham cracker, ginger snap, or other cookie for a bit of crispy crunch!*

*See page 36 for sweetener options.

**NUTRITION INFORMATION PER SERVING:** Calories 85 | Carbohydrate 15g (Sugars 6g) | Total Fat 1g (Sat Fat 0g) | Protein 6g | Fiber 2g | Cholesterol 0mg | Sodium 80mg | Food Exchanges: 1 Vegetable, 1 Lean Meat, ½ Carbohydrate | Carbohydrate Choices: 1 | Weight Watcher Smart Point Comparison: 1

# 15-Minute Coconut Cream Candy Bar Pie

*THERE IS NOTHING QUITE AS SPECIAL AS A HOMEMADE PIE, but this one is super special. Not only does it have all of the creamy coconut-y lusciousness one expects from a coconut cream pie, it packs a double dose of chocolate! It can also be made in as little as 15 minutes (yep, you read that right). And, as if that were not enough, it has less than one-third of the usual calories, carbs, and sugar of a regular coconut cream pie. If you love coconut and chocolate, this is a must-try pie!*

**MAKES 8 SERVINGS**

4 tablespoons sweetened flaked coconut

1⅓ cups low-fat milk

1 (4-serving size) package sugar-free instant vanilla pudding

1¾ cups light whipped topping, thawed

1 teaspoon coconut extract

1 chocolate graham cracker or Oreo premade piecrust

1 tablespoon sugar-free chocolate ice cream topping

1. In a medium skillet, add coconut and toast over medium heat, while stirring, for 3 to 4 minutes, or until lightly browned. Let cool slightly.

2. In a medium bowl, whisk the pudding mix into the milk until mixture is smooth and no lumps remain. Stir in 2 tablespoons toasted coconut and the coconut extract. Lightly fold in the whipped topping (do not overmix).

3. Spoon the filling into the crust and smooth the top. Drizzle with the chocolate ice cream topping and sprinkle with remaining 2 tablespoons of toasted coconut. Refrigerate 2 hours or more before serving. (I like this pie served very cold and often place it in the freezer for about 30 minutes before serving. It can also be served frozen.)

**DARE TO COMPARE:** One slice of Marie Callender's Coconut Cream Pie has 649 calories, 37 grams of fat, 72 grams of carbs, and 42 grams of sugar!

**NUTRITION INFORMATION PER SERVING:** (1 piece) Calories 190 | Carbohydrate 22g (Sugars 12g) | Total Fat 10g (Sat Fat 4.5g) | Protein 3g | Fiber 1g | Cholesterol 0mg | Sodium 220mg | Food Exchanges: 1½ Carbohydrate, 2 Fat | Carbohydrate Choices: 1½ | Weight Watcher Smart Point Comparison: 8

# Grilled Peach Sundaes with Caramel Sauce and Almonds

*I HAVE TO ADMIT, I NEVER CONSIDERED GRILLED PEACH HALVES A SENSATIONAL dessert—until I saw a recipe in the* New York Times *featuring them as part of a sundae. Warm peaches, cold and creamy ice cream, crunchy nuts, and gooey caramel sauce—now that is what I call dessert! The original recipe called for 19 different ingredients and a whopping 1,120 calories per serving. My knock-off has 6 ingredients and 150 calories. Enjoy!*

MAKES 4 SERVINGS

Canola oil

2 large slightly firm peaches cut in half, pits removed

4 teaspoons brown sugar

1 cup no-sugar-added vanilla ice cream

4 tablespoons sugar-free caramel sundae topping, warmed

4 tablespoons sliced toasted almonds

1. Lightly brush a preheated grill with canola oil. Place peaches cut-side down on the hot grill. Grill for 3 to 5 minutes, depending on temperature of grill, until peaches have softened and have grill marks. Remove from heat and place on a plate, grill-side up. Sprinkle immediately with brown sugar (approximately 1 teaspoon per peach half).

2. Place each peach half on a plate. Top with ¼ cup ice cream, 1 tablespoon topping, and 1 tablespoon nuts.

**DARE TO COMPARE:** The Grilled-Peach Sundaes with Salted Bourbon Caramel Sauce recipe (as in the *New York Times*) that inspired me served a full peach and came with a generous 1,120 calories, 83 grams of fat (including 2 days' of sat fat), and a staggering 20 teaspoons of added sugar! If desired, add a tablespoon of bourbon into the caramel sauce when you warm it and top with a pinch of salt.

**NUTRITION INFORMATION PER SERVING:** (1 peach half) Calories 150 | Carbohydrate 22g (Sugars 9g) | Total Fat 5g (Sat Fat 0g) | Protein 3g | Fiber 5g | Cholesterol 55mg | Sodium 55mg | Food Exchanges: 1 Carbohydrate, ½ Fruit | Carbohydrate Choices: 1 | Weight Watcher Smart Point Comparison: 4

# No-Churn Fruity Frozen Yogurt

*LET'S FACE IT, A DESSERT OF FRESH FRUIT IS A HEALTHY CHOICE, but it isn't always exciting. What's more, many of the most tempting fruits are either poor quality or pricy when not in season. With 3 grams of fiber, 5 grams of protein, and half your daily requirement for vitamins A and C, this creamy two-minute mix of freshly frozen fruit and protein-rich yogurt will satisfy your body and dessert-loving sweet tooth—any time of year!*

**MAKES 3 SERVINGS**

1 cup frozen strawberries

1 cup frozen mangoes

1/2 medium frozen banana, sliced

1/2 cup nonfat plain Greek yogurt

1 to 2 tablespoons low-fat milk

1 to 2 tablespoons sugar, honey or granulated no-calorie sweetener (optional)*

1. Place all the ingredients into a food processor. Pulse and purée until smooth, adding additional milk if necessary. Serve immediately or cover and freeze. Once frozen, thaw for 15 minutes before eating for best texture.

**Marlene Says:** *I find two tablespoons of sweetener brings the sweetness level up to that of most frozen yogurts. Here are what other options "cost" per **serving** for every tablespoon added: Each tablespoon of honey adds 20 calories (5 grams of sugar), each tablespoon of sugar adds 16 calories (4 grams of sugar), 1/2 tablespoon of Truvia Baking Blend (which adds the sweetness of 1 tablespoon of sugar) costs 5 calories (1 gram of sugar), and a tablespoon of granulated sucralose adds 2 calories (0 sugar).*

*See page 36 for sweetener options.

**NUTRITION INFORMATION PER SERVING:** (1/2 cup) Calories 100 | Carbohydrate 20g (Sugars 18g) | Total Fat 0g (Sat Fat 0g) | Protein 5g | Fiber 3g | Cholesterol 0mg | Sodium 0mg | Food Exchanges: 1/2 Lean Meat, 1 Fruit | Carbohydrate Choices: 1 | Weight Watcher Smart Point Comparison: 4

# No-Bake Red, White, and Blue Dome Cake

*PERFECT FOR ENTERTAINING WITH EASE, this cake looks ravishing, but is a breeze to make. You simply line the inside of a bowl with strawberry slices (which easily hold each other in place), add ice cream and a layer of jam-laced lady fingers, and in minutes you have a stunning no-bake ice cream "cake". When served with warm blueberry sauce, the frosty, creamy, cakey combination is simply stellar— to look at, and to eat!*

SERVES 10

3/4 pound fresh strawberries

1.5-quart container no-sugar added vanilla ice cream, softened

3 tablespoons low sugar strawberry jam

1 (3-ounce) package soft ladyfingers (12 split fingers)

1 recipe (blueberry) Fast Fix Berry Sauce, warm

1. Line a 1½-quart stainless steel or glass bowl, with the plastic wrap, letting the plastic edges overhang outside of the bowl, and set aside.

2. Rinse strawberries and slice off tops and tips. Slice each strawberry into 3 to 4 thin circles. Arrange strawberry slices in a single layer on the inside of the bowl, starting in the bottom center and working out to the top edges. Scoop softened ice cream over the top of the strawberries and smooth until the surface is flat.

3. Place strawberry jam in a small bowl and heat in the microwave on high for 30 seconds to warm. Split ladyfingers and spread strawberry jam between them. Sandwich back together and press them onto the top of the bowl (breaking some apart, if necessary, to cover most of the surface). Cover the bowl with plastic wrap, press down once more on the ladyfingers (a pot lid works well) and and place in freezer for at least 6 hours or until firm.

4. To serve. Remove the plastic wrap from the top of the bowl, place a serving plate over the cake and flip. Pour 1 cup of the sauce onto the middle of the top of the cake, and serve each piece with the remaining sauce

**Marlene Says:** *Make this the day before you serve it to ensure the ice cream is firm for cutting. It will hold for several weeks in the freezer.*

**NUTRITION INFORMATION PER SERVING:** (1 slice plus sauce) Calories 165 | Carbohydrate 30 (Sugars 14) | Total Fat 5 (Sat Fat 3) | Protein 4g | Fiber 7g | Cholesterol 0g | Sodium 115 mg | Food Exchanges: 1 Carbohydrate, ½ Fruit, ½ Fat | Carbohydrate Choices: 1½ | Weight Watcher Smart Point Comparison: 6

# Chocolate-Covered Crispy Peanut Butter Bon Bons

*FOR THOSE OF YOU WHO HAVE WRITTEN AND ASKED FOR A CANDY RECIPE, here you go. These sweet peanutty balls dipped in chocolate remind me of the classic buckeye candy we used to get when I lived in Ohio—with only a speck of the original sugar. Crispy rice cereal adds a lovely crunch, but please note they soften after a day or so (which most certainly did not keep me from nibbling on them for the next week!).*

MAKES 16 SERVINGS

½ cup creamy peanut butter

¼ cup granulated sweetener*

3 tablespoons light cream cheese

1 tablespoon brown sugar

½ teaspoon vanilla extract

1 cup crispy rice cereal

½ cup semi-sweet chocolate chips

½ teaspoon canola oil

1. Place a sheet of wax paper on a large plate or small sheet pan and set aside. In a large mixing bowl, place the first 5 ingredients (peanut butter through vanilla) and, with an electric mixer, cream together until smooth. Gently fold in the rice cereal.

2. Scoop 1 tablespoon mounds of the mixture, roll into balls, and transfer to the prepared plate or sheet pan. In a small microwave-safe bowl, place the chocolate chips and oil, and microwave 2 minutes, or until melted, stirring every 30 seconds.

3. Dip half of each bon bon into the melted chocolate, or if you prefer, simply drizzle each with ½ teaspoon of chocolate. Refrigerate or freeze until chocolate firms.

**DARE TO COMPARE:** A classic recipe for buckeyes calls for more than 4 cups of powdered sugar with each buckeye containing 183 calories, 20 grams of carbohydrate, and 16 grams of sugar.

*See page 36 for sweetener options.

**NUTRITION INFORMATION PER SERVING:** (1 bon bon) Calories 75 | Carbohydrate 5g (Sugars 3g) | Total Fat 5g (Sat Fat 1.5g) | Protein 3g | Fiber 1g | Cholesterol 0mg | Sodium 65mg | Food Exchanges: 1 Medium Fat Meat, 1 Fat, ½ Carbohydrate | Carbohydrate Choices: 0 | Weight Watcher Smart Point Comparison: 3

# 2-Minute Chocolate "Cup" Cake for One

*YOU'LL GET ONLY SWEET SATISFACTION when you make this almost-instant chocolate cake—and it's all for you! I tried a lot of horrible homemade "mug" cake recipes to create this one and I am thrilled to report that after many messy mugs, I perfected it. A mixture of on-hand ingredients quickly goes into a coffee mug, and after one short minute in the microwave, you've got cake. Warm, fudgy, dark chocolate cake! It goes without saying than you can top it with a dollop of light whipped cream. WARNING: Making these can become habit-forming.*

MAKES 1 SERVING

1½ teaspoons butter or margarine

1 tablespoon low-fat milk

2 tablespoons granulated sweetener (or 3 packets)

1 tablespoon liquid egg substitute or egg white

1 teaspoon brown sugar

¼ teaspoon vanilla extract

2 tablespoons all-purpose flour

1 tablespoon cocoa powder, preferably Dutch-process

1/8 teaspoon baking soda

1. Measure the butter in a microwave-safe coffee cup (1¼ to 1½ cup capacity is best), and microwave for 10 seconds. Whisk in the next 5 ingredients (milk through vanilla). Add the flour, cocoa, and baking soda and stir until just mixed.

2. Microwave on high power for 1 minute, or until the top puffs up and the center is barely set. Remove from microwave and let cool for 1 to 2 minutes (if you can). (The cake will continue to cook slightly after being removed from the microwave.)

**Marlene Says:** *Microwaves vary greatly in time and power, so keep an eye on your "cup" cake as it cooks. You may need to add 5 to 10 seconds to the cook time. The texture is best when made with packets of sucralose or Truvia, 1 tablespoon Truvia Baking Blend, or 2 tablespoons granulated sugar. If you use 2 tablespoons of sucralose based no-calorie granulated sweetener, add ½ tablespoon more milk.*

*See page 36 for sweetener options.

**NUTRITION INFORMATION PER SERVING:** (1 "cake") Calories 130 | Carbohydrate 19 g (Sugars 4g) | Total Fat 6g (Sat Fat 2g) | Protein 5g | Fiber 2g | Cholesterol 0mg | Sodium 220 mg | Food Exchanges: 1 Carbohydrate, 1 Fat | Carbohydrate Choices: 1 | Weight Watcher Smart Point Comparison: 4

# No-Bake Cherry-Topped Cheesecake Cupcakes

*SMALLER VERSIONS OF FAVORITE DESSERTS ALWAYS MAKE PEOPLE SMILE and this one is no exception. Simply place a vanilla wafer into a cupcake liner, top with the no-bake cheesecake filling, and top that with ready-made cherry topping. Done! Once set, you have twelve slimmin' 110-calorie cheesecake cupcakes perfect for any occasion. This recipe can easily be halved to make just half a dozen.*

**MAKES 12 SERVINGS**

8 ounces light cream cheese

8 ounces nonfat cream cheese

1/2 cup light sour cream

1/3 cup granulated sweetener*

1/4 teaspoon almond extract

2 tablespoons powdered sugar

1/2 teaspoon lemon zest

1/2 cup light whipped topping, thawed

12 vanilla wafers

1 1/2 cups light cherry filling**

1. Line 12 muffin cups with foil liners and lightly coat with cooking spray. In a large bowl, with an electric mixer, beat the first 7 ingredients (cream cheese through lemon zest) until smooth. Gently fold in the whipped topping.

2. Place a vanilla wafer in each foil liner (flat-side down). Top each wafer with 3 tablespoons of cheesecake filling, gently smoothing the top. Refrigerate for at least 3 hours. Top each cheesecake with 2 tablespoons of cherry filling before serving.

**Marlene Says:** **A 15-ounce can of cherry pie filling contains about 2 cups. To top these cupcakes use all of the cherries (which will leave about 1/2 cup of jel that you can either discard or add berries to and use it to top pancakes, waffles, or ice cream). Extra vanilla wafers can be used to make a Vanilla Crumb Crust (see page 321).*

* See page 36 for sweetener options.

**NUTRITION INFORMATION PER SERVING:** (1 cupcake) Calories 110 | Carbohydrate 11g (Sugars 7g) | Total Fat 4g (Sat Fat 2.5g) | Protein 6g | Fiber 0g | Cholesterol 10mg | Sodium 190mg | Food Exchanges: 1 Carbohydrate | Carbohydrate Choices: 1 | Weight Watcher Smart Point Comparison: 4

# Chocolate Hazelnut (Nutella®) Mousse

*THIS DELECTABLE COMPANY-WORTHY MOUSSE IS SO GOOD, IT'S DOWNRIGHT DANGEROUS. Made with Nutella® (the utterly delicious chocolate hazelnut spread) and cream cheese, it has a luscious texture and a sinful taste. Give it extra-special treat status by serving it in stemmed glasses with fresh raspberries, a shaving of chocolate, and a dollop of whipped topping. (Psst. . . there's no need to tell your guests that a ½-cup serving has the same number of calories and essentially the same amount of fat and carbs as just 2 tablespoons of the spread.)*

MAKES 4 SERVINGS

¼ cup Nutella®

¼ cup light tub-style cream cheese, at room temperature

¼ cup fat-free cream cheese, at room temperature

¼ cup no-calorie granulated sweetener (or 4 packets)*

2 tablespoons low-fat milk

¼ teaspoon hazelnut extract

1½ cups light whipped topping, thawed

1. In a large bowl, using an electric mixer, beat the Nutella and cream cheeses. Add the sweetener, milk, and hazelnut extract. Beat until smooth.

2. Gently fold in the whipped topping, a half cup at a time (do not beat it in or the mousse will be too dense). Divide into four serving dishes. Chill for at least 30 minutes, or until ready to serve.

**DARE TO COMPARE:** Beware of "better-for-you" headline myths. I recently found a recipe for a "slimming" chocolate mousse in a very popular physician's health magazine. It had twice the calories, three times the fat, and four times the saturated fat as this equally decadent-tasting mousse.

* See page 36 for sweetener options.

**NUTRITION INFORMATION PER SERVING:** (½ cup) Calories 200 | Carbohydrate 19g (Sugars 10g) | Total Fat 11g (Sat Fat 5g) | Protein 5g | Fiber 1g | Cholesterol 10mg | Sodium 220mg | Food Exchanges: 2 Fat, 1 Carbohydrate | Carbohydrate Choices: 1 | Weight Watcher Smart Point Comparison: 8

# MORE EASY & EFFORTLESS DESSERTS

## more easy & effortless desserts

# { BAKING BASICS }

In this chapter, you'll find plenty of marvelous recipe shortcuts to produce mouthwatering desserts in mere minutes. That said, when it comes to baking—unlike cooking—some rules simply can't be broken. When you bake, not following certain rules (or the recipe to a tee) can mean the difference between fabulous and a flop! Here are eight tried and true baking steps not worth shortcutting.

## EIGHT STEPS TO BETTER BAKING

1) Ensure ingredients are at the proper temperature. If the temperature of the ingredients is imperative, it will be noted in the recipe. Otherwise, as a rule, eggs are best close to room temperature (and can be warmed quickly in a bowl of warm water), and pie and pastry dough are best kept cold.

2) Preheat the oven. Some ovens preheat in minutes while others (like mine) are very slow, so plan accordingly. Baking anything in an oven that is not up to temperature can result in uneven or improper cooking.

3) Place the baking rack in the proper position. The top and bottom of an oven cook differently. If it's not specified in the recipe, position the rack in the center slot.

4) Use the specified-sized baking pan. Baking batter in too small a pan can cause overflow and the center may not cook properly. Baking batter in too large a pan will affect the height and be prone to overbaking. A 9-inch square pan is 33% larger than an 8-inch square pan!

5) Grease, flour, and/or line your baking pans per the recipe. Spraying the inside of a cupcake liner will keep the "cake" from sticking to the wrapper.

6) Pay attention when mixing by using the visual clues in addition to the specified time. When the recipe states light and fluffy it means light and fluffy, and just mixed means just mixed, regardless of the time it takes. Don't rush here, as over- or undermixing will affect your baked goods.

7) Keep an eye on baking goods. To be safe, especially the first time you make a recipe, check it several minutes before the suggested baking time comes to an end. Use the alternate methods of determining doneness given in the recipe. Never rely on time alone.

8) Respect timing. Baking can't be hurried. Never frost cakes and cupcakes that aren't fully cooled, and factor refrigeration, freezer, or warming times into the timing of when you want to serve your dessert.

# Blueberry Cheesecake Pie Cups

*AFTER DISCOVERING HOW FANTASTICALLY EASY-TO-MAKE AND DELICIOUS the filling for my Easiest-Ever Fresh Blueberry Pie (page 290) turned out to be, I immediately made it into single serving pie cups. But I couldn't stop there. No siree, I decided to add a lusciously sweet cream cheese layer. Ever so lightly scented with orange, it mingles perfectly with the fresh blueberry top. Some days in the test kitchen are especially sweet. I highly recommend these delectable blueberry beauties.*

### MAKES 12 SERVINGS

1 package refrigerated pie crust

1 recipe Blueberry Filling (page 290)

1/4 cup light cream cheese

3 tablespoons light sour cream

1 1/2 tablespoons reduced-sugar orange marmalade

1. Preheat the oven to 400° F. Place one piecrust on a cutting board and roll out lightly to an 11-inch diameter. Using a 4-inch round cutter, cut out 6 rounds. Discard scraps, and repeat with the second piecrust.

2. Lightly press the pastry rounds into 12 muffin cups, pressing the dough into the bottom and up the sides. Prick the bottoms and sides with a fork and bake for 10 minutes, or until nicely browned. While the crusts are baking, prepare the blueberry pie filling.

3. In a small bowl, mix together the cream cheese, sour cream, and marmalade. Spoon 2 teaspoons of the mixture into the bottom of each cooled pie cup and top with 1/4 cup of the blueberry filling. Refrigerate for at least one hour before serving.

**DARE TO COMPARE:** Oh my! A regular piece of Marie Callendar's Blueberry Pie has 600 calories, 78 grams of carb (or more than an entire meals' worth), 31 grams of fat, and 37 grams of sugar.

**NUTRITION INFORMATION PER SERVING:** (1 pie cup) Calories 140 | Carbohydrate 19 g (Sugars 9g) | Total Fat 6g (Sat Fat 2g) | Protein 2g | Fiber 2g | Cholesterol 5mg | Sodium 130mg | Food Exchanges: 1/2 Starch, 1/2 Fruit | Carbohydrate Choices: 1 | Weight Watcher Smart Point Comparison: 5

# Easiest-Ever Fresh Blueberry Pie

*THIS IS NOT ONLY THE EASIEST BLUEBERRY PIE RECIPE EVER. IT'S ONE OF THE BEST! Instead of baking, you simply coat plump fresh blueberries with a scrumptious blueberry-studded glaze (that takes just five minutes to make) and spoon the mixture into a baked pie shell. That's it! I find this pie irresistible when it's made with a traditional crust, but for a tempting no-bake pie, just spoon the filling into a premade shortbread or graham cracker crust. With its fabulous fresh flavor, the better the berries, the better the pie!*

MAKES 8 SERVINGS

½ package refrigerated piecrust

Blueberry Filling:

2 tablespoons cornstarch

2 tablespoons lemon juice

1 cup frozen blueberries

6 tablespoons granulated sweetener*

2 tablespoons granulated sugar

½ teaspoon lemon zest

3 cups fresh blueberries

1. Prepare a 9-inch baked one-crust piecrust according to package directions. Let cool while preparing the filling.

2. In a small bowl, whisk together the cornstarch, lemon juice, and 2 tablespoons water until smooth. Set aside. Place the frozen blueberries and ⅔ cup water in a medium saucepan and bring to a low simmer over medium-high heat. Cook for 3 to 4 minutes, stirring and smashing some of the berries, until berries have softened and sauce slightly thickens.

3. Add the cornstarch mixture to the saucepan along with the sweetener, sugar, and zest. Bring to a simmer, cook for 1 minute, or until the mixture clears. Remove from heat and stir in the fresh berries. Spoon the filling into the piecrust and chill for 2 hours before serving.

**Marlene Says:** *Because frozen blueberries break down more easily than fresh, they are better for the glaze, as is a small amount of real sugar to keep it clear. If all-natural Truvia Baking Blend is your preferred sweetener, eliminate the sweetener and the sugar and simply use ¼ cup of the baking blend.*

**NUTRITION INFORMATION PER SERVING: (1 piece)** Calories 160 | Carbohydrate 25g (Sugars 11g) | Total Fat 5g (Sat Fat 2g) | Protein 2g | Fiber 2g | Cholesterol 5mg | Sodium 75mg | Food Exchanges: 1 Starch, ½ Fruit | Carbohydrate Choices: 1½ | Weight Watcher Smart Point Comparison: 4

# 3-Ingredient Shortcut Strawberry Soufflés

**AIR FRY!**
SEE PAGE **325**

*THREE INGREDIENTS PLUS 15 SHORT MINUTES EQUALS SWEET STRAWBERRY HEAVEN!*
*If you have eggs, sugar, and jam in the house you are minutes away from serving up two sweet, billowy strawberry soufflés—each with only 125 slim calories. If you have never made a soufflé, don't worry, these are delectable and effortless. Simply whip the egg whites and sugar, fold in the jam, and bake. It couldn't be easier!*

MAKES 2 SERVINGS

2 large egg whites

2½ tablespoons granulated sugar

¼ cup low-sugar strawberry preserves (like Smucker's)

1. Preheat the oven to 400°F. Spray two 1-cup ramekins with non-stick cooking spray and set aside.

2. In a large bowl, with an electric mixer, add the egg whites and whip on medium speed until frothy. Sprinkle in the sugar and continue until egg whites just reach stiff peak form. Gently fold in the strawberry jam. Divide the soufflé mixture into the prepared ramekins and smooth the tops.

3. Bake for 8 minutes, reduce the oven to 350°F, and bake for 3 minutes longer, or until the tops are lightly browned and the soufflés have puffed up. Serve immediately.

**Marlene Says:** *With just 3 ingredients, regular granulated sugar and low-sugar preserves (not "sugar-free") are required to stabilize these sweet soufflés. Looking for a last minute dessert with less sugar or carbs? Try the Two-Minute Chocolate "Cup" Cake on page 281 or Two-Minute Microwave Pumpkin Pie on page 273.*

**NUTRITION INFORMATION PER SERVING:** (Each) Calories 125 | Carbohydrate 28g (Sugars 26g) | Total Fat 0g (Sat Fat 0g) | Protein 4g | Fiber 0g | Cholesterol 0mg | Sodium 70mg | Food Exchanges: 2 Carbohydrate | Carbohydrate Choices: 2 | Weight Watcher Smart Point Comparison: 6

# Almond Tea Cakes

*THESE NUTTY GEMS ARE THE PERFECT TEATIME TREAT. Because they are made with more almonds than flour, they are naturally low in carbs and high in healthy fats, making them heart-smart and blood sugar friendly. If you would like to make them gluten-free, simply swap your favorite gluten-free flour for the all-purpose flour. I like to keep a batch of these in the freezer so I can grab one (or two) when my inner cookie monster strikes.*

MAKES 18 COOKIES

1 cup whole almonds

1/2 cup all-purpose flour

3 tablespoons butter, softened

1/2 cup granulated sweetener*

2 tablespoons sugar

1 large egg

1/2 teaspoon almond extract

1 tablespoon powdered sugar

1. Preheat the oven to 350°F. Place the almonds in a food processor and pulse until a coarse meal, but not powdery or oily. Pour ground almonds into a small mixing bowl, and whisk in the flour. Set aside.

2. In a large bowl, using an electric mixer, beat the butter, sweetener, and sugar until well combined (mixture will not be creamy). Add egg and almond extract and beat until light and fluffy. Add the flour mixture and gently stir until all ingredients are well blended.

3. Roll level tablespoons of dough into balls and place 1¼ inches apart on a baking sheet. Bake 9 to 10 minutes, rotating pan halfway through, until cookie bottoms are golden brown (tops will remain pale). Remove and cool on rack. Dust with powdered sugar.

**Marlene Says:** *Recipes that use less wheat flour are the easiest to make gluten-free. A couple of good gluten-free flours are Cup4Cup and Bob's Red Mill 1:1 Baking Flour.*

*See page 36 for sweetener options.

**NUTRITION INFORMATION PER SERVING:** (1 cookie) Calories 90 | Carbohydrate 6g (Sugars 2g) | Total Fat 6g (Sat Fat 1g) | Protein 3g | Fiber 1g | Cholesterol 15 mg | Sodium 25mg | Food Exchanges: 1 Fat, 1/2 Carbohydrate | Carbohydrate Choices: 1/2 | Weight Watcher Smart Point Comparison: 3

# Easy Apple Pie Pastry Squares

*FLAKY, BUTTERY FROZEN PUFF PASTRY HAS LONG BEEN A STAPLE in my last-minute entertaining arsenal. Admittedly, it's a high-fat indulgence, yet these apple pie squares clock in at a mere 100 calories. If you're wondering how, I thinly roll out the dough and pile on slender apple slices. This little trick minimizes the amount of pastry in each serving while still offering a wonderfully satisfying dessert or snack that looks and tastes like it came from a fine bakery.*

**MAKES 12 SERVINGS**

1 tablespoon all-purpose flour

1 sheet frozen puff pastry, thawed (like Pepperidge Farms)

3 medium apples (about 1 pound)

$\frac{1}{2}$ medium lemon, juiced

2 tablespoons granulated sugar, divided

$\frac{1}{2}$ teaspoon ground cinnamon

2 tablespoons reduced-sugar apricot jam

1. Position an oven rack in the lower third of the oven, and preheat oven to 400°F. Sprinkle the flour on a flat surface and lay the pastry sheet on it. Roll out the pastry lightly to make a 10 x 14-inch rectangle. Transfer pastry to a baking sheet, and refrigerate while preparing the apples.

2. Peel, core, and thinly slice the apples (about $\frac{1}{8}$ inch thick), and place in a medium bowl. Add the lemon juice and gently toss to coat the apples. Sprinkle the chilled pastry evenly with 1 tablespoon sugar. Arrange the apples over the pastry in rows, slightly overlapping the slices and leaving a $\frac{1}{2}$-inch pastry border around the outer edge.

3. In a small bowl, combine the cinnamon and remaining sugar, and sprinkle over the apples. Bake for 25 to 30 minutes, or until golden brown. Remove from oven. In a small microwave-safe bowl, stir the jam with 1 teaspoon water and heat on high for 15 seconds. Brush over the apples and crust. Cut into 12 squares and serve immediately, or set aside and serve at room temperature.

**Marlene Says:** *Another name for this dessert is Apple Slab Pie. If you cut the finished pastry in three equal parts on the short side and four on the long side, you will have twelve 3-inch squares. For a "pie"-sized serving; simply cut it into 6 portions and double all of the nutritional information. Serve a la mode if desired.*

**NUTRITION INFORMATION PER SERVING:** (1 square) Calories 100 | Carbohydrate 15g (Sugars 7g) | Total Fat 5g (Sat Fat 1g) | Protein 1g | Fiber 1g | Cholesterol 0mg | Sodium 65mg | Food Exchanges: $\frac{1}{2}$ Carbohydrate, $\frac{1}{2}$ Fruit | Carbohydrate Choices: 1 | Weight Watcher Smart Point Comparison: 4

# Quick and Easy Chocolate Cake Mix Cookies

*WITH JUST SIX INGREDIENTS, THESE ARE THE EASIEST, QUICKEST CHOCOLATE COOKIES I have ever made. After baking more batches than I care to count, we discovered that adding a bit of cocoa powder to the cake mix created a richer chocolate flavor, that light sour cream was an amazing low-fat replacement for oil (see Marlene Says, below) and that a touch of cinnamon on the outside pairs wonderfully with the soft chocolate inside. My chocolate, snickerdoodle- loving boys gobbled these gems up in no time flat. Good thing they are quick 'n easy!*

MAKES 24 COOKIES

1 (16-ounce) package sugar-free or regular chocolate cake mix

2 tablespoons cocoa powder

2 large eggs

¼ cup light sour cream

2 tablespoons granulated sugar

2 teaspoons cinnamon

1. Preheat the oven to 375°F. Spray a cookie sheet with non-stick cooking spray.

2. In a medium bowl combine the cake mix, cocoa powder, sour cream, eggs, and 2 tablespoons of water (use only 1 tablespoon with a regular mix). Mix with a spoon until smooth (dough will be sticky). Mix sugar and cinnamon in a small bowl. With moist hands, roll dough by the tablespoonful into balls. Roll the balls in sugar mixture, place on cookie sheet, and flatten with the bottom of a drinking glass.

3. Bake cookies for 7 to 8 minutes. Remove from pan and cool on rack.

**Marlene Says:** *Both sugar-free and regular cake mix produce delicious cookies. Using a regular mix adds 20 calories, 1 gram of fat, and 3 carbs per cookie. For a fudgier cookie, use 2 tablespoons each of light sour cream and canola oil. To make just a dozen cookies, use 1¾ cups dry mix and halve all the other ingredients. (Note: If you are sensitive with sugar-free chocolates, I recommend you use regular cake mix).*

**NUTRITION INFORMATION PER SERVING:** (1 cookie)  Calories 65 | Carbohydrate 12g (Sugars 1g)  |  Total Fat 1g (Sat Fat .5g)  |  Protein 2g  |  Fiber 1g  |  Cholesterol 15mg  |  Sodium 125mg  |  Food Exchanges: 1 Starch | Carbohydrate Choices: 1 | Weight Watcher Smart Point Comparison: 2

# Double Strawberry Cheesecake Bars

*WITH A DOUBLE DOSE OF STRAWBERRY FLAVOR the taste of these super creamy bars belies their healthy status. Creamed low-fat cottage cheese and nonfat Greek yogurt lend a hefty 8 grams of protein per bar while the strawberries contribute 30% of one's daily requirement for vitamin C—but you'll only be thinking of yum when you eat'm! I've made them with both regular and chocolate graham cracker crumbs and love them either way. The nutritional content remains the same.*

MAKES 9 SERVINGS

1 cup regular or chocolate graham cracker crumbs

3 tablespoons plus ½ cup granulated sweetener, divided

3 tablespoons margarine or butter, melted

¾ cup low-fat cottage cheese

4 ounces light cream cheese

4 ounces nonfat cream cheese

¼ cup reduced-sugar strawberry jam

⅔ cup nonfat plain Greek yogurt

2 cups sliced strawberries

1. Preheat the oven to 325°F. Lightly coat an 8 x 8-inch square pan with cooking spray. In a small bowl, combine the graham cracker crumbs, 3 tablespoons sweetener, and margarine. Press into pan and bake for 5 minutes. Set aside to cool.

2. Using a food processor or immersion blender, blend the cottage cheese until smooth. Transfer to a bowl and add the cream cheeses and remaining ½ cup sweetener.

3. Place jam in a small microwave-safe bowl and heat on high for 20 seconds. Stir jam well (it should be just warm, not hot), and then stir it into cream cheese mixture. Fold in yogurt and pour onto the prepared crust. Gently top with sliced strawberries and refrigerate for at least one hour before cutting.

**Marlene Says:** *If you make this a day ahead of time, or would like your strawberries to look at their freshest, top the bars with the berries just before serving.*

**NUTRITION INFORMATION PER SERVING:** (1 bar) Calories 160 | Carbohydrate 19g (Sugars 12g) | Total Fat 5g (Sat Fat 2g) | Protein 8g | Fiber 1g | Cholesterol 10mg | Sodium 270 mg | Food Exchanges: 1 Low Fat Meat, ½ Carbohydrate, ½ Fruit | Carbohydrate Choices: 1 | Weight Watcher Smart Point Comparison: 6

# Small Batch Chocolate Caramel Cheesecake Stuffed Cupcakes

*CHOCOLATE, CARAMEL, AND CHEESECAKE—NEED I SAY MORE? For this recipe, I take one-bowl fudgy cupcakes, fill them with creamy cheesecake, and then top them with caramel sauce! Perhaps even more fun, they each clock in with a slim 150-calorie, diabetes-friendly price tag. Making only six at a time quickens the process (as does not having to make frosting) and allows you to enjoy a treat without too many temptations on hand. Of course, the recipe can be doubled if six is just not enough :).*

**MAKES 6 CUPCAKES**

⅓ cup light tub-style cream cheese

2 teaspoons powdered sugar

7 tablespoons granulated sweetener, divided*

1½ teaspoons vanilla extract, divided

3 tablespoons cocoa powder

1 tablespoon brown sugar

¼ cup low-fat milk

1 large egg

¼ cup light mayonnaise

⅔ cup all-purpose flour

½ teaspoon baking powder

¼ teaspoon baking soda

3 tablespoons sugar-free caramel ice cream topping.

1. Preheat the oven to 325°F. Line 6 muffin cups with liners and spray with non-stick cooking spray (foil liners do not need to be sprayed). In a small bowl, mix together the cream cheese, powdered sugar, 1 tablespoon sweetener, and ½ teaspoon vanilla. Set aside.

2. Place cocoa powder in a medium bowl. Add ¼ cup warm water and whisk until smooth. Whisk in remaining 6 tablespoons sweetener, 1 teaspoon vanilla, brown sugar, milk, egg, and mayonnaise. Sift in flour, baking powder, and baking soda, and whisk again just until smooth.

3. Scoop scant ¼ cup of batter into each muffin cup. Place 2 teaspoons of cream cheese mixture into the center of each, pressing about ¾ into the cupcake. Bake for 15 minutes or until the cake near the center springs back when touched. Remove from oven and cool on wire rack.

4. Just before serving, warm the topping and drizzle 1½ teaspoons over each cupcake.

> **DARE TO COMPARE:** A Chocolate Caramel Muffin at Starbucks has 410 calories and 35 grams (or 9 teaspoons) of sugar, while a piece of Chocolate Cake Cheesecake at the Cheesecake Factory has 1,200 calories and over 50 grams of fat. These "small batch" cupcakes are big in savings!

**NUTRITION INFORMATION PER SERVING: (1 cupcake)** Calories 150 | Carbohydrate 22g (Sugars 4g) | Total Fat 6g (Sat Fat 2g) | Protein 4g | Fiber 2g | Cholesterol 35 mg | Sodium 240mg | Food Exchanges: 1½ Carbohydrate, 1 Fat | Carbohydrate Choices: 1½ | Weight Watcher Smart Point Comparison: 5

# PB&J Thumbprint Cookies

*YOU'D BE HARD PRESSED TO FIND ANOTHER FOOD THAT CONJURES up more memories of childhood than peanut butter and jelly. Here this beloved flavor pair is featured in a better-for-you, old-fashioned thumbprint cookie—which is great news for kids of all ages! Equally newsworthy is that these cookies come together quickly and can be baked in as little as five minutes, so you can enjoy them in a flash. Get your glass of milk ready!*

**MAKES 24 COOKIES**

1⅓ cups all-purpose flour

1 teaspoon baking soda

½ teaspoon baking powder

¾ cup creamy peanut butter

¾ cup granulated sweetener*

¼ cup brown sugar

1 large egg

3 tablespoons low-fat milk

2 teaspoons vanilla extract

4 tablespoons reduced-sugar jam

1. Preheat the oven to 350°F. In a small bowl, whisk together the flour, baking soda, and baking powder; set aside.

2. In a medium bowl, with an electric mixer, add the next 6 ingredients (peanut butter through vanilla), and beat well. Stir in the flour mixture. Dough will be stiff.

3. Scoop dough by rounded tablespoons onto prepared pan. Flatten cookies with your fingers, and use your thumb to make a large indentation. Spoon ½ teaspoon of jam into each indentation. Bake for 5 to 7 minutes, or until just set. Remove from pan and cool on rack.

*See page 36 for sweetener options.

**NUTRITION INFORMATION PER SERVING: (1 cookie)** Calories 85 | Carbohydrate 9g (Sugars 4g) | Total Fat 4g (Sat Fat 1g) | Protein 3g | Fiber 1g | Cholesterol 10mg | Sodium 10mg | Food Exchanges: 1 Fat, ½ Carbohydrate | Carbohydrate Choices: ½ | Weight Watcher Smart Point Comparison: 3

# Heavenly Chocolate Cupcakes with Mocha Topping

*LIKE MY HEAVENLY ANGEL CUPCAKES WITH LUSCIOUS LEMON FROSTING in* Eat More of What You Love, *these foolproof cupcakes start with the convenience of angel food cake mix—only this time it's the classic "mocha" combo of chocolate and coffee that will have you giving thanks. Instead of the dusting of cocoa powder, a drizzle of chocolate sauce and/or a teaspoon of sliced almonds is lovely atop the mocha topping. The plain cupcakes freeze well and should be topped after thawing.*

**MAKES 12 CUPCAKES**

1 cup, plus 2 tablespoons dry angel food cake mix (one-half 16-ounce box)

½ cup plus 2 tablespoons water

2½ tablespoons unsweetened cocoa powder, preferably Dutch-process, divided

1½ cups light whipped topping, thawed

1¼ teaspoons instant coffee powder

1. Preheat the oven to 350°F. Place foil cupcake liners in 12 muffin cups and set aside. In a medium bowl, with an electric mixer, beat the angel food mix with the water for 30 seconds on low speed, then increase speed to high and beat for 1 minute.

2. Sift 2 tablespoons cocoa powder over the batter and gently fold it into the batter just until mixed. Do not overmix. (It's okay if a few streaks remain.) Scoop batter into muffin cups (about ¼ cup each). Bake for 15 to 17 minutes or until just set. Place muffin tin on a baking rack to cool.

3. To make the topping, dissolve coffee powder in 1 teaspoon warm water. Let cool, then fold coffee mixture into the whipped topping. Top each cupcake with about 2 tablespoons of coffee topping and dust with additional cocoa powder.

**DARE TO COMPARE:** An average mocha cupcake from a cupcake bakery has 425 calories, with 20 grams of fat and 60 grams of carbohydrate.

**NUTRITION INFORMATION PER SERVING: (1 cupcake)** Calories 90 | Carbohydrate 18g (Sugars 13g) | Total Fat 1g (Sat Fat 1g) | Protein 2g | Fiber 0g | Cholesterol 0mg | Sodium 170mg | Food Exchanges: 1 Carbohydrate | Carbohydrate Choices: 1 | Weight Watcher Smart Point Comparison: 4

# One-Bowl Mandarin Orange Cake

*IF YOU'RE FROM THE SOUTH, YOU'RE MORE THAN LIKELY FAMILIAR WITH THIS TYPE of moist, citrusy cake which goes by a variety names, such as Pig Pickin' Cake, Pig Lickin' Cake, Pig Eatin' Cake, and Sunshine Cake—just to name a few! Though it traditionally starts with a boxed cake mix, I find starting from scratch just as easy (not to mention a major reduction in fat and sugar!). I prefer it topped with just a dusting of powdered sugar or a dollop of light whipped topping, but I've included the oft-used pineapple whipped topping frosting below, just in case it's a Pig Lickin' must-have for y'all.*

MAKES 8 SERVINGS

2 large eggs

2/3 cup granulated sweetener*

1 (11-ounce) can mandarin oranges, in light syrup

1½ teaspoons vanilla extract

¼ teaspoon salt

1¼ cups all-purpose flour

1 teaspoon baking powder

½ teaspoon baking soda

1 teaspoon orange zest

1. Preheat oven to 350°F. Coat an 8-inch round cake pan with nonstick baking spray.

2. In a large mixing bowl, with an electric mixer, beat eggs and sweetener for 1 minute, or until lightened and fluffy. Pour the syrup from the oranges into the mixture (I hold the orange slices back with the can lid), along with vanilla, zest, and salt, and beat for 10 seconds to incorporate.

3. Sift the flour, baking powder, and baking soda directly into the bowl, and stir with a spoon just until smooth. Fold in the mandarin oranges and pour batter into the prepared pan. Bake for 20 to 25 minutes or until top springs back when touched. Cool and serve.

**Marlene Says:** *To make Pineapple Whipped Cream topping, sprinkle 1 tablespoon of instant sugar-free vanilla pudding over 1½ cups of thawed light whipped topping and stir to combine. Stir in one 8-ounce can crushed pineapple in light juice and continue to stir until it has frosting consistency. (The topping adds 45 calories, 8 grams of carb, and 1.5 grams of fat.)*

* See page 36 for sweetener options.

**NUTRITIONAL INFORMATION PER SERVING:** (1 piece) Calories 115 | Carbohydrate 20g | Total Fat 1g (Sat Fat 0g) | Protein 2g | Fiber 1g | Cholesterol 45mg | Sodium 235mg | Food Exchanges: 1 Carbohydrate, ½ Fruit | Carbohydrate Choices: 2 | Weight Watcher Smart Point Comparison: 4

# My Unbelievable One-Bowl Chocolate Cake

*BECAUSE I FIRMLY BELIEVE EVERYONE DESERVES CHOCOLATE CAKE, this signature recipe is now an Eat What You Love tradition. And while I love that it takes only a whisk and a bowl and 10 minutes to whip up, I am even more delighted at the number of readers who have taken the time to share how much they love this recipe. (I can't even keep track of how many birthday parties it has attended!) With its moist light crumb and dark chocolate taste, it's hard to believe this easy-to-make, unbelievable cake has less of anything.*

MAKES 9 SERVINGS

1/4 cup canola oil

1 large egg

1 teaspoon vanilla

1/4 cup packed brown sugar

1 cup granulated sweetener*

1 cup low-fat buttermilk

1 1/4 cups cake flour

1 teaspoon baking soda

1 teaspoon baking powder

1/4 cup Dutch-process cocoa powder

2 teaspoons powdered sugar

1. Preheat oven to 350°F. Spray an 8 x 8-inch baking pan with non-stick baking spray.

2. In a large bowl, whisk together the oil and egg for 1 minute, until the mixture is frothy and thick. Add the vanilla, brown sugar, and sweetener. Beat for 2 more minutes until the mixture is smooth and the sugars have been thoroughly incorporated. Add the buttermilk and continue to mix.

3. Sift in the flour, baking soda, baking powder, and cocoa powder. Whisk for 1 to 2 minutes until the batter is smooth. Add 1/4 cup hot water to the batter and whisk again until the batter is smooth (batter will be thin). Pour the batter into the prepared cake pan and tap the pan on the counter to level the surface and remove any air bubbles.

4. Bake for 18 to 20 minutes or just until the center springs back when touched and a toothpick comes out clean. Do not over-bake. Place pan on a rack to cool. Dust with powdered sugar just before serving.

* See page 36 for sweetener options.

**NUTRITION INFORMATION PER SERVING:** (1 piece) Calories 160 | Carbohydrate 22g (Sugars 8g) | Total Fat 7g (Sat Fat 1g) | Protein 3g | Fiber 1g | Cholesterol 25mg | Sodium 180mg | Food Exchanges: 1 1/2 Carbohydrate, 1 Fat | Carbohydrate Choices: 1 1/2 | Weight Watcher Smart Point Comparison: 6

# QUICK & EASY BASICS

# quick & easy basics

# Homemade Ranch Dressing

*AS THE COMMERCIAL SAYS, "Hidden Valley brand is what ranch is supposed to taste like." That's why I am happy to say that this ranch dressing perfectly mimics its flavor and even happier that it does so with significantly less sodium, fat, and calories (only 35 per serving!). I even think the flavor is better than any commercial brand—bottled or made from a mix. Made with everyday, on-hand ingredients, this recipe is also easy on the wallet.*

MAKES 8 SERVINGS

1/3 cup low-fat milk

1/3 cup light mayonnaise

1/3 cup plain nonfat Greek yogurt

1 teaspoon dried parsley

1/2 teaspoon garlic powder

1/2 teaspoon onion powder

1/4 teaspoon salt

1/4 teaspoon black pepper

1. In a medium bowl, add all ingredients and whisk to combine.

**DARE TO COMPARE:** Hidden Valley Ranch bottled dressing has 140 calories per 2-tablespoon serving, including 14 grams of fat and 260 milligrams of sodium. Step into Subway, and the ranch dressing topping your "light" salad will cost you 220 calories and 400 milligrams of sodium.

**NUTRITION INFORMATION PER SERVING:** (2 tablespoons) Calories 35 | Carbohydrate 2g (Sugars 1g) | Total Fat 3g (Sat Fat 0g) | Protein 1g | Fiber 0g | Cholesterol 0mg | Sodium 140mg | Food Exchanges: 1/2 Fat | Carbohydrate Choices: 0 | Weight Watcher Smart Point Comparison: 1

# Buttermilk Scallion Dressing

*A GENEROUS CHEF COLLEAGUE SHARED THIS RECIPE WITH ME for the Bibb and Blue Salad on page 142, and it has quickly become a new staple in my dressing repertoire—and his. With a texture and taste similar to that of my Homemade Ranch Dressing (see facing page), this one, made with fresh green onion, offers a touch more tang and a fresh onion flavor.*

MAKES ABOUT 2/3 CUP

1/3 cup low-fat buttermilk

2 tablespoons light mayonnaise

2 tablespoons plain nonfat Greek yogurt

1 teaspoon cider vinegar

1/8 teaspoon salt

1/8 teaspoon black pepper

1 large green onion, minced

1. In a small bowl, whisk together all of the ingredients, except the green onion, until smooth. Add the green onion and whisk just to incorporate.

**Marlene Says:** *I enjoy this dressing so much that I used it as the base for the creamy horseradish dressing for the Steakhouse Salad on page 158. It's also versatile—just add a teaspoon of sugar and turn it into a great dressing for your next coleslaw!*

**NUTRITION INFORMATION PER SERVING:** (2 tablespoons) Calories 30 | Carbohydrate 2g (Sugars 1g) | Total Fat 2g (Sat Fat 0g) | Protein 1g | Fiber 0g | Cholesterol 0mg | Sodium 150mg | Food Exchanges: 1/2 Fat | Carbohydrate Choices: 0 | Weight Watcher Smart Point Comparison: 1

# Creamy Caesar Dressing

*CONTRARY TO POPULAR BELIEF, the "Caesar" in Caesar salad has nothing to do with Julius Caesar, but everything to do with Tijuana, Mexico, where Caesar Cardini, an Italian chef, invented the salad. This creamy version of the wildly popular dressing is one I make regularly. While lightened up, it still includes all of the classic ingredients (sans coddled egg) that gives Caesar dressings their wonderful Parmesany, garlicky bite.*

MAKES 1/2 CUP

2 tablespoons lemon juice

3 1/2 tablespoons plain low-fat Greek yogurt

1 teaspoon Dijon mustard

1 1/2 teaspoons minced garlic (3 cloves)

1 teaspoon Worcestershire sauce

1/2 teaspoon anchovy paste* (optional)

2 tablespoons extra-virgin olive oil

2 tablespoons grated Parmesan cheese

1/2 teaspoon ground black pepper, or to taste

1. In a food processor, combine the first 6 ingredients (lemon juice through anchovy paste) and pulse briefly.

2. With the processor running, slowly add in the olive oil until the dressing is creamy and smooth. Add the Parmesan and pepper and pulse briefly.

**Marlene Says:** *Although I do not particularly care for anchovies, I always add anchovy paste to my Caesar dressing. It imparts an authentic Caesar taste without a trace of fishy flavor. Look for anchovy paste in a tube next to the canned seafood. It keeps for at least a year in the refrigerator.*

**NUTRITION INFORMATION PER SERVING:** (1 tablespoon) Calories 50 | Carbohydrate 1g (Sugars g) | Total Fat 4.5g (Sat Fat 1g) | Protein 1g | Fiber 0g | Cholesterol 0mg | Sodium 150mg | Food Exchanges: 1 Fat | Carbohydrate Choices: 0 | Weight Watcher Smart Point Comparison: 2

# DIY Taco Seasoning

*THERE ISN'T A MORE VERSATILE SEASONING BLEND THAN TACO SEASONING. It makes quick work of preparing tacos, but it also comes in mighty handy for quickly seasoning soups, chilies, casseroles, and even pasta dishes (as you will find in this book!). Less expensive than purchasing a packet, and with far less sodium, this full-flavored blend of south-of-the border spices can be used in any recipe calling for taco seasoning. 1 recipe = 2 tablespoons = 1 store-bought packet. You can double or even triple the recipe!*

**MAKES ABOUT 2 TABLESPOONS**

2 teaspoons chili powder

1 teaspoon cumin

1/2 teaspoon paprika

1/2 teaspoon dried oregano

1 teaspoon garlic salt with parsley

1/2 teaspoon onion powder

1/8 teaspoon cayenne pepper

1/2 teaspoon brown sugar

1. Place all ingredients in a medium bowl and whisk to combine. Transfer to a small jar and store in a cool, dry place.

**Marlene Says:** *To season ground beef or chicken for tacos or nachos, brown one pound of your choice of protein with 1 recipe (2 tablespoons) DIY Taco Seasoning. When well browned, sprinkle 2 teaspoons instant flour into the meat, stir, and then add 1/3 cup of water and one tablespoon ketchup. Cook on medium low heat, stirring occasionally, until mixture is thickened.*

**NUTRITION INFORMATION PER SERVING: (2 teaspoons)** Calories 10 | Carbohydrate 2g (Sugars 1g) | Total Fat 0g (Sat Fat 0g) | Protein 0g | Fiber 1g | Cholesterol 0mg | Sodium 230mg | Food Exchanges: Free Food | Carbohydrate Choices: 0 | Weight Watcher Smart Point Comparison: 0

# Favorite Pumpkin Pie Seasoning

*TO BE HONEST, I HAVE NEVER BEEN A FAN OF COMMERCIAL PUMPKIN PIE SPICE, instead preferring to tailor the mixture of warm spices often found in pumpkin pie to a given recipe (be it a beverage, a cake, or French toast!). Perhaps I just never found the right blend for my palate. Well, now I have! Rich in cinnamon, ginger, and cloves (as is Libby's famous pumpkin pie recipe) and with the addition of nutmeg, this richly flavored, perfectly balanced autumn-hued spice mixture is as wonderful as pumpkin pie.*

**MAKES 7 TEASPOONS**

1½ tablespoons cinnamon

2 teaspoons ground ginger

½ teaspoon ground cloves

½ teaspoon nutmeg

1. Place all ingredients in a medium bowl and whisk to combine. Transfer to a small jar and store in a cool, dry place.

**Marlene Says:** *There are a several recipes in this book where you can use this spice mix including Pumpkin Pie French Toast (page 73), 2-Minute Microwave Pumpkin Pie (page 273), and the Skinny Pumpkin Spice Latte (page 48). It will also work well in your own favorite recipes.*

**NUTRITION INFORMATION PER SERVING: (1 teaspoon)** Calories 5 | Carbohydrate 1g (Sugars 0g) | Total Fat 0g (Sat Fat 0g) | Protein 0g | Fiber 1g | Cholesterol 0mg | Sodium 0mg | Food Exchanges: Free Food | Carbohydrate Choices: 0 | Weight Watcher Smart Point Comparison: 0

# Everyday Marinara Sauce

*WHEN IT COMES TO QUICK AND EASY COOKING, few pantry staples are as popular as jarred marinara—and for good reason. Whether you use it as is, or doctor it as I do for my 15-Minute Shrimp and Penne Pasta with Marsala Marinara (see 170), ready-made marinara is the perfect go-to for fast-fix Italian meals. This simple-to-make stovetop recipe is richer in flavor and lower in sodium and sugar than most jarred brands.*

**MAKES 6 CUPS**

1 tablespoon olive oil

1 medium white onion, chopped (about 1¼ cups)

3 cloves garlic cloves, minced, or 1 tablespoon jarred

½ cup dry red wine or reduced-sodium beef broth

1 (28-ounce) can crushed tomatoes

1 (8-ounce) can tomato sauce

1 (6-ounce) can tomato paste

2 teaspoons sugar

1½ teaspoons dried basil leaves

1½ teaspoons dried oregano leaves

1. In a large pot, heat oil over medium-high heat. Add the onion and cook for 6 to 8 minutes, or until softened. Stir in garlic and cook for 2 minutes. Pour in the wine and cook for 4 to 5 minutes, or until most of the liquid is evaporated.

2. Stir in all of the remaining ingredients, crushing the basil and oregano with your fingers as you add it to the pot. Stir in 1 cup of water. Reduce the heat, cover, and cook for 20 to 30 minutes, stirring occasionally. Remove from heat and let cool completely before refrigerating.

**Marlene Says:** *A single recipe makes the equivalent of approximately two 28-ounce jars. It keeps well for about a week in the fridge and for several months in the freezer.*

**NUTRITION INFORMATION PER SERVING:** (½ cup) Calories 60 | Carbohydrate 11g (Sugars 3g) | Total Fat 1.5g (Sat Fat 0g) | Protein 2g | Fiber 2g | Cholesterol 0mg | Sodium 220mg | Food Exchanges: 1½ Vegetable | Carbohydrate Choices: ½ | Weight Watcher Smart Point Comparison: 1

# Easy Red Enchilada Sauce

*HERE'S SOME EXCITING NEWS: In not much more time than it takes to open a can, you can make a deeper, richer-tasting enchilada sauce for a fraction of the cost (and the sodium content)! To prove to myself that this sauce was better than any I could buy, I set up a blind taste test for my husband and sons against my "old-favorite" canned brand. My sauce won, hands down! Try it and prove to yourself that it's absolutely worth the extra minute or two.*

MAKES 2 CUPS

½ teaspoon garlic powder

1½ tablespoons chili powder

1 teaspoon ground cumin

1 teaspoon sugar

¼ teaspoon dried oregano

⅛ teaspoon salt, or to taste

1 (8-ounce) can tomato sauce

1. Place a small saucepan over medium heat and add all the ingredients except the tomato sauce. Stir until fragrant, about 30 seconds.

2. Pour in the tomato sauce and 1 cup of water over the spice mixture, stir well, and simmer 2 minutes to blend the spices into the sauce.

**Marlene Says:** *Use this sauce spooned over poached eggs, to make homemade chicken enchiladas, or or for my Chicken Enchilada Tacos (page 130)!*

**NUTRITION INFORMATION PER SERVING:** (¼ cup) Calories 15 | Carbohydrate 3g (Sugars 2g) | Total Fat 0g (Sat Fat 0g) | Protein 1g | Fiber 1g | Cholesterol 0mg | Sodium 230mg | Food Exchanges: Free Food | Carbohydrate Choices: 0 | Weight Watcher Smart Point Comparison: 0

# Easy Cheese Sauce

*I AM ALWAYS TINKERING WITH MY CHEESE SAUCE RECIPES in an effort to deliver the biggest creamy, cheesy bang for the lowest fat and calorie buck. This is my latest rendition and I hope you agree that it is both as delicious and as easy as can be. I use this for macaroni and cheese, but it's perfect for pouring over steamed vegetables or nachos. Add the green chilies (or chopped fresh jalapeño, if you wish) for an amazing reduced-fat Mexican queso dip.*

**MAKES ABOUT 1½ CUPS**

¾ cup low-fat evaporated milk

½ cup reduced-sodium chicken broth

2 teaspoons cornstarch

¾ teaspoon dry mustard

½ teaspoon garlic salt with parsley

1 cup shredded reduced-fat sharp cheddar cheese

Pinch of pepper (optional)

1 (4-ounce) can fire roasted green chilies (optional)*

1. In a medium saucepan, whisk together the first 4 ingredients over medium heat, until the mixture thickens and bubbles form.

2. Turn off heat and stir in the cheese until melted and creamy. Add a tiny pinch of black pepper or the fired roasted green chilies (drained of excess juice if there is any), if desired.

> **DARE TO COMPARE:** One-quarter cup of a traditional cheese sauce, made with whole milk and regular cheddar, has 210 calories and 16 grams (or four times) the fat and twice the sodium of this versatile sauce.

* With added green chilies, the queso dip is 15 calories per tablespoon (or 60 calories per quarter cup).

**NUTRITION INFORMATION PER SERVING: (¼ cup)** Calories 80 | Carbohydrate 0g (Sugars 0g) | Total Fat 3.5g (Sat Fat 2g) | Protein 8g | Fiber 0g | Cholesterol 15mg | Sodium 220mg | Food Exchanges: 1 Lean Meat, ½ Fat | Carbohydrate Choices: 0 | Weight Watcher Smart Point Comparison: 2

# Fast-Fix Berry Sauce

*BERRIES, FROZEN AT THEIR PEAK, make this multipurpose sauce a snap to make—all year round. Moreover, frozen berries make a quicker, better sauce as they release their juices more readily than fresh. This is a spectacular topper for the No-Bake Red, White, and Blue Dome Cake (page 278), or you can pour it over plain yogurt, ice cream, pancakes, cheesecake. . . . At just 35 calories per quarter cup, the sky's the limit!*

**MAKES ABOUT 2½ CUPS**

2⅓ cups frozen berries

⅓ cup granulated sweetener*

4 teaspoons granulated sugar or corn syrup

½ cup cold water

1 tablespoon cornstarch

1½ tablespoons lemon juice

Pinch of salt (optional)

1. Place the berries in a heavy, non-aluminum saucepan. Add remaining ingredients and stir until cornstarch dissolves. Place over medium heat and bring to a simmer. Cook for 2 to 3 minutes, or until mixture thickens and clears.

**Marlene Says:** *You may need to adjust the amount of sweetener, depending on the type of berries you are cooking. Boysenberries, for example, may need a touch more sweetener and strawberries may need a touch less.*

\* See page 36 for sweetener options.

**NUTRITION INFORMATION PER SERVING:** (¼ cup) Calories 35 | Carbohydrate 8g (Sugars 5g) | Total Fat 0g (Sat Fat 0g) | Protein 0g | Fiber 2g | Cholesterol 0mg | Sodium 10mg | Food Exchanges: ½ Fruit | Carbohydrate Choices: ½ | Weight Watcher Smart Point Comparison: 1

# Double Dark Chocolate Sauce

*DEEP, DARK, AND DANGEROUSLY DELICIOUS, this thick, glossy chocolate sauce is doubly chocolate good. With only 60 calories and 5 grams of carbohydrate per serving it's also heart-healthy and blood sugar–friendly, but it's the taste that will keep you coming back for more. Feel free to use it anywhere I list sugar-free fudge topping for drizzling, or serve it warmed as a dipping sauce for strawberries for a last-minute dessert.*

**MAKES 7 SERVINGS**

¼ teaspoon cornstarch

¼ cup Dutch-process cocoa powder

⅓ cup granulated sweetener*

⅓ cup nonfat half-and-half

¼ cup water

1 tablespoon light corn syrup

⅓ cup dark or semi-sweet chocolate chips

1 teaspoon vanilla extract

Pinch of salt (optional)

1. In a small saucepan, whisk together cornstarch and 1 teaspoon water until smooth. Whisk in the next 5 ingredients (cocoa through corn syrup) and place pan over low heat. Whisk over low heat until mixture barely simmers and thickens slightly.

2. Remove from heat, add chocolate chips and vanilla, and whisk until chocolate melts and sauce is smooth.

**Marlene Says:** *For my Chocolate Caramel Biscuit Donuts a stickier sauce works best, like Smucker's Sugar-Free Ice Cream Topping or my Chocolate Fudge Glaze from* Eat What You Love Everyday.

* See page 36 for sweetener options.

**NUTRITION INFORMATION PER SERVING:** (2 tablespoons) Calories 60 | Carbohydrate 9g (Sugars 5g) | Total Fat 2g (Sat Fat 1.5g) | Protein 1g | Fiber 1g | Cholesterol 0mg | Sodium 45mg | Food Exchanges: ½ Starch | Carbohydrate Choices: ½ | Weight Watcher Smart Point Comparison: 3

# Vanilla Crumb Crust

*I LOVE THE COMBINATION OF A SHORTBREAD CRUST WITH THE CREAMY LEMON FILLING in my Luscious Lemon Pie (see 270). I also know that compared to premade graham cracker crusts, ready-made shortbread crusts (I use Keebler brand) are not readily available, so I am sharing an oldie but goodie recipe of mine for a similar-tasting crust made with good ol' vanilla wafers. And, surprisingly, even though it's made with cookies, this easy crust clocks in with no more carbs or calories than a reduced-fat pastry crust. How yummy is that?*

MAKES 1 CRUST

1 generous cup crushed vanilla wafers (30 wafers)

1 tablespoon granulated sweetener*

2 teaspoons margarine or butter, melted

1 tablespoon egg white

1. Preheat oven to 350°F. Lightly coat a 9-inch pie pan with non-stick cooking spray.

2. Combine crumbs in a small bowl or food processor (pulse to make crumbs from wafers). Add sweetener and margarine, and stir or pulse. Add egg white and stir well, or pulse again.

3. Pour crumb mixture into pie plate. With your fingers, the back of a spoon, or with a sheet of plastic wrap, press down on the crumbs until they coat the bottom and sides of the pie plate. Bake 8 to 10 minutes.

> **Marlene Says:** *Place a sheet of plastic wrap over the crumbs and press down on it to make sure the crust sticks to the pan and not your hand.*

* See page 36 for sweetener options.

**NUTRITION INFORMATION PER SERVING (⅛ crust):** Calories 90 | Carbohydrate 11g (Sugars 5g) | Total Fat 5g (Sat Fat 1g) | Protein 1g | Fiber 0g | Cholesterol 0mg | Sodium 60mg | Food Exchanges: 1 Starch, 1 Fat | Carbohydrate Choices: 1 | Weight Watcher Smart Point Comparison: 2

# AIR FRYER FAVORITES

# *air fryer (convection oven) favorites*

# For the Love of
## { HOT AIR }

Being able to deliver the culinary quartet of quick, easy, healthy, and tasty was what got me the most excited when I originally wrote this book. Now I am doubly excited, as this brand-new chapter not only delivers on that original promise, it tops it—thanks to hot air!

To be honest, something happened that I truly did not expect—I fell in love with my air fryer. Like convection ovens (for which I have also provided cooking instructions), air fryers cook by circulating hot air. The result is more heat concentration and even cooking on the exterior of foods and shorter cooking times. The super-heated intensely circulated air of an air fryer however takes this to the next level. In doing so, air fryers can cook and produce extra crispy goodness and more, with less fat, in record time. And they do so with less fuss, less mess, and faster clean up. I'm in love...

### HERE ARE EIGHT TIPS ON ACHIEVING SUCCESS WITH MY RECIPES.

1) **ADJUST COOKING TIMES** and batching based on your air fryer specifications. The recipes in this book were tested in a 5.3-quart air fryer with 1700 watts of power.

2) **PREHEAT YOUR AIR FRYER.** Two to three minutes is all that is required for most air fryers.

3) **DO NOT OVERCROWD THE BASKET** with too much food! Most foods cook best when placed in a single layer, or with just a small amount of overlap.

4) **CHECK FOR DONENESS** by opening your air fryer as needed. This is an air fryer bonus. Simply pull the drawer out, take a quick peek, and resume cooking if needed.

5) **SHAKE OR TURN THE FOOD AS DIRECTED** for best results. Not all recipes will require this.

6) **SPRAY FOOD LIGHTLY WITH COOKING SPRAY** if crumbs look dry or you would like the food to crisp or brown more.

7) **CLEAN THE DRAWER AND THE BASKET** after each use. You can dry them by simply placing them back in the fryer and turning it on for 2 – 3 minutes if desired.

8) **WHEN USING THE CONVECTION OVEN INSTRUCTIONS**, follow the air fryer instructions for preparation, turning and or adding additional cooking spray to the food, and checking for doneness, unless directed differently. Cooking times will be a tad longer, the results equally delicious.

# { MORE QUICK & EASY AIR-FRYER RECIPES }

Across my four *Eat What You Love* cookbooks you will find lots of easy recipes that can be cooked in your air-fryer. Foods that are oven, skillet, or pan-fried, are grilled or roasted with high heat, or lift with air (like soufflés), are particularly well suited to air frying. They "fry" up fabulously with less fat—most often in half the usual time—and clean up is a breeze! Here are some now quicker-than-ever recipes from this book to get you started!

### BUFFALO CAULIFLOWER BITES *(page 87)*

Preheat air fryer to 380°F. Add cauliflower bites and air fry for 9 to 10 minutes, shaking once, with an additional light spray of cooking spray. Coating should be well-browned and crispy.

### "FRIED" MACARONI & CHEESE *(page 88)*

Preheat air fryer to 400°F. Spray basket with cooking spray, add coated macaroni & cheese triangles and air fry for 7 to 8 minutes, or until coating is well-browned and crispy (do not turn or shake). Let cool 1-2 minutes.

### EASIEST EVER GLAZED CARROTS *(page 183)*

Preheat air fryer to 400°F. Add seasoned carrots and air fry for 10-12 minutes, or until tender, shaking once or twice. Toss cooked carrots with marmalade, black pepper and salt as directed.

### COCONUT COCONUT CHICKEN *(page 206)* and TERIYAKI FRIED CHICKEN *(page 213)*

Preheat air fryer to 360°F. Spray basket with cooking spray. Air fry coated chicken breasts for 10 to 8 minutes respectively, turning halfway, or until coating is browned and crispy and chicken is fully cooked.

### ANYTIME TURKEY MEATBALLS *(page 221)*

Preheat air fryer to 380°F. Add meatballs to basket and air-fry for 10 minutes, shaking once after 6 minutes. (Add 2 to 3 minutes for refrigerated meatballs or, until interior is no longer pink.)

### CHICKEN FRIED FISH WITH BUTTERMILK SCALLION DRESSING *(page 249)*

Preheat air fryer to 360°F. Add 2 tsp. of the listed oil to the coating mix. Air fry fish for 7 to 8 minutes, turning once, and lightly coating once with cooking spray, or until coating is browned and crispy.

### STEAK-STYLE PORTOBELLOS *(page 265)*

Preheat air fryer to 400°F. Place mushrooms in basket gill side up. Air-fry for 10 minutes, turn over, and brush with marinade. Air-fry for 5 more minutes, or until lightly charred in appearance and tender to a fork.

### 3-INGREDIENT SHORTCUT STRAWBERRY SOUFFLÉS *(page 292)*

Preheat air fryer to 320°F. Place ramekins in the air fryer and air fry soufflés for 8 to 9 minutes, or until they have risen tall and tops are well browned. Let cool for 2 minutes.

*Note: A 5.3-quart air fryer with 1700 watts of power was used to test these recipes. Adjust cooking times as needed for your air fryer. See page 324 for more cooking tips.*

# Krispy Cinnamon French Toast

*SWEET, CINNAMONY, CRISPY-TOPPED FRENCH TOAST—made start to finish in less than 15 minutes! And as if that were not enough, this dressed-up French toast delivers just one-third of the calories and 90% less saturated fat than an unadorned order at most restaurants. While delicious as is, feel free to embellish it even further with a drizzle of your favorite pancake topper or syrup.*

**MAKES 2 SERVINGS**

1 teaspoon cinnamon, divided

2 teaspoons granulated sugar

1 large egg

2 large egg whites

2/3 cup low-fat milk

3/4 teaspoon vanilla

1/2 teaspoon baking powder

4 slices sourdough (or light wheat bread*)

2/3 cup crispy rice cereal

1 teaspoon powdered sugar (optional)

1. Preheat the air fryer to 360°F. In a small cup, mix together ½ teaspoon cinnamon and the sugar.

2. In a shallow bowl, whisk together the egg, egg whites, milk, vanilla, baking powder, and remaining ½ teaspoon cinnamon. Dip the bread into egg mixture (dipping only as many slices as will fit immediately into your air fryer), turning once to coat both sides.

3. Spray the air fryer lightly with cooking spray. Place soaked bread in the air fryer and top each piece with 2 rounded tablespoons of rice cereal (slightly crushing them with your hands as you press them on top the bread). Sprinkle each with ½ teaspoon of the cinnamon sugar and air-fry for 6 to 7 minutes, or until lightly puffed and browned. Repeat with remaining bread. Dust with powdered sugar before serving, if desired.

\* Dip bread briefly. Adds 8 grams of fiber and reduces carbs by 4 grams per serving.

**COUNTERTOP CONVECTION OVEN:** Place a baking sheet in the oven and preheat to 380°F. When oven is ready, dip all 4 slices of bread into the egg mixture, remove baking pan, spray with nonstick cooking spray where bread will sit, and place bread onto the pan. Top according to directions, and bake for 12 to 14 minutes.

**NUTRITION INFORMATION PER SERVING:** Calories 230 | Carbohydrate 36 g (Sugars 8 g) | Total Fat 4 g (Sat Fat 1g) | Protein 14 g | Fiber 0 g | Cholesterol 90 mg | Sodium 390 mg | Food Exchanges: 2½ Starch, 1 Lean Meat | Carbohydrate Choices: 2 ½ | Weight Watcher Smart Point Comparison: 6

# Egg, Bacon, and Cheese Chimichanga (Burrito)

*Of all the things I tested in my air fryer, my son Stephen loved this crispy breakfast burrito best. Usually, delicious, deep-fried burritos, known as chimichangas, are notoriously high in fat and calories, but this one comes out perfectly crisped using only circulating hot air and a touch of cooking spray. For lunch or dinner, try stuffing the tortilla with the chicken and bean filling on page 000 (simply double up the filling). So amazingly crispy—so incredibly good!*

MAKES 1 SERVING

1 large egg

1 large egg white

Salt and pepper (optional)

2 tablespoons shredded light Mexican cheese blend

1 (8-inch) reduced-carb high fiber flour tortilla (recommend Mission brand*)

1 tablespoon salsa or taco sauce

2 teaspoons real bacon bits

1. Preheat the air fryer to 380°F.

2. Whisk the egg and egg white in a small bowl. Spray a small non-stick skillet with cooking spray and place over medium-low heat. Add eggs to pan and cook, stirring gently, for 2 to 3 minutes or until almost set, seasoning with salt and pepper as desired. Top with cheese and cover pan.

3. Microwave the tortilla for 20 seconds, or until soft and pliable. Place scrambled eggs in the middle of the tortilla, top with salsa, and sprinkle on bacon bits. Fold bottom of tortilla over filling, fold in the sides, and then roll to create a burrito and secure the seam with a toothpick. Spray chimichanga with cooking spray, and place seam side down in the air fryer. Air-fry for 6 minutes, flip chimichanga, lightly spray top, and air-fry 3 to 4 minutes, or until golden brown. Let cool for 2 to 3 minutes and enjoy!

*Mission brand Carb Balance flour tortillas crisp beautifully, as do their Gluten-Free tortillas. Not all high-fiber tortillas (like La Tortilla Factory, which I love for soft burritos), crisp well.

**COUNTERTOP CONVECTION OVEN:** Preheat oven to 400°F. Once assembled, place chimichanga on a baking sheet. Bake for 10 minutes, flip, and bake 5 more minutes or until golden brown.

**NUTRITION INFORMATION PER SERVING:** Calories 225 | Carbohydrate 18 g (Sugars 2g) | Total Fat 10g (Sat Fat 5g) | Protein 20 g | Fiber 6g | Cholesterol 190 mg | Sodium 530 mg | Food Exchanges: 2 Medium-Fat Meat, 1 Starch | Carbohydrate Choices: 1 | Weight Watcher Smart Point Comparison: 4

# Bacon-Wrapped Shrimp with Honey Mustard Sauce

*Everything is better with bacon—and shrimp are no exception. What makes this ridiculously easy appetizer (or dinner) really soar, however, is the sauce. The trio of sweet honey mustard, salty bacon, and succulent shrimp is nothing short of amazing (as is the fact that each wrapped-and-sauced beauty is only 30 calories). Wrap the shrimp ahead of time and your first batch will be ready in 7 minutes!*

**MAKES 6 SERVINGS**

6 strips center-cut bacon

18 extra-large shrimp, peeled, tails on (about 3/4 pound, 21 to 24 count)

1 tablespoon Dijon mustard

1 tablespoon light mayonnaise

1 tablespoon honey

2 teaspoons vinegar

1. Slightly stretch strips of bacon (to a length of about 12 inches) and cut into 3 pieces. Tightly wrap a piece of the bacon around the middle of each shrimp and place on a plate seam side down.

2. Preheat the air fryer to 400°F. While heating, in a small bowl, whisk together the remaining ingredients. Set aside.

3. Place half of the shrimp, or as many as fit flat without touching each other, in the air fryer seam side down (pressing down to keep bacon in place). Air-fry for 4 minutes, turn the shrimp, and air-fry for 3 additional minutes or until most of the bacon is crispy. Place the shrimp on a plate and top each with 1/2 teaspoon of the sauce. (Caution: Wait about 1 minute before eating, as shrimp will be hot!) Repeat with remaining shrimp.

**COUNTERTOP CONVECTION OVEN:** This recipe is an exception. No method in my countertop convection oven worked to my satisfaction, but a nonstick skillet did! Simply heat a large nonstick skillet over medium-high heat, lay the shrimp in the pan, and cook for 3-4 minutes or until underside of the bacon is crisp. Turn shrimp and cook until bacon is crisp and shrimp are cooked through.

**NUTRITION INFORMATION PER SERVING (3 shrimp):** Calories 90 | Carbohydrate 3g (Sugars 3g) | Total Fat 3g (Sat Fat 1g) | Protein 11g | Fiber 1g | Cholesterol 90mg | Sodium 270mg | Food Exchanges: 1 1/2 Lean Meat, 1/2 Fat | Carbohydrate Choices: 0 | Weight Watcher Smart Point Comparison: 2

# 15-Minute Crispy Chicken Tacos

*EVERYBODY LOVES CRUNCHY-EDGED TACOS. Just ask Jack in the Box; they sold 554 million of their beloved deep-fried tacos last year. It is exactly that texture that entices my two taco-loving boys, and has them loving these! The fact these fast-fix tacos are not oil-laden, and the flavorful creamy filling is packed with protein instead of filler, is an irresistable waist- and taste-winning bonus. The tacos assemble quickly, but can also be prepped ahead. Cover filled tacos tightly with plastic wrap and refrigerate until ready to cook.*

**MAKES 4 TO 6 SERVINGS**

½ (16-oz) can refried black beans, fat-free

¼ cup chopped green onions

¼ cup salsa

1 tablespoon DIY Taco Seasoning (page 312) or ½ store-bought packet

2 cups cooked shredded chicken breast

¼ cup light sour cream

¼ cup fresh cilantro, finely chopped

12 thin corn tortillas

Shredded iceberg lettuce

¾ cup Light Mexican blend or other cheese

Hot sauce, salsa, or guacamole (optional)

1. Preheat the air fryer to 380°F degrees. Add beans to a medium microwave-safe mixing bowl. Stir in green onion, salsa, and taco seasoning. Microwave for 1 ½ minutes, or until warm. Gently fold in the chicken, taking care not to break it down, then stir in the sour cream and cilantro.

2. Slightly wet 3 or 4 tortillas at a time and place in the micro-wave. Heat on high for 20 to 30 seconds or until softened. Place 3 full tablespoons of filling on one side of tortilla, fold empty half of tortilla over filling, and press slightly to seal. Repeat with remaining tortillas and filling.

3. Lightly spray top of tacos with cooking spray. Place half of the tacos (or as many fit with a small overlap or flat) in air fryer and air-fry for 5 minutes or until the edges are well crisped. Serve stuffed or topped with lettuce, cheese, and additional garnishes, as desired.

**DARE TO COMPARE:** Two Jack In the Box tacos have 340 cal-ories, including 18 grams of fat and 12 grams of protein. These crispy tacos have 78% less fat and almost double the protein.

**COUNTERTOP CONVECTION OVEN:** Preheat oven to 400°F. Place tacos flat on a baking sheet, spray lightly with cooking spray, and bake for 8 to 9 minutes or until edges are crisped.

**NUTRITION INFORMATION (Per taco):** Calories 110 | Carbohydrate 13 g (Sugars 1g) | Fat 2 g (Sat Fat 1g) | Protein 10g | Fiber 2g | Cholesterol 20mg | Sodium 225 mg | Food Exchanges: 1 Lean Meat, 1 Carbohydrate | Carbohydrate Choices: 1 (2 Tacos = 1 ½ carb choices) | Weight Watcher Smart Point Comparison: 1

# Chicken Spinach Artichoke Sandwich

*WHO SAID AN OOEY, GOOEY, CREAMY, CHEESY SANDWICH couldn't be waist whittling? Not me! What's even better is this slimming sandwich also delivers a cheesy toasty crunch. Even better yet, no turning, pressing, or butter is required! Simply place it in the air fryer, wait 6 short minutes, and brace yourself for a taste-and-texture treat.*

SERVES 2

2/3 cup finely chopped spinach

1/4 cup finely chopped artichoke hearts

1/3 cup light mozzarella cheese

3 tablespoons light mayonnaise

1/4 teaspoon garlic powder

1/4 teaspoon onion powder

1/8 teaspoon black pepper

1/2 cup cooked shredded chicken breast

4 slices sourdough or light wheat bread

4 teaspoons grated Parmesan cheese

1. Preheat the air fryer to 340°F.

2. In a small bowl, mix together the first 7 ingredients (spinach through black pepper). Lightly spray two slices of bread with cooking spray, turn them over, and spread 1/2 cup of the "dip" onto the bread. Top each with 1/4 cup shredded chicken and another slice of bread.

3. Place sandwich(s) into the air fryer sprayed side down, lightly spray tops with cooking spray (butter-flavored works well here), and sprinkle each with 2 teaspoons of Parmesan cheese. Air-fry for 6 minutes (spraying once more with cooking spray if needed), or until tops are golden brown, and cheese looks melted when sandwiches are lightly pressed on. Repeat if needed.

**COUNTERTOP CONVECTION OVEN:** Preheat oven to 340°F. Spray a baking tray with cooking spray under where you will place sandwiches. Place sandwiches on tray and bake for 10 to 12 minutes.

**NUTRITION INFORMATION PER SERVING (1 sandwich):** Calories 260 | Carbohydrate 27g (Sugars 1g) | Total Fat 8g (Sat Fat 3g) | Protein 19g | Fiber 3g | Cholesterol 90mg | Sodium 635mg | Food Exchanges: 2 1/2 Lean Meat, 2 Starch, 1/2 Vegetable | Carbohydrate Choices: 2 | Weight Watcher Smart Point Comparison: 6 (5 with light wheat bread)

# Meat-Lovers Portobello "Pizza"

*MEAT-LOVING PIZZA FANS, THIS ONE'S FOR YOU! Meaty portobello mushrooms provide heft without the carbs and calories of a traditional pizza crust in this half-pound cheesy, saucy, meaty "pizza" that delivers the great flavors of both pepperoni and sausage. A coating of breadcrumbs adds a nice crispy crunch to the mushroom (substitute cornmeal for half the breadcrumbs for extra crispiness). A cool mixed green salad, like the one on page 000, is a perfect accompaniment.*

**MAKES 2 SERVINGS**

1 egg white, beaten

¼ cup breadcrumbs

2 large portobello mushrooms

4 ounces Italian-seasoned lean ground turkey

½ teaspoon fennel seeds, finely chopped

¼ cup diced green pepper

¼ cup pizza sauce or marinara

⅓ cup reduced fat mozzarella

½ teaspoon dried oregano

6 slices turkey pepperoni

1. Preheat the air fryer to 370°F. Rinse the mushrooms if needed, dry them, and remove and reserve stems. Scrape gills from the underside of the mushrooms, turn them over, and coat with beaten egg white. Roll through or sprinkle well with breadcrumbs and set aside.

2. Place the turkey, fennel seed, and green pepper in a small bowl. Grate mushroom stems into bowl and combine. Gently spray the bottoms of the mushrooms with cooking spray and lightly pat 1/2 of the meat filling into each mushroom cap. Top with 2 tablespoons pizza sauce.

3. Place mushroom(s) into the air fryer and air-fry for 10 minutes, or until mushroom has started to soften. Sprinkle mushroom(s) with cheese and oregano and top with pepperoni. Air-fry for 4 to 5 more minutes or until cheese is melted and mushroom is tender.

**DARE TO COMPARE:** Two slices of a medium Pizza Hut Meat-lovers™ pizza clocks in at 600 calories with 32 grams of fat (half of it saturated), 1,720 mg of sodium, and 20 points!

**COUNTERTOP CONVECTION OVEN:** Preheat oven to 400°F. Place stuffed mushrooms on a baking pan and bake for 14 minutes, or until mushroom is starting to soften. Add cheese, oregano, and pepperoni as in step 3, and cook until cheese is melted and mushroom is tender.

**NUTRITION INFORMATION PER SERVING (1 pizza):** Calories 220 | Carbohydrate 15g (Sugars 3g) | Total Fat 7g (Sat Fat 3g) | Protein 23g | Fiber 3g | Cholesterol 60mg | Sodium 680mg | Food Exchanges: 2½ Lean Meat, 1½ Vegetable, ½ Starch | Carbohydrate Choices: 1 | Weight Watcher Smart Point Comparison: 5

# Tilapia Parmesan for Two

*I ALWAYS KEEP TILAPIA LOINS OR FILLETS in my freezer (see page 000) for more keep-on-hand frozen favorites). In addition to their mild taste, I love how quickly the individually portioned pieces thaw; making last-minute dinner decisions a breeze. After a 10-minute thaw this dish is on the table in a mere 15 minutes! Bring a pot of water to boil before you preheat the air fryer and the One-Pot Spaghetti and Spinach (page 195) will be ready as a side dish just in time.*

**MAKES 2 SERVINGS**

3 tablespoons finely shredded Parmesan cheese

3 tablespoons Panko breadcrumbs

¼ teaspoon dried oregano

⅛ teaspoon Italian seasoning

Pinch of black pepper

1 large egg white

1 tablespoon light mayonnaise

2 (5-ounce) tilapia loins or fillets

½ cup store-bought or DIY marinara (or page 315)

1. Preheat the air fryer to 370°F.

2. In a shallow bowl, combine the first 5 ingredients (Parmesan through pepper). In another shallow bowl, beat the egg white and mayonnaise until smooth. Smear a thin layer of the egg white mixture across the top of each of the fillets and then top with the crumb mixture.

3. Place the fillets in the air fryer and air-fry for 10 minutes, or until top is brown and fish flakes easily when tested with a fork. While fish is cooking, heat marinara on the stovetop or in the microwave. To serve, spoon ¼ cup of marinara on a plate, and top with the fish.

**COUNTERTOP CONVECTION OVEN:** Preheat oven to 380°F. Place topped fillets on a baking sheet coated with cooking spray and bake for 12 to 14 minutes. Continue with directions in step 3.

**NUTRITION INFORMATION PER SERVING (1 fillet plus sauce):** Calories 225 | Carbohydrate 9g (Sugars 3g) | Total Fat 6g (Sat Fat 2g) | Protein 35g | Fiber 1g | Cholesterol 35mg | Sodium 390mg | Food Exchanges: 4½ Lean Meat, ½ Starch, ½ Vegetable | Carbohydrate Choices: ½ | Weight Watcher Smart Point Comparison: 2

# Zesty Fried Zucchini Sticks

*ZUCCHINI, DUE TO ITS HIGH WATER CONTENT, usually requires a heavy coating and/or a lot of fat to get the crispy crave-worthy texture everyone loves, but that's not the case here! My repeated efforts to get these right was confirmed when my husband and son, who had already finished dinner, dutifully tasted, and then gobbled the entire batch of these crispy crunchy flavorful "fries".*

**MAKES 2 TO 3 SERVINGS**

⅓ cup breadcrumbs

¼ cup Panko breadcrumbs

½ teaspoon garlic salt

¼ teaspoon dried oregano

¼ teaspoon Italian seasoning

⅛ teaspoon black pepper

1 large egg white

1 large zucchini (about ½ pound), cut into 24 ½-inch sticks

1 tablespoon Wondra flour (preferred), or all-purpose

Garlic Mayo Dip (optional, see Marlene Says)

1. In a shallow bowl, combine the first 6 ingredients (breadcrumbs through black pepper). In a separate bowl, whip the egg white until very frothy.

2. Preheat the air fryer to 380°F. Dust zucchini sticks with the flour. Dip one at time through the froth of the egg white (whisking again as needed) and roll through the breadcrumb mixture. Place zucchini sticks on a plate and spray lightly with cooking spray.

3. Add the sticks to the air fryer (in one layer or layering cross ways) and air-fry for 6 minutes. Turn, spray lightly with cooking spray, and air-fry for 2 more minutes or until well browned. Sprinkle with salt, as desired. (Caution: Let cool briefly. Interior of the fries will be very hot.)

**Marlene Says:** *These fries are flavorful as is, but even better with this GARLIC MAYO DIP: Whisk together 2 tablespoons of each light mayonnaise and nonfat Greek yogurt, 1 tablespoon water, ½ teaspoon yellow mustard, 1/4 teaspoon garlic powder, and a pinch of salt and pepper. (Makes 5 tablespoons. 15 calories and 1 gram of fat per tablespoon)*

**COUNTERTOP CONVECTION OVEN:** Place sheet pan into the oven and preheat oven to 400°F. Spray hot pan lightly with cooking spray, and add zucchini sticks in a flat layer to pan. Cook for 8 minutes, or until underside is browned, turn, spray again and cook 6 minutes or until well browned.

**NUTRITION INFORMATION PER SERVING (1/3 of batch):** Calories 70 | Carbohydrate 7g (Sugars 2g) | Total Fat 2g (Sat Fat 1g) | Protein 5g | Fiber 1g | Cholesterol 5mg | Sodium 160mg | Food Exchanges: ½ Vegetable, 1/4 Starch | Carbohydrate Choices: ½ | Weight Watcher Smart Point Comparison: 2

# Sirloin Steak with Peppers, Onions, and Mushrooms

*ONE OF MY FAVORITE RECIPES IN THIS BOOK is the steak marinade on page 229, so I simply could not resist using it again for my steak recipe in this new chapter. It's just that good (as is the air fryer for cooking steak!). To elevate the juicy, flavorful steak to greater heights—in taste and healthfulness—I've adorned it with the craveable combination of peppers, onions, and mushrooms.*

SERVES 4

1 recipe steak marinade
(page 229)

1 ¼ pounds lean sirloin steak,
about 1 inch thick

1 large red pepper, cut in
½-inch strips

1 medium onion, cut in
½-inch strips

1 8-ounce package sliced
mushrooms

2 tablespoons light soy sauce

¼ teaspoon black pepper

1 teaspoon oil or butter

1 scant teaspoon dried thyme

1. Preheat the air fryer to 400°F. Place the marinade in a dish (reserving one tablespoon), add the steak, and turn to coat. Using a fork or meat tenderizer pierce the meat to allow marinade to penetrate it, and let set for 20 to 30 minutes.

2. In a large bowl, toss the pepper and onion with reserved marinade and place them in the air fryer, spray with cooking spray, and air-fry for 10 minutes, shaking once, until peppers and onions are softened (some of the onion tips may be charred). Place them back in the bowl and place steak in the air fryer. Add remaining ingredients to the bowl, crushing the thyme leaves in with your fingers, and toss well. Cover, and set aside.

3. Air-fry the steak for 5 minutes, turn, and cook 5 to 7 minutes, or until the steak is done to your liking. (See temperature chart on page 228.) Remove steak from the air fryer; add the vegetables back into the air fryer and air-fry for 7 to 8 minutes or until mushrooms are tender, shaking once or twice. Slice the steak thinly across the grain and serve topped with roasted vegetables.

**COUNTERTOP CONVECTION OVEN:** Preheat oven to 450°F. Place peppers and onions on a baking pan, spray with cooking spray, and cook for 15 minutes, or until softened, turning once or twice. As soon as you pull them, in a sauté pan over very high heat (that fits in your oven if possible), sear the steak well on both sides and then place the steak in the hot oven. Follow the directions in step 2 for the peppers and onions. Cook the steak for 5 minutes or until done to your liking (see above). Dump the vegetables back on the baking pan. Place in the oven and follow instructions in step 3.

**NUTRITION INFORMATION PER SERVING (1/4 of the meat + 1/2 cup topping):** Calories 225 | Carbohydrate 9 g (Sugars 5g) | Total Fat 8g (Sat Fat 2.5g) | Protein 28g | Fiber 2g | Cholesterol 55 mg | Sodium 450 mg | Food Exchanges: 4 Lean Meat, 1½ Vegetables | Carbohydrate Choices: ½ | Weight Watcher Smart Point Comparison: 4

# Southern-Style Chicken Strips with Ranch Dressing

*AFTER TRYING LOTS OF COATINGS, MY SON JAMES (a fried chicken tender aficionado), declared this simple mixture of two different types of breadcrumbs and a few flavorful seasonings as the "best." A quick dip in buttermilk and savory poultry seasoning add a bit of Southern flair to these crispy restaurant-worthy tenders and the homemade Ranch dressing sends them over the top. Pair these with Parmesan Garlic Steak Fries (page 340) for a far-better-than-fast-food fix.*

SERVES (?)

½ cup buttermilk

1 large egg white

½ teaspoon baking soda

1 ¼ pounds chicken tenders (about 8)

⅓ cup Panko breadcrumbs

⅓ cup dry breadcrumbs

½ teaspoon seasoned salt

½ teaspoon black pepper

¼ teaspoon poultry seasoning

Homemade Ranch Dressing (page 308), optional

1. Preheat air fryer to 360°F.

2. In a large shallow bowl, whisk together buttermilk, egg white, and baking soda. Add the chicken to the buttermilk mixture and let set for 5 minutes.

3. In another shallow bowl, combine the next 5 ingredients (Panko through poultry seasoning). Drizzle one tablespoon of the buttermilk mixture on top and mix well. Remove chicken one piece at a time and roll into crumb mixture coating all sides.

4. Spray chicken strips with cooking spray and places pieces into the air fryer in a flat layer (in batches if necessary). Air-fry chicken strips for 8 to 9 minutes, or until nicely browned, turning once and lightly spraying with cooking spray again after 5 minutes. Serve with Ranch dressing.

> **DARE TO COMPARE:** An order of fast-food chicken tenders with 32 grams of protein, like these, has 500 calories with twice as much sodium, and 10 times the fat!

**COUNTERTOP CONVECTION OVEN:** Preheat oven to 400°F. Spray a sheet pan with cooking spray. Place prepared breadcrumb-coated chicken strips on pan and bake for 7 minutes. Turn the strips, spray lightly with cooking spray and bake for 5 more minutes or until nicely browned.

**NUTRITION INFORMATION PER SERVING (2 strips without dressing):** Calories 185 | Carbohydrate 11g (Sugars 2g) | Total Fat 2g (Sat Fat 0g) | Protein 32g | Fiber 3g | Cholesterol 0mg | Sodium 435mg | Food Exchanges: 4 Lean Meat, 1 Starch | Carbohydrate Choices: ½ | Weight Watcher Smart Point Comparison: 2

# Parmesan Garlic Steak Fries

*"FRIES" OF ALL KINDS AND AIR FRYERS ARE A PERFECT FIT; they can be made with less oil—and in less time. Baking potatoes (particularly russets) are the best for producing crispy on the outside; creamy on the inside french fries. My method of popping the freshly cut potato wedges into the microwave for a few minutes jump-starts the cooking, and also replaces the need to blanch or soak the potatoes for them to crisp well. A single large potato is perfect for two; simply double the recipe if cooking for four.*

SERVES 2

1 large russet potato
(about 10 ounces)

1 teaspoon olive oil

3/4 teaspoon garlic salt with
parsley, divided*

1/4 teaspoon onion powder

1/8 teaspoon black pepper

2 tablespoons finely
shredded Parmesan cheese

1. Scrub the potato and cut in half lengthwise. Lay cut side down, and cut each half into 6 equal wedge-shaped fries. Place the fries on a large microwave-safe plate and microwave on high for 4 minutes, or until barely tender when checked with a fork. (If you double the recipe, do this twice.)

2. While the potatoes are cooking, preheat the air fryer to 400°F.

3. Remove potatoes from microwave, drizzle with olive oil, sprinkle with 1/4 teaspoon garlic salt, onion powder, and pepper, and toss to coat. Drop the fries into the air fryer (cut side down in a single layer browns best) and air-fry for 4 minutes. Shake the basket, and cook 4 minutes, or until golden brown. Spray fries lightly with cooking spray, sprinkle with Parmesan cheese and remaining 1/2 teaspoon of garlic salt and air-fry for 1 to 2 minutes or until Parmesan is lightly browned. (Let cool for a couple of minutes before eating, as the inside will be very hot!)

**COUNTERTOP CONVECTION OVEN:** Preheat convection oven to 440°F. Place seasoned potato wedges onto a baking sheet and place in oven. Bake for 7 to 8 minutes, or until underside is browned, turn, and bake for 4 more minutes. Spray fries lightly with cooking spray, sprinkle on Parmesan cheese and remaining 1/2 teaspoon of garlic salt and bake for 2 to 3 more minutes.

**DARE TO COMPARE:** With 23 grams of fat, a medium order of garlic fries from McDonald's serves up 420 calories (and 13 points)!

**NUTRITION INFORMATION PER SERVING (1/2 recipe):** Calories 155 | Carbohydrate 28g (Sugars 0g) | Total Fat 3g (Sat Fat 1g) | Protein 4g | Fiber 3g | Cholesterol 0mg | Sodium 290mg | Food Exchanges: 1½ Starch, ½ Fat | Carbohydrate Choices: 1½ | Weight Watcher Smart Point Comparison: 4

# Apple Pie "Fries" with Caramel Drizzle

*THESE MUST-TRY FRIES ARE, WELL, AS SWEET AS PIE! Crushed graham crackers create a crunchy "crust" coating over a warm, soft, apple pie textured middle. Instead of ketchup, they're drizzled with caramel sauce! What's more, you can whip up this apple-licious dessert for two in less than 15 minutes. Enjoy them alone or serve with a small scoop of vanilla ice cream or light whipped topping. Your sweet tooth is sure to thank you.*

SERVES 2

1 large apple (about 8 ounces)

1/3 cup graham cracker crumbs

2 teaspoons granulated sweetener or sugar*

1/2 teaspoon cinnamon

1/4 teaspoon nutmeg (optional but nice)

1 large egg white

1 tablespoon sugar-free caramel ice cream topping, warmed

1. Preheat the air fryer to 330°F. Peel apple and cut into quarters. Remove core from each and cut into 3 equal wedges. (The apple should yield 12 wedges.) Set aside.

2. In a shallow bowl, combine crumbs, sweetener, cinnamon, and nutmeg, if desired. In another small bowl, whip the egg white until frothy. Lightly dip each apple wedge into egg white to coat and then roll into the crumbs using your hands as needed to coat the wedges.

3. Lightly spray the apple fries with cooking spray and place into the air fryer. Air-fry for 5 minutes, turn, lightly spray again, and air-fry for 3 more minutes, or until crumbs are nicely browned. Place fries on a plate and drizzle with caramel topping. (Let cool for a couple of minutes before eating, as the middle will be very hot.)

* See page 36 for sweetener options. One teaspoon of a sweetener/ sugar blend works nicely here.

**COUNTERTOP CONVECTION OVEN:** Preheat convection oven to 375°F. Place coated apples onto a sheet pan lightly coated with cooking spray and bake for 7 minutes, turn, lightly spray again, and bake for 5 more minutes or until crumbs are crisped.

**NUTRITION INFORMATION PER SERVING (6 "fries"):** Calories 145 | Carbohydrate 29 g (Sugars 18g) | Total Fat 2g (Sat Fat 0g) | Protein 2g | Fiber 2g | Cholesterol 0mg | Sodium 120mg | Food Exchanges: 1 Starch, 1 Fruit | Carbohydrate Choices: 2 | Weight Watcher Smart Point Comparison: 3

# Anytime Cherry Berry Pocket Pies

*FOOLPROOF REFRIGERATED PIE DOUGH and easy-to-keep-on-hand frozen fruit make these plump home-style fruit pies an anytime treat. I love the mixture of berries and dark sweet cherries, but any type or blend of frozen berries will do. You can also roll out the pastry circles ahead of time, cover with plastic wrap, and place them back in the fridge. When your craving for pie strikes, simply fill them with the berry mix and pop them the air fryer. Nine minutes later, you've got pie!*

MAKES 6 SERVINGS

1 ¼ cups frozen mixed berries and cherries

1 teaspoon cornstarch

3 tablespoons granulated sweetener*

½ package refrigerated pie crust (I like Pillsbury brand)

1 lightly beaten egg or 1 tablespoon milk

1 teaspoon granulated sugar

1. Place the frozen berry mix in a small bowl and toss with the cornstarch and sweetener. Set aside. Place the pie crust on a cutting board or flat surface. Using a 4-inch round cutter, cut out 4 rounds of dough. Press the scraps together and cut two more 4-inch circles. Lightly roll each round out to a 5- to 5 ½-inch diameter.

2. Preheat the air fryer to 350°F. Spoon about 3 tablespoons of berry mix onto half of a pastry round and carefully fold empty pastry over the top to form a half moon (packet will be plump). Press edges together and tightly crimp with a fork. Brush lightly with egg or milk, and sprinkle with a scant ¼ teaspoon of sugar.

3. Place the pies in the air fryer and air-fry for 9 minutes, or until crusts are golden brown.

**Marlene Says:** *To create a fruit drizzle for the pies, place 2 tablespoons reduced-sugar jam and 1 teaspoon of water in a microwave-safe bowl, heat on high for 20 seconds, and stir. Let cool slightly until desired drizzling consistency.*

* See page 36 for sweetener options.

**COUNTERTOP CONVECTION OVEN:** Preheat convection oven to 375°F. Place pies on a baking sheet and bake for 15 minutes, or until crusts are golden brown.

**NUTRITION INFORMATION PER SERVING (1 pie):** Calories 150 | Carbohydrate 20g (Sugars 5g) | Total Fat 8g (Sat Fat 3g) | Protein 2g | Fiber 1g | Cholesterol 90mg | Sodium 160mg | Food Exchanges: 1 Carbohydrate, 1 Fat, ¼ Fruit | Carbohydrate Choices: 1 | Weight Watcher Smart Point Comparison: 5

# Chocolate Soufflés for Two

*A WARM CHOCOLATY SOUFFLÉ NEVER FAILS TO IMPRESS. Fortunately, for us air fryer lovers; airy soufflés love being baked in warm circulating air. Soufflés also have a reputation for being difficult, but trust me when I say, they are actually very simple to make. You can even prep them hours ahead of time (see step 4). I love the warm soufflés served with a just a light dusting of powdered sugar and a dollop of light whipped topping. My the-more-chocolate-the-better husband has been known to add a drizzle of Double Dark Chocolate Sauce (page 320) :).*

MAKES 2 SERVINGS

1 tablespoon cocoa powder, divided

¼ cup semisweet chocolate chips

1 large egg, separated

½ teaspoon vanilla

1 large egg white

⅛ teaspoon cream of tartar (optional)

1 tablespoon granulated sugar

1. Lightly spray two 6-ounce ramekins with baking spray, and sprinkle each with ½ teaspoon cocoa powder. Set aside.

2. Place the chocolate chips in a small microwave-safe bowl and heat for 1 to 1½ minutes or until they start to melt. Remove and whisk until smooth. Whisk egg yolk with 1½ tablespoons of water and then whisk it into the chocolate with the vanilla and remaining 2 teaspoons of cocoa powder. Preheat air fryer to 330°F.

3. In a separate bowl, with an electric mixer, beat the egg whites and cream of tartar, if desired, (it helps keep the egg whites stiff), until foamy. Gradually add the sugar and beat to stiff, but not dry, peaks. Gently fold half of the chocolate mixture into the egg whites (taking care not to deflate them), and then fold in the remaining chocolate mixture.

4. Divide the batter between the ramekins. (Note: Ramekins can be covered and kept in the refrigerator for several hours at this point.) Place the ramekins in the air fryer and air-fry for 8 to 9 minutes or until they have risen nicely and tops are dry. Garnish as desired and serve immediately.

**COUNTERTOP CONVECTION OVEN:** Preheat convection oven to 375°F. Place soufflés on a baking sheet and bake for 10 minutes or until they have risen nicely and tops are dry.

**NUTRITION INFORMATION PER SERVING (1 soufflé):** Calories 175 | Carbohydrate 20g (Sugars 16g) | Total Fat 9g (Sat Fat 4g) | Protein 6g | Fiber 2g | Cholesterol 90mg | Sodium 70mg | Food Exchanges: 1 Carbohydrate, 1 Fat, ½ Medium Fat Meat | Carbohydrate Choices: 1 | Weight Watcher Smart Point Comparison: 5

# QUICK & EASY
## MENUS FOR ENTERTAINING

# Sunday Brunch

This company-worthy menu serves up to six—and can be on the table in sixty minutes, or less. Pour a cup of coffee (that's my kick start on a lazy Sunday morning) and then immediately pre-heat the oven for the muffins. As soon as they are prepped, pop them in the oven and prepare the Cheesy Spinach Breakfast Bake. As soon as the muffins are done, reduce the heat to 350°, and place the spinach bake in the oven. While it bakes, heat the sausage, slice the tomatoes, and place the berries in a pretty bowl. You can also bake the muffins the night before for an even simpler start to your day. Simply re-warm them before serving.

✦ Fresh Berries

✦ Small Batch Bakery-Style Blackberry Muffins *(page 54)*

✦ Cheesy Spinach Breakfast Bake *(page 66)*

✦ Sliced Tomatoes

✦ Turkey Sausage Breakfast Patties*

* There are several store brands. Or, if you own the first *Eat What You Love* cookbook ("the pink one"), you will find a recipe for Turkey Breakfast Sausage on page 107.

**Marlene Says:** *Colorful fruit and veggies bring this protein packed brunch to life. Low in sugar and total grams of refined carbs, it serves up 33 grams of belly-filling protein and 10 grams of fabulous fiber—all for less than 450 calories.*

# Company's Coming
# Make-Ahead Lunch

There is no easier way to entertain than having everything done before the guests arrive (even if the guests are your own family!). Every part of this make-ahead meal is easy to make and guaranteed to please. Prepare the Strawberry Pretzel salad the day before you plan to serve it, saving the crushed pretzels for just before serving time. The dip and the pie can be made up to two days' ahead of time, or simply prepare them as soon as the beef is in the slow cooker—they both whip up in a flash! Veggies for dipping, can be prepped ahead, or purchased ready to go. Add colorful napkins and paper plates for a festive feel with little cleanup.

✦ Avocado Ranch Dip with Assorted Veggie Dippers *(page 80)*

✦ Upside-Down Strawberry Pretzel Salad *(page 150)*

✦ Slow-Cooker Balsamic BBQ Beef *(page 236)*

✦ Whole Wheat Buns

✦ 15-Minute Minute Coconut Cream Candy Bar Pie *(page 275)*, or Luscious Lemon Pie with Shortbread Crust *(page 270)*.

# Fast-Fix Summertime Supper

When fragrant tomatoes, fresh corn, juicy watermelon and blueberries bursting with flavor hit the market, I hit the kitchen! This menu is as carefree as a lazy summer day—no oven is required and not a single recipe takes more than 15-minutes to make. And the combination of tastes, textures and colors, well, its as glorious as it gets. Prep the pie using a store-bought graham cracker (or shortbread) crust and place it in the refrigerator at least 2 hours before serving. I serve the pizza salad as an appetizer and the tomato salad with the meal; corn on the cob fills in as the starchy side. When grilling the chicken, plan on adding an extra minute or so to the cooking time. But be sure to cook it last, it will take no more than 2 to 3 minutes to cook!

✦ Watermelon Feta "Pizza" Salad *(page 147)*

✦ Easiest Ever Corn on the Cob *(page 189)*

✦ Any Time Tomato Salad *(page 141)*

✦ 2-Minute Greek Lemon Chicken *(page 215)*

✦ Easiest Ever Fresh (No-Bake) Blueberry Pie *(page 290)*

**DARE TO COMPARE:** This menu delivers ten times the protein and four times the fiber with 20% less calories, carbs, and sugar, and 60% less fat than a single *piece* of Marie Callender's Blueberry pie. Great taste and good health is as easy as pie when you eat what you love!

# A Lovely Dinner—
# Just for Two

A lovely meal is the tastiest way I know of to say I love you. This menu is special enough and yet easy and quick enough to satisfy any occasion—be it a birthday or a weeknight date night! I prepared it recently for my husband and he loved the steakhouse quality (I didn't mention it has a mere fraction of the usual steakhouse heft!). The dressing can be made early in the day or even the day before. I like to plate my salads ahead of time and set them in the fridge. Measure out the ingredients for the soufflés and the steak entrée, and set them aside, then prepare the potatoes. As soon as they are in the hot oven, cook the broccolini while searing the steak. Complete the entrée course by preparing the pan sauce. When finished, have your beloved clear the table. In the time it takes to do so, the soufflés will be in the oven!

✦ Bagged Mixed Green Salad with Creamy Caesar Dressing *(page 310)*

✦ Pan-Seared Filet Mignon with Rosemary Red Wine Sauce *(page 235)*

✦ Last-Minute Roasted Reds *(page 192)*

✦ Pan-Roasted Broccolini *(page 194)*

✦ 3-Ingredient Shortcut Strawberry Soufflés *(page 292)*

**Marlene says:** *Omitting the salad or buying the dressing or dessert is perfectly fine. It's your night too!*

# ACKNOWLEDGMENTS

While this cookbook is filled with quick and easy recipes, writing a cookbook is never quick nor easy. But every bit of effort is worth it when you hear that your book(s) make life easier (and tastier!) for others. My sincere gratitude for helping me make this book possible goes out to:

Jennifer Kasius and Jeanne Emanuel with Running Press for your generous editorial and sales assistance and most of all, ongoing support. Kristin Kiser, Publisher, for jumping on board with my mission, and Susan Van Horn for designing yet another beautiful book.

Rick Rodgers, chef extraordinaire. From concept to the development of delicious fare, your expertise and kindness were most appreciated. And to my stellar kitchen crew; Megan Westersund and chefs Judy LaCara and Tricia Davey—from recipe collaboration to cooking to copywriting and cleanup, I could not have asked for more. Your patience and unwavering positive energy, flexibility, and support are beyond measure.

PJ Dempsey, my longtime colleague and sidekick, for your ongoing editorial as well as personal support. Caroline Gottesman Kaufman MS, RDN, for your thorough research and engaging copy contributions, and to Gabi Moskowitz and Jerome Fuchs for your flair with the written word.

Sensational food stylists Carol Haffey and Lisa Cherkasky, photographer Steve Legato, and prop stylists Mariellen Melker and Kristi Hunter for bringing another *Eat What You Love* book to life. Additional thanks go to John Haffey, Harley Blaisdell, Bonne DiTomo, and Danielle Devine.

The wonderful folks at QVC: especially Christina Pennypacker, Michelle Phillips, Candace Stitt and the stellar hosts, with an extra big hug for my favorite foodie, Mr. David Venable. Thank you David for your extraordinary professionalism, kindness, warmth, and support.

Chuck, Stephen, and James, forever friend Nancie Crosby, and the rest of my family and friends. Your love and support means the world to me. And for making every day easier, my sincere gratitude and thanks go to the best "roommate" ever, Perla Uy Mendoza.

Last, but not least, my fabulous "kochbook" fans. Your ongoing support lifts my spirits, inspires me daily, and provides me with the fuel to keep doing what I do. This book is for you!

# INDEX